LOW.ENERGY.DESIGN

PRINTING AND COPYRIGHT

Published by

Interface Publishing,
3 Station Lane, Greenfield,
Oldham, OL3 7EL

© Richard Nicholls 2002

First published September 2002

ISBN 0-9539409-2-6

Printed in Great Britain by Browns Colour Printers, Oldham. Tel. 0161 627 0010

FURTHER COPIES

Further copies of this book are available for purchase by contacting the publishers at the above address or by telephone or email: Tel. 01457 878987, email sales@interface-publishing.co.uk

ACKNOWLEDGMENTS

Thanks are due to Michael Buckley who assisted with organisation and editing. I would also like to thank Ian Butterss, Roger Hitchin, David Loe, James Honour and Mike Brookes from Action Energy who gave constructive comments on how the text could be improved.

The writing and development of this publication was undertaken by Richard Nicholls of the Department of Architecture, Huddersfield University with funding from Action Energy, a programme run by the Carbon Trust and funded by the Department for Environment, Food and Rural Affairs, The Scottish Executive, Invest Northern Ireland and The National Assembly for Wales It has been published and distributed by Interface Publishing.

PUBLISHERS NOTE

Neither the DTI, Author, Publisher nor any person or organisation acting on their behalf makes any warranty or representation, express or implied with respect to the information contained in the publication; nor assumes any liability with respect to the use of or damages resulting from this publication.

The information given in this book is for general guidance only. It is not intended to be exhaustive or definitive. All relevant standards, regulations and codes of practice should be consulted before any work is carried out.

00 CONTENTS

04 - FABRIC

05 - VENTILATION

06 - DAYLIGHT

07 - ARTIFICIAL LIGHT

08 - RENEWABLE ENERGY

09 - HEATING

10 - COOLING

11 - ENERGY MANAGEMENT

IP - INFORMATION PANELS

12 - INDEX

FURTHER INFORMATION

Throughout this book reference is made to various publications produced by Action Energy that are related to energy efficiency in buildings. These documents are identified by letters and a number. The number relates to different publications in the same seriese the letters refer to the document seriese as follows:

ECG - Energy Consumption Guides - Compare energy use in specific processes, operations, plant and building types.

GIR - General Information Report. Gives an overview of the issues related to a specific topic within low energy design. (sometimes GIL - general information leaflet, a smaller document)

GPCS - Good Practice Case Study. Gives a case study of a building that demonstrates the application of energy efficiency concepts.

GPG - Good Practice Guides. Guide to energy efficiency.

NP - New Practice. Monitors first commercial application of new energy efficiency measures.

FP - Future Practice. Reports on joint R&D ventures into new energy efficiency measures.

FE - Fuel Efficiency Booklets. Gives detailed information on specific technologies and techniques.

IEE - Introduction to Energy Efficiency. Helps new energy managers understand the use and cost of energy.

These documents are available free by

Downloading them from the internet. The site is www.actionenergy.org.uk.

or

Contacting Action Energy on 0800 58 57 94

General information on buildings can be obtained from the website www.info4study.com

01 INTRODUCTION

In this chapter we will find that;

- Energy consumption in buildings accounts for 80 Million kWh (45%) of the total UK energy consumption of 177M kWh.

- Of the energy consumed in buildings 64% is used by housing, 9% by industrial buildings and 27% by office buildings.

- Energy is consumed in buildings for space and water heating, lighting, ventilation, air conditioning systems and general electrical services.

- Different buildings have different patterns of energy consumption.

- Some fuels are more expensive than others per unit of energy, electricity being the most expensive.

- Some fuels are more polluting than others per unit of energy, electricity generated from fossil fuels being the most polluting.

- Energy consumption results in acid rain, global warming and air pollution.

- The occupants of low energy buildings suffer from less ill health, greater thermal comfort and, in the workplace are more productive.

- Low energy local authority housing is valued by prospective tenants and is more easy to let.

- Energy conservation is the most practical and cost effective method for reducing the total amount of energy consumed in the UK.

- To be effective, low energy strategies must be based on predicted energy flows and consider the building and its services holistically.

1.0 Energy Consumption in Buildings

All developed societies including the United Kingdom (UK) are dependent on energy for their existence. In the UK the three sectors that are the main consumers of energy are industry, transportation and buildings. In 1994 these three sectors accounted for 21%, 33% and 45% of the total UK primary energy consumption respectively (figure 1.1). Farming and street lighting made up the remaining 1%. Unfortunately, the consumption of energy is costly and degrades the environment and so its use should be reduced. Since buildings account for the largest proportion of UK energy consumption they assume a high importance in the quest to reduce the overall UK energy consumption.

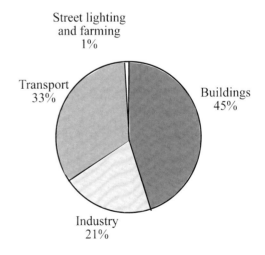

Figure 1.1 *Breakdown of UK energy consumption*

Energy is used by the building services installed within buildings to create a comfortable, safe, healthy and productive environment.

To achieve this the following systems are used.

- Space heating
- Domestic hot water heating
- Lighting
- Mechanical ventilation
- Air conditioning
- General electrical services such as lifts and escalators

Space and water heating require heat. This is produced by converting the chemical energy in gas, oil or coal to thermal energy by combustion in a heating appliance. The remaining services in the above list require electricity. Electricity can also be used to provide space and water heating. In the UK the majority of electricity is produced in power stations from steam or gas turbines driven by the combustion of fossil fuels. Smaller quantities are generated from nuclear power and renewable energy sources (see chapter 8).

The environmental damage caused by carbon dioxide (CO_2) released during energy use, combined with the more basic issue of cost has made energy conservation the central theme of sustainable architecture. This chapter will consider the consumption of energy by buildings, the cost and environmental consequences of energy consumption and strategies for low energy design. Throughout, the need for an integrated approach to low energy design will be stressed.

1.0.1 Patterns of Energy Use

Buildings enclose a wide range of human activities. They are places of education, work, entertainment and living. Within each category there are sub divisions for example, places of living may be student accommodation, hostels, hotels or individual homes.

Each individual building will have a different pattern of energy consumption throughout each day of the year. To restrict this variation for the purposes of this book we will concentrate on two broad categories of building to demonstrate methods for energy reduction. These are domestic buildings and non domestic buildings. The former category is also referred to as housing and the latter category is also referred to as commercial buildings. Of the 177M kWh of energy used each year

in buildings, 64% (113M kWh) is used in housing and 36% (64M kWh) is used in commercial buildings.

Where the energy goes in these buildings is illustrated in figures 1.2, 1.3 and 1.4 which show the breakdown of the total energy consumption of a typical domestic property, a naturally ventilated office building and a mechanically cooled and ventilated office building respectively[1].

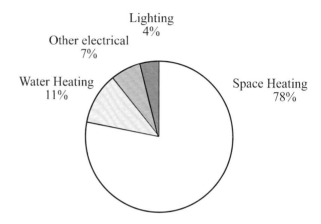

Figure 1.2 *Breakdown of domestic energy consumption*

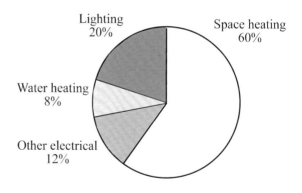

Figure 1.3 *Breakdown of naturally ventilated office energy consumption.*

The diagrams show that space heating energy consumption, which is derived from gas, is the largest portion of the total energy consumption in all three types of building, comprising 78%, 60% and 48% of the total for the domestic, naturally ventilated office and air conditioned office respectively. It can be seen that the portion of the total energy used for space

IP1 - Energy

We use energy in building services systems to do work for us. The basic scientific unit of energy is the Joule (J). But this unit is too small for describing the quantities of energy used in buildings. Instead we normally use the unit, Watt hour. This is still small so we use thousands(kilo (k)) of Watt hours i.e. kilowatt hours (kWh). 1kWh is equivalent to 36,000,000 Joules! or 0.036 Gigajoules (GJ). The energy used in buildings is found in a number of forms:

Chemical energy such as coal, oil or gas. Often referred to as fuels. The energy forms part of the fuel until it is released by combustion. Fuels are useful as they are a store of energy and can be used to move energy from one location to another simply be transporting the fuel. The amount of energy contained within a certain amount of fuel is known as its calorific value. The calorific values of gas, coal and oil are;

Calorific value of gas = 10.5 kWh/m^3
Calorific value of coal = 9.02 kWh/kg
Calorific value of oil = 10.4 kWh/litre

Mechanical energy which is the energy within an object due to it being in motion. One example is the energy in a rotating fan blade. Mechanical energy is useful for making other things move in turn for example the fan blade gives up some of its energy to air next to the blade causing that to move. Hopefully the air movement goes to provide a useful function in the building such as extracting fumes.

Thermal energy is also known as heat. Heat can be put into objects and this increases their temperature such as heating room air or domestic hot water. Heat can also be removed from objects and this decreases their temperature such as removing heat from water to create chilled water. Human beings detect thermal energy as warmth. It is an essential requirement for human survival and comfort.

Electromagnetic energy is a form of radiant energy eminating from within the atomic structure of matter. One of the properties of electromagnetic energy is its wavelength. The wavelength varies depending on the energy content. Human beings are sensitive to some wavelengths for example the wavelengths known as infra red are felt as heat by the skin. Another shorter wavelength band is detected by the human eye as light.

Electrical energy is the energy contained within moving electrons. Moving electrons are detected as an electrical current in wires. The electrical current on its own is not much use but the effects of it are. These are; heating effect - can be used for space heating or creation of light and electromagnetic effect - can be used in electric motors to create movement.

Energy cannot be created or destroyed but as hinted at in the description of electrical energy it can be converted from one form to another. For example chemical energy can be burned to produce heat, and mechanical energy can be used in a generator to produce electricity.

PRIMARY AND DELIVERED ENERGY

Energy use in buildings can be described in terms of primary energy or delivered energy. Primary energy is that which is found within the fossil fuels in the ground. Delivered energy is that which is delivered to the building. For coal, oil and gas delivered energy is very similar to primary energy as little is lost during extraction. However, the delivered value of electricity is provided by a much larger quantity of primary energy as a great deal of the energy in the coal, oil or gas is wasted in the power station during generation. For a typical coal fired power station for every 100kWh of primary energy taken in as coal only 33kWh will be output as delivered electricity. The rest goes to waste.

INPUT AND OUTPUT ENERGY

The efficiency of combustion devices is less than 100% since hot dangerous flue gases need to be exhausted. This means that not all of the input energy to a combustion device appears as thermal energy on the output side. For example a gas boiler may have an efficiency of 80%. This means that if an output of 100kWh is required 125kWh of energy in the form of gas needs to be input to the boiler. The extra amount is to make up for the losses from the boiler.

heating diminishes as the building complexity increases. This reduction can be attributed to the additional electricity consumed to provide higher standards of lighting in office buildings and, in the air conditioned office the electricity consumption of the chillers and fans. In section 1.3.2 these patterns of energy consumption are used to inform the low energy strategy of the building type to which they relate.

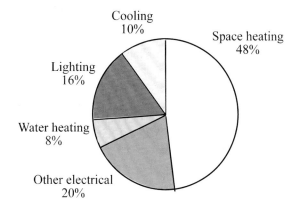

Figure 1.4 *Breakdown of air conditioned office energy consumption*

The pie charts have been drawn the same size to illustrate where the energy goes and to allow a comparison between the different building types. The area does not represent the amount of energy used. If the area did represent quantities of energy used, the mechanically ventilated and air conditioned chart would be the biggest followed by the naturally ventilated office with the domestic chart being the smallest. This is because the total energy consumption in any building depends on climate, installed services, the building fabric and the floor area being treated by the services.

To normalise energy consumption for the purpose of allowing a comparison to be made between building types it is usual to divide the total annual energy used by the building by its treated floor area. This gives an energy consumption in kilowatt hours per square metre per year ($kWh/m^2/y$). For our three building types typical energy consumption's per square metre are;

Domestic	$150kWh/m^2/y$
Naturally ventilated office	$205kWh/m^2/y$

Mechanically ventilated a/c office $460kWh/m^2/y$

It is the aim of low energy design to reduce these values to, or below, good practice values that have been found by carrying out research into energy efficient buildings. For comparison the target good practice energy consumption's per square metre are;

Domestic	$88kWh/m^2/year$
Naturally ventilated office	$110kWh/m^2/year$
Mechanically ventilated a/c office	$260kWh/m^2/year$

1.1 Why Save Energy?

There are four reasons why it is important to reduce the amount of energy consumed by buildings, three of them will be considered in this chapter and are:

- Cutting Costs
- Protecting the Environment
- Producing Better Buildings

The fourth reason is political. Countries that are self sufficient in fuel are not dependent on other countries for their essential energy supplies. This is important since fuel supplied from other countries can be affected by the internal politics of that country or regional conflicts. However, whilst this is a serious topic, the politics of energy consumption will not be considered in this book.

1.1.1 Cutting Costs

Different forms of energy have different costs per unit of energy. Table 1.1 shows the cost to a domestic consumer of 1kWh (1 unit) of different forms of energy. It can be seen that coal is the cheapest form of fuel, followed by oil then gas. Electricity is significantly more expensive per unit of energy than the fossil fuels. This is because the unit cost depends on both the extraction costs and any conversion costs.

This is best illustrated using electricity as an example. Electricity seems an ideal fuel. Of every 100kWh of electrical energy used by a heating appliance, 100kWh of thermal energy is released. In other words at the point of use it is 100% efficient. However, we must not forget that electricity is generated primarily from fossil fuels in power stations. Figure 1.5 shows the energy flows in a typical power station. It can be seen that of every 100kWh of fossil fuels input to the power station, approximately 5% is lost during electrical transmission (heating up of wires whilst overcoming resistance) and 60% is lost jointly in waste gases in the flue and as steam in the cooling towers. This results in a conversion efficiency which varies between 31.5 and 37% depending on operating conditions. This wasteful method of production makes electricity costs high in relation to other fuels such as gas that are simply extracted and used with little processing.

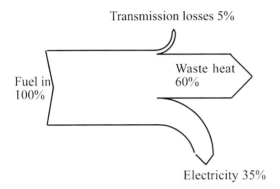

Figure 1.5 *Energy flows in a typical power station.*

Fuel Type	Cost relative to gas
Gas	1.00
Oil	0.93
Coal	0.47
Electricity	4.73

Table 1.1   *Cost of 1kWh of various fuels relative to gas.*

GREEN ELECTRICITY

It is possible to purchase electricity that has been generated from renewable sources such as windfarms and hydropower. This is known as green electricity because it releases no carbon dioxide or other products of combustion into the atmosphere.

In reality, the electricity you take from the grid may be from a local nuclear power station. However, the utilities are required to prove that they are buying and supplying the same amount of renewable electricity to the grid as is supplied to customers on green electricity tariffs. Green electricity does cost approximately 8% more per unit than 'standard' electricity generated from traditional power stations.

COMMERCIAL FUEL PRICES

The relative unit energy costs shown in table 1.1 are for domestic customers. Commercial users of energy are able to negotiate a favourable contract price for fuels from competitive suppliers due to the large quantities they consume. This tends to make unit costs lower, although there may be a complex arrangement of additional standing charges associated with energy demand throughout the year. In recent years fuel price competition has also been available to domestic customers

WHOLE BUILDING ENERGY COSTS

The cost of energy used is worked out by multiplying the number of energy units consumed by the unit cost of fuel. For comparative purposes, annual energy costs are usually stated as a cost per square metre (of treated floor area) per year ($£/m^2/y$). Ultimately the amount of energy consumed will depend on the floor area of the building, its construction, the type of services installed and its climatic location.

COMPARATIVE COSTS

The importance of energy costs in commercial buildings can only be illustrated by making a comparison with other running costs associated with buildings such as staff costs.

Staff costs in a typical office building are approximately £2,500 per square metre per year ($£/m^2/year$) (based on £25000 staff cost per year and an occupancy of 1 person per $10m^2$) whereas total energy costs for the highest energy consuming building type, the prestige office, are a modest $£25/m^2/year$. There are two conclusions to be drawn from this comparison. The first is that financial savings are most easily made by employing fewer staff than saving energy. Secondly, since the staff of a particular business are its most valuable asset it would be unwise to risk a fall off in productivity by making the staff thermally uncomfortable during the quest to save energy. Energy savings should be made without making people thermally or visually uncomfortable.

Energy costs are of a similar size to other non-staff running costs such as security, cleaning, water supply and maintenance. For example typical annual costs for maintenance and cleaning are £26 and £12/m^2/year respectively. This situation has meant that energy costs reductions have a similar priority to other operating costs in the day to day operation of a business.

ENERGY CONSERVATION INVESTMENTS

The decision on whether or not to include an energy saving feature in a building is usually decided by calculating and assessing a rate of return on the investment. The most basic way of calculating this is to use the simple payback period. This is the number of years required to recoup the initial capital cost from the value of energy savings made.

The payback period is calculated from the following formula:

Payback = Capital cost of energy saving feature (£)
period (y)   Value of energy savings per year(£/y)

Industry usually requires a payback period of less than 3 years for expenditure on energy saving features to be seen as worthwhile. From the formula it can be seen that the payback period will become longer if the capital cost of the equipment increases or the value of saved fuel decreases. The biggest change in these two factors over recent years has been fuel cost reductions, reducing the value of energy saved. This has arisen after the privatisation of the energy utilities and the introduction of price competition first to commercial customers and recently to domestic customers. Reduced prices are a benefit to the balance book but makes the installation of energy saving features more difficult to justify on financial grounds.

Price falls have been as large as 40% in commercial gas and 11% in commercial electricity prices over recent years. As a result energy managers have seen their role change from savers of energy to fuel price negotiators where substantial cost savings can be made even if energy use stays the same or in some cases increases!

It has been estimated that for each 10% fall in fuel prices there is a 4% rise in energy consumption. However, fuel prices are variable and the most recent trend has been towards increasing prices and so the pressure towards increased consumption simply because it has become cheaper is likely to be reversed.

Many energy saving features can be justified on cost grounds because they carry little or no additional cost if installed during construction or major upgrades such as replacing old boilers and controls for new versions. However, if installation takes place as an addition it is becoming increasingly difficult to justify such works using financial payback periods. If this is the case our attention must now focus on justification on environmental grounds. Section 11.7 considers this subject in more detail.

1.1.2 Protecting the Environment

The chemical reaction, called combustion, that takes place between fossil fuels and oxygen to release heat, also produces a number of gaseous by-products. Typically these are carbon dioxide (CO_2), sulphur dioxide (SO_2), nitric oxide(NO) and nitrogen dioxide (NO_2). The latter two are collectively known as nitrous oxides (NO_x).

Pollutant gas output is quoted as a mass of gas, measured in kilograms(kg) per kilowatt hour (kWh) of delivered energy. Carbon dioxide output is also specified in terms of a weight of carbon per unit of delivered energy (kg/kWh). It is possible to convert between the two quoted values by considering the atomic weight of carbon and oxygen. Carbon has an atomic weight of 12, oxygen has an atomic weight of 16. So the molecular weight of CO_2 is (12+16+16) 44. Therefore the fraction of carbon in carbon dioxide is 12/44ths or 3/11ths. To convert a mass of carbon dioxide to a mass of carbon multiply it by 3/11. To convert a mass of carbon to a mass of carbon dioxide divide it by 3/11.

Different fuels have different pollution outputs per unit

of energy. The pollutant gases given out depends on the elements present in the fuel before combustion such as carbon and sulphur. Table 1.2 shows the output of carbon arising from the use of 1kWh of energy for various fuels. From the table it can be seen that natural gas has the lowest pollution output per unit of energy. Gas produces 53% less carbon than electricity and 28% and 38% less than from using oil and coal respectively.

Delivered fuel	Carbon emission factor (kgC/kWh)
Natural gas	0.053
LPG	0.068
Biogas	0
Oil (all grades)	0.074
Coal	0.086
Biomass	0
Electricity	0.113
Waste heat	0

Table 1.2 Output of carbon per kWh of delivered energy.

The most polluting fuel, electricity is generated from a mix of coal and oil fired power stations, nuclear power and a very small proportion of renewables. It can be seen that electricity has by far the greatest output of carbon per kWh. This is a direct result of inefficiencies in power generation from fossil fuels as mentioned earlier. In 1988 71% of UK emissions of sulphur dioxide, 33% of CO_2 emissions and 32% of Nitrous Oxides (NOx) emissions came from power stations[2].

It should be noted that the proportions of pollutants output from the use of 1kWh of electricity is set to be reduced. The early 90's saw the "dash for gas" in power generation. Many new combined cycle gas fired power stations were constructed. These power stations have an efficiency of 42 - 45% and are therefore more efficient than coal fired stations. In addition the pollution output of the primary fuel, gas, is lower. For example, a coal fired power station produces between 64.9 and 76.2g of CO_2 per MJ of electricity generated. A combined cycle gas turbine power station produces between 28 and 33.3g of CO_2 per MJ of electricity[3].

Each of the gases arising from combustion is known to cause environmental damage. Carbon dioxide is a greenhouse gas, sulphur and carbon dioxide combine with moisture in the air to create acid rain, Nitric oxides add to poor air quality and ozone depletion.

ACID RAIN

Rain is naturally acidic due to the presence of dissolved carbon and sulphur dioxides from the atmosphere. However, the release of additional quantities of these gases from the burning of fossil fuels has made the rain more acidic.

The more accurate term is acid deposition since burning fossil fuels in buildings and power stations results in both wet and dry deposits. Dry deposition in the form of dust and gas generally occurs close to the source. The wet deposits, acid rain or snow, can be carried long distances in the atmosphere. Fuel combustion in one country can cause environmental damage in a neighbouring country.

Life forms have developed in an environment with a particular acidity level. Altering this natural state will distress the vegetation and freshwater life in those ecosystems. Acid rain also causes damage to buildings by reacting with the materials from which they are made. Historic buildings and statues made from stone are particularly vulnerable to attack.

The degree of acidity of a solution is indicated using the pH scale. pH7 is neutral, lower pH values represent increasing acidity down to pH1. pH values higher than 7 are more alkaline up to pH14. Table 1.3 shows examples of the range of acidities and alkalinities encountered in every day life.

PH		Example
13.0	strong alkaline	dilute sodium hydroxide
11.0		bathroom cleaner
7.0	neutral	distilled water
5.3	slightly acidic	normal rain
4.5		acid rain
3.0		Vinegar
1.0	strong acid	dilute nitric acid

Table 1.3 *pH Values of some common liquids.*

Research has shown that the acidity of lakes in some parts of Norway has increased from pH5.8 in 1940 to pH4.8 in 1990. Fish cannot live in lakes and rivers with water below pH4.5. Many north European deciduous forests are showing signs of leaf damage which is thought to be due to acid rain.

GLOBAL WARMING

The earth's atmosphere is transparent to short wave infra red (heat) radiation from the sun. This radiation is absorbed by the earth and is re-radiated at a longer wavelength. The atmosphere is not transparent to this long wave radiation and so the heat is trapped.

This warming effect is essential to life on earth. Without it the earth would be 30°C cooler. The degree to which heat is trapped in the atmosphere depends on its mixtures of gases. There are a number of greenhouse gases, natural ones such as methane and man made ones such as the chlorofluorocarbons (CFCs). The greenhouse gas which exists in the largest quantities is carbon dioxide (CO_2) this occurs both naturally and as a result of man's activities. Scientists have noted that the concentration of CO_2 is increasing in the atmosphere as a result of fossil fuel combustion and deforestation. It is now accepted by the scientific community that increased global warming is now occurring due to man's activities. The continuing disagreement amongst scientists is over the magnitude of the effects of global warming. It is predicted that atmospheric temperatures will increase, sea levels will rise, weather patterns will change and agriculture will be affected.

Estimates of temperature increase and the likely consequences vary depending on the mathematical model of the climate being used. Various catastrophic scenarios have been detailed such as melting of the ice caps and expansion of the oceans leading to widespread flooding and changes in weather patterns. However, there is a conflicting opinion that some of the worst effects may be limited by processes which arise due to global warming itself, resulting in negative feedback. The first factor is increased plankton growth in the warm oceans that would consume more CO_2. Plankton are tiny plants found in the upper layers of the sea. As they grow they consume carbon dioxide. The second factor is reflection of solar energy back into space from cloud cover which is predicted to increase as a consequence of global warming.

Models will continue to be refined to determine more accurately the consequences of global warming. What is known is that man made CO_2 increases are detrimental to climatic processes and all efforts should be made to limit unnecessary CO_2 output.

AIR QUALITY

The products of combustion from heating systems and power stations contribute to poor air quality. Nitrous oxides are known to be a lung irritant and as such they can cause breathing difficulties in adults and asthma problems in children.

CONSERVING FOSSIL FUELS

One of the most difficult aspects of fossil fuel usage is to predict the longevity of supplies. Fossil fuels were created from prehistoric forests and so the amount is finite. Modern societies are consuming this finite resource so it should be possible to predict how long reserves will last by dividing the quantities available by the rate of consumption. Various predictions have been made in this way. For example oil is estimated to last a further 40 years, gas 65 years and coal 300 years. These predictions vary due to a number of factors which are;

- new reserves being found due to exploration

- previously uneconomic reserves being brought into production due to increases in fuel costs

- variations in demand for example, due to economic growth and recession.

These factors cause variation in the number of years before fossil fuel is estimated to become exhausted but the orders of magnitude remain the same. Fossil fuels will eventually run out. Energy conservation will slow down the rate of consumption which, being optimistic, will give society time to research, develop and implement alternative sustainable energy sources.

1.1.3 Better Buildings

A number of research projects have shown that low energy buildings tend to be more desirable to the occupants than an equivalent higher energy consuming building. In housing the effect is seen as an immediate reduction in gas and electricity bills. However, the reductions in bills are often not as large as predicted. This is because the building occupants use the opportunity for lower fuel bills to obtain an improvement in thermal comfort conditions. The home can be better heated but still have lower fuel bills. Improvements in temperatures also have an effect on health. In the UK many elderly people die each year due to hypothermia in poorly heated homes. In addition many accidents occur due to a reduction in mobility with low temperatures. Warmer homes can prevent much of this and also aid in respiratory illnesses by driving away the dampness that can lead to mould growth and dust mite infestations. The spores from the former and detritus from the latter can cause allergic reactions leading to asthma especially in young children.

Many studies have shown that the workforce in low energy commercial buildings is more productive. This may be due to an overall corporate staff management system which not only values the environment but the employees also. It may also be due to the fact that many low energy office buildings are well daylit, naturally ventilated by openable windows and may incorporate planted atria and other spaces which inspire and add to occupant well-being.

Another benefit of low energy buildings is that maintenance costs are reduced since there will be less energy consuming plant installed and that which is will run for fewer hours during a shorter heating season.

1.2 Reducing Energy Consumption

From the preceding sections it can be seen that there are many benefits to be gained by reducing the energy consumption of buildings.

A number of methods are available that either induce, reward, assist or encourage the saving of energy. The methods available can be broadly categorised as either fiscal, legislative or technical.

FISCAL

Taxation can be used to penalise the use of energy or reward the purchase of energy saving devices.

The climate change levy is a new tax that has been added to energy costs incurred by industry, commerce, agriculture and public sector services. The aim is to discourage energy use by increasing the cost of fuels. It also makes purchases of energy saving devices and systems more cost effective. The tax will be added to energy bills at a rate of 0.43p/kWh for electricity, 0.15p/kWh for gas, 1.17p/kWh for coal and 0.096p/kWh for LPG. It can be seen that these sums reflect the pollution output of the various fuels (table 1.2). The more polluting the fuel the greater is the levy. Part of the revenue collected from this tax will go to reducing employers national insurance contributions, making it cheaper to employ staff. Part will also be used to fund energy efficiency schemes and renewable energy systems.

Some fuels are exempt from the levy such as renewable energy and combined heat and power output. For some users the levy is being reduced for example energy intensive industries who are implementing energy reduction strategies.

Taxation is a punitive method of encouraging energy efficiency but there are also enhanced capital tax allowances available for energy efficiency equipment such as chp systems, efficient boilers, pipe insulation, variable speed drives and low energy lighting systems. These enhanced allowances allow the full cost of the devices to be written off over one year instead of over approximately eight years which is normal for most capital items.

LEGISLATION

In recognition of the need to save energy. Conservation of fuel and power is included within the building regulations which are enforceable by law. The building regulations are regularly reviewed. In the past the regulations have concentrated on reducing the space heating energy use of buildings. They now include lighting, ventilation and air-conditioning with an expected tightening of standards in future years.

TECHNICAL

There are a number of new, re-discovered or improved technologies which can be used to reduce energy consumption and reduced CO_2 output whilst maintaining existing levels of thermal comfort, ventilation and lighting.

Reforestation - One of the causes of rising CO levels is the destruction of forests. The planting of new forests will help to absorb atmospheric CO_2 during their growth periods. Forests also help to promote bio-diversity by providing an habitat for wild life. However, it is estimated that reforestation in the UK will only contribute a small proportion to the target CO_2 reductions set by the UK government.

Improve electrical generation efficiencies. Higher efficiencies can be obtained from new coal fired generation and even higher efficiencies from gas generation. This is proven technology which is already contributing to reducing CO_2 output. However, there are commentators who believe gas should be reserved for distributed heating and CHP plant where efficiencies of 80-90% can be achieved and that more effort should be expended in producing cleaner coal fired electricity since coal reserves are more extensive than gas.

Renewable energy - Wind, solar, bio-mass and hydro electric power stations can be used to displace fossil fuel and nuclear generation. At the moment renewables are not cost competitive when compared to fossil fuel generated electricity. In many cases they also have their own environmental concerns. For example, windfarms are often rejected for their visual intrusion on hill tops and tidal barrages interfere with estuarine life.

Building energy efficiency - It is generally accepted that cost effective energy savings as great as 40% can be made in existing buildings with poor fabric and services and that savings of 10-20% can be made on average across the whole buildings sector. These

savings can be achieved often at little or no extra cost if energy efficiency methods are integrated during re-furbishment or at the design stage.

From the above it is clear that low energy design in both refurbishment of old and construction of new buildings, is the method which is likely to have the largest impact on energy consumption and pollutant gas emissions within the UK. This also makes real sense since rather than provide new forms of supply, it is far more cost effective to reduce demand. This may also increase the viability of renewable energy schemes in the future which at current rates of generation can only supply a small fraction of UK electricity needs.

1.3 Low Energy Design

Virtually every aspect of a building's design, construction and services has an effect on its energy consumption. In order to reduce the energy consumption to a minimum, whilst maintaining comfort standards, we must first identify the role these design aspects play in energy performance. This knowledge will then indicate the methods we can use to restrict energy use. This can be by careful design, adoption of new or improved technologies and materials or utilisation of traditional architectural techniques.

- **Siting and climate**
  Energy is used to create a comfortable internal environment when the external environment is too severe for comfort. It follows that the more severe the external climate the more energy is used. Landscaping can be used to create a less severe microclimate in which to place a building.

- **Form of the building (internal and external)**
  The form of the building dictates the size of the surface area and volume. These two factors in turn are directly proportional to the fabric and ventilation heat loss rates respectively. Form also dictates the ability with which natural energy can be collected and used such as solar heat, light and natural ventilation.

- **Building fabric**
  The heat transfer characteristics of the external

envelope determine fabric heat loss rates. Low density materials, insulators, can be used to slow the passage of heat. Dense, thermally massive materials can be used internally to help cool a building in summer.

- **Building ventilation**
  Uncontrolled infiltration involves cold air entering a building and warm air being lost from it. The motors in mechanical ventilation systems consume electricity. Infiltration should be minimised and mechanical systems should operate efficiently and only as necessary.

- **Natural daylight**
  Natural light can be used to displace the use of artificial light created using electricity. The glazed openings of a building have the strongest influence on natural light utilisation.

- **Artificial lighting**
  Artificial lighting consumes electricity and so should be produced efficiently and only used as required.

- **Passive solar heating**
  Passive solar heating can be used to displace the use of mechanical heating created from burning fossil fuels. This requires well thought out controls that allow full advantage to be made of natural energy flows.

- **Heating systems**
  Mechanical heating systems consume fossil fuels to create heat and so should be operated efficiently and only as required.

- **Cooling**
  Mechanical cooling systems consume electricity to create coolth. To avoid this means of cooling, passive methods such as shading and exposing mass with night time ventilation should be used as a first option. Where passive cooling is inadequate efficient mechanical systems should be chosen and operated only as required.

- **General services**
  Lifts, escalators, emergency lighting and other systems consume electricity and so efficient systems should be chosen and used only as required

- **Post occupancy energy management**
  Loss of adjustment in controls or faults can cause energy consuming equipment to operate inefficiently. Building energy consumption can increase if it is not monitored and managed to remain on target.

The topics listed above exert have varying relevance depending on the building type and its services. For example, air-conditioning is rarely used in domestic buildings and some equipment intensive office buildings may only use space heating at the perimeter. The emphasis in any low energy strategy must be driven by a knowledge of predicted energy flows as introduced in section 1.0 and further developed in the next section.

1.3.1 General Low Energy Strategy

A general low energy strategy is indicated in Figure 1.6. The approach is to first reduce the demand for energy then make use of natural energy flows and finally supply the energy that is needed in an efficient and well controlled manner. The order to elements of the strategy is therefore:

1. Site and orientate the building in a "kind" microclimate by choosing an appropriate site or using landscaping techniques to modify the climate.

2. Minimise fabric and ventilation heat loss rates.

3. Optimise any "free" sources of energy such as solar gains, daylight or natural ventilation.

4. Select the energy consuming plant to be as energy efficient as possible.

5. Control the energy consuming plant so that it operates only when required and to the level required.

6. Recover waste energy where viable.

Figure 1.6 General low energy strategy.

FOCUSSING THE STRATEGY

The diagrams in section 1.0 showed the percentage of the total energy consumption taken by various demands in three types of building. However, if this energy were free, limitless and non-polluting its use would be of no concern. Unfortunately, this is not the case and so we are interested in reducing the effects of energy consumption i.e. its cost and environmental impact. To be better informed about this diagrams 1.2, energy consumption for a typical house and 1.4, energy consumption for an air conditioned office, have been simplified and redrawn as figures 1.7 and 1.8 to show only total gas and electrical consumption's. Also shown is the percentage of the total CO_2 output emitted due to the gas and electricity consumption.

Figure 1.7 shows that in housing the largest energy consumption is in the form of gas which is also the largest source of CO_2. In the air conditioned office (figure 1.8) gas consumption is still the largest energy flow but when considering CO_2 output the electrical component is the largest contributor. Cost tends to follow a similar pattern to CO_2 output. It follows therefore that if we are interested in reducing costs and environmental impact then;

- In domestic buildings space heating reductions remain a priority. In this case considerations should be made to reduce heat losses, optimise the use of passive solar space heating and provide efficent

heating systems and adequate controls. Following this the electrical consumption of the lighting and domestic appliances should be reduced as should energy used for water heating.

- In office buildings electricity reductions through reduced artificial lighting, ventilation and cooling is the priority. In this case effort should be made to maximise the use of natural ventilation, passive cooling and natural light.

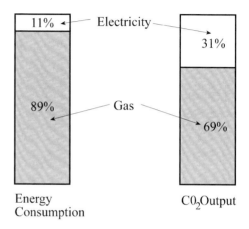

Figure 1.7 Percentage of total delivered energy use and CO_2 output attributed to gas and electricity consumption in housing.

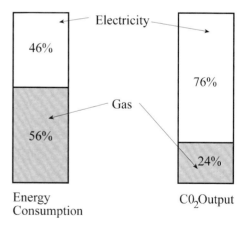

Figure 1.8 Percentage of total delivered energy use and CO_2 output attributed to gas and electricity consumption in an air-conditioned office.

An example of a strategy to supplement space heating in housing using a passive solar strategy is described below.

SOLAR STRATEGY

For passive solar design to work effectively a number of elements need to be considered simultaneously (figure 1.9). This will ensure that optimising one element does not cause detrimental effects elsewhere. Many of the methods used to optimise solar energy collection can lead to an increase in energy consumption or discomfort if not applied carefully.

The first stage in the strategy is to consider the usefulness of the solar gains. In a commercial building solar gains may be rejected as they would simply add to other gains and cause over heating. This also applies to domestic buildings in hot climates. If solar gains are considered to be of benefit then the following issues should be addressed - note the warnings shown in *italics*.

Figure 1.9 *Elements of a passive solar space heating strategy.*

1. Siting - Allow good solar access to the site.

Make sure buildings that are collecting solar energy for themselves do not overshadow nearby buildings to the north. The spacing out of buildings to avoid overshadowing of neighbouring buildings can allow local wind speeds to increase which would increase ventilation heat losses.

2. Form - Extend south facing facade to increase the

area for solar collection. Plan rooms so that habitable spaces are to the south and service rooms to the north.

Increasing the surface area of a building increases the area through which fabric heat losses occur.

3. Fabric - Increase the glazed area on the south side and reduce it on the north side.

At night and on overcast days solar gains will be non existent or minimal but heat losses will continue through the thermally weak glazing. During the day glare will occur if a bright window appears in the field of view. The building should be highly insulated but this, combined with solar heat gains, can result in overheating in summer. Reductions in the size of north facing glazing can lead to inadequate daylight levels.

4. Services - The heating system should be responsive, modulating its output in response to solar gains.

Savings in energy will not be made and discomfort will be caused if the output of the mechanical heating system is not reduced in response to solar heat gain.

5. Cooling - Provide shading devices on windows and thermal mass in the interior to avoid summertime overheating.

Shading devices should be selective, allowing gains in winter but rejecting them in summer. Blinds and Shades should not significantly reduce daylight levels.

Low energy design principles must be applied with care. There are numerous interactions that take place between form, fabric and services. A successful low energy design considers the building holistically, carefully assessing the impact any decisions have on the buildings overall performance.

1.4 Conclusion

There are three factors that necessitate the increased use of low energy principles in everyday design decisions. These are;

- Professional responsibility - given the value of low energy design principles to producing better buildings and reducing environmental impact, it is the duty of professionals in the construction industry to recommend low energy solutions whenever alternative choices occur.

- Increasing legislation - Governments, in recognition of the importance of energy issues have introduced legislation that aims to reduce building energy consumption. This legislation must be complied with.

- Client pressure - Many businesses have green policies covering the products sold or services provided. In many cases this now extends to the headquarters from which these businesses are run. As a result, many clients are now demanding a high level of energy efficiency from their new or refurbished corporate headquarters.

The government's target is to reduce UK greenhouse gas emissions to a level that is 12.5% less than 1990 levels by 2008 - 2012, with a desire of extending this to a 20% reduction if possible. Architects, building services engineers and other construction specialists can assist in meeting these targets by making energy conservation a consideration in all design decisions.

REFERENCES

1. Energy Consumption Guide 19: Energy Use in Offices. 1998

2. Department of the Environment. Digest, Environmental Protection and Water Statistics. No 12 1989.

3. British Gas, Gas and the Environment. Publication produced by British Gas Corporation Affairs, Grosvenor Road, London, 1992.

FURTHER READING

1. Chartered Institution of Building Services Engineers (CIBSE). Guide F: CIBSE Energy Efficiency Guide. 1998

02 SITE & CLIMATE

In this chapter we will find that;

- Energy is required to provide comfort inside a building by changing the uncomfortable external climate. It follows that the more severe the climate the more energy is required.

- When the interior is heated and it is cold outside, the temperature difference drives heat out through the external shell of the building.

- In the UK, sites at northern latitudes and those at high altitude have lower average external temperatures than southern and low lying areas.

- Degree days are a good method of expressing the severity of the climate in relation to space heating.

- The external temperature on the east, south and west faces of a building can be raised by providing good solar access to the site.

- Fabric heat loss rate can be reduced using thermal insulation.

- Some locations such as coasts, hilltops and flat open areas are more severely exposed to the wind than inland, urban sites.

- Wind speed drives the rate of ventilation heat loss, wind direction determines where ventilation air enters and leaves the building.

- Wind can be slowed down by wind barriers.

- Wind driven heat losses can be reduced by modifying the building form, modifying the arrangement of groups of buildings and by adding draught-proofing to the building.

- Driving rain can wet masonry and lower its insulating properties.

- Good solar access is necessary for passive solar heating.

- Avoidance of external obstructions near windows is essential to provide good levels of daylight.

- Buildings situated on sites polluted by noise and traffic fumes will have difficulty implementing passive ventilation strategies.

- Energy usage for commuting to out of town sites will be greater than for an inner city location with public transport facilities.

2.0 Introduction

Buildings are constructed so that humans can carry out their various activities in an appropriate environment, efficiently, safely and in thermal comfort. The shell of a building is a barrier between the varying external environment which can be uncomfortably cold or hot and the stable, comfortable internal environment. The building fabric acts as a moderator of climate but it is usual, during seasonal extremes, to use energy to maintain internal conditions. It follows therefore that the greater the deviation of the external environment from the required internal conditions the greater is the need for energy consumption.

In this chapter we will consider how the climate at a particular site is determined by geographic and topographic factors and how this climate affects the energy consumption of a building. We will consider how excess energy consumption can be limited by firstly modifying the site using landscaping and then enhancing the building itself.

2.1 Climate and Energy

The energy used to heat a building does not remain in the building but is lost from it in two ways known as fabric and ventilation heat losses. This section will consider these two forms of heat loss and introduce the effect of the climate on them.

Fabric heat losses arise when heat is transferred from the warm interior to the cold exterior through the external fabric. This occurs by a combination of three heat transfer mechanisms; conduction through the solid materials such as masonry, convection across air spaces such as cavities, and radiation across cavities and from the external masonry surface. Thermal properties of the fabric are discussed more fully in information panel 2 (IP2).

Ventilation heat losses occur when the warm air inside the building leaves and is replaced by cool air from outside.

The speed with which heat is lost in these two ways is known as the heat loss rate, measured in Joules per second (J/s) or Watts (W). The equations that are used to calculate the steady state heat loss rate from buildings for both fabric (Q_f) and ventilation (Q_v) heat loss rate are shown on page 23.

EFFECT OF CLIMATE

Figure IP3.1 on page 23 show the variables involved in determining the fabric and ventilation heat loss rates. Some of these are constants, determined by the building form and fabric, others are variable depending on the external climate.

Constants. The area, volume and internal temperature are all constant. The first two determined by the building form the latter by the building services that function to maintain a constant internal temperature.

Variables affected by the climate. In the following sections we will find that; the ventilation rate increases as the wind speed increases. The temperature difference between inside and outside increases as the external temperature falls and the U-value of masonry walls increases when wind and rain exposure increases. Each of these increases will result in larger heat loss rates. These affects will be discussed more fully in the sections below.

2.1.1 Macroclimate and Microclimate

Climatological processes arising from variations in solar energy deposition on the earth dictate the patterns of weather we encounter. The variation in solar energy deposition repeats annually. As a consequence the climatic variables including temperature, wind-speed and direction, solar intensity and humidity can be anticipated each year, on a national scale, with a degree of predictability.

At this stage the distinction between weather and climate must be made clear. The weather is the conditions prevailing at a particular time including wind speed, wind direction, insolation, air temperature, relative humidity and precipitation. Climate on the other hand is a statistical set of data based on weather records taken over a number of years. For example, a standard set of data used by building scientists is based on the period 1961 to 1990. From these records patterns can be determined. For example the most common wind direction in December in the UK is from the south west. This gives us information on which to make a good prediction of what the wind direction is likely to be in December. In reality on any given day in December the wind can come from any direction due to variations in the weather. Weather data is gathered by meteorological offices in the major cities in the UK. From this, tables of data are prepared giving us a good indication of what the climate is most likely to be for each month of the year. This is known as macroclimatic data since it is relevant for large regions of the UK.

The physical processes that dictate macroclimates can be modified on a local scale by variations in topography. For example the presence of coasts, valleys, dense woodland or hills all interact with the general climate of the region and cause local variations.

Buildings and other large natural features can further modify the local climate by wind channelling, solar trapping and overshadowing. These variations create a small region of distinctly different climatic conditions known as the microclimate.

CHOICE OF SITE

It is impractical to suggest choosing a site for a new development because it is most conducive to low energy consumption. This is because in practice little choice is available. Planning restrictions, the need to build at a particular location say for transport or closeness to commerce, land availability, cost of land or use of an existing site all limit the choices available. However, much can be achieved by considering the building and its relationship with the site to minimise the effect of climate on energy consumption.

Four areas of knowledge are required to minimise the effect of climatic conditions on energy consumption;

•   A knowledge of how climate varies with location. The location of a site has a profound effect on the climate it experiences. Site knowledge through local monitoring or meteorological office data will enable the more extreme climatic variables to be identified.

•   A knowledge of how climate affects heat loss. Wind, rain, solar intensity and external temperature all have a direct affect on a buildings heat loss or gain rate. An understanding of climate related heat loss processes is a necessary precursor for suggesting methods for preventing such heat loss.

•   A knowledge of how the landscape can be designed to minimise the effects of climate. A range of techniques are available that modify the general climate to create a "kind" micro-climate.

•   A knowledge of how the building fabric and its form can be enhanced so that it acts as a climatic moderator.

The above areas of knowledge will be addressed during discussions of each of the environmental variables affecting heat loss.

2.2 External Temperature

The space heating energy consumption of a building

is directly proportional to the difference between inside and outside environmental temperatures. Assuming we input heat to the building to maintain a constant internal temperature then the factor that determines the magnitude of the temperature difference is the size of the external temperature. The lower the outside temperature the greater the rate of heat loss for both fabric and ventilation routes.

UK TEMPERATURE PROFILE

There are two factors that strongly influence the temperature at a particular location in the UK these are the altitude and latitude of the site.

•   At a fixed altitude (fixed height above sea level) temperatures decrease with increasing latitude. Figure 2.1 shows the average daily external temperature at sea level for the UK measured over the heating season. It can be seen that the further north one goes the lower the average outside temperatures. This is further illustrated in Table 2.1 which shows the average monthly temperatures for Southampton, Manchester and Aberdeen. On average the temperature in Aberdeen is 1.5°C cooler than Manchester and 2.3°C cooler than Southampton.

•   At a fixed latitude, (fixed angular distance from the equator) temperatures decrease with increasing altitude. Typically the reduction in temperature is $0.6°C$ per 100m increase in altitude[1].

There are local variations in addition to these general rules. For example, the west coast experiences higher temperatures on average than the rest of the UK due to the effect of warm sea currents. Absorption of solar energy can create warm islands and depressions in the land experience lower than average outside temperatures due to cold air sinking and collecting in them.

DEGREE DAYS

The severity of the outside temperatures related to heating energy consumption is illustrated using a system known as degree days[2]. This is a method of expressing the depth and length of time the outside air temperature fell below a certain threshold. The

IP2 - Thermal Properties of Construction Materials

Heat moves naturally from a warm place to a cold place by a combination of the three heat transfer mechanisms; conduction, convection and radiation. Figure IP2.1 shows these mechanisms in relation to an insulated cavity wall.

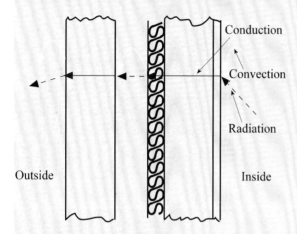

Figure IP2.1 Heat transfer mechanisms through an insulated cavity wall

Conduction is the heat transfer process through the solid parts of the external envelope. Conduction can be thought of as heat being passed from one molecule of the material to the next in the direction of decreasing temperature. It follows that conduction will occur more easily in dense materials i.e. those where the molecules are packed closely together. Conduction will be much more difficult in low density materials where the molecules are spaced further apart. This is witnessed in construction materials where dense products such as concrete conduct heat well and lightweight materials such as foamed plastics conduct heat poorly. We tend not to call dense materials conductors but we do refer to lightweight materials as insulators. Most buildings are made up of a mixture of the two types of material. The hard dense materials providing structural strength and the light-weight materials preventing heat transfer out of the building.

Convection is the mechanism of heat transfer through gases. Air in contact with a surface hotter than itself will become warmed. This warm air will rise and move away from the wall as it becomes less dense, carrying energy away with it. If this airstream comes in to contact with a surface that is cooler than itself then heat will be transferred from the air to the surface. It is by this mechanism that heat is transferred to and from surfaces in contact with air and across cavities in walls or double glazing systems.

Radiation does not require solid materials or air for heat exchange to take place. The exchange of thermal radiation takes place between the surfaces of a hot body and a cold body. The quantity of energy transferred depends on the temperature of the surfaces and the emissivity of the source surface and absorptivity of the receiving surface. Emissivity (E) is an indication of the ability of a surface to emit thermal radiation in comparison to a perfect emitter. The scale of values runs between 0 in which no energy will be radiated and 1 which indicates the surface is a perfect radiator. Most building materials have an emissivity of 0.9 indicating they are strong radiators of heat. Polished aluminium has an emissivity of 0.5. Absorptivity (A) is a similar concept but indicates the ability of a surface to absorb thermal radiation. For most building materials the value of the absorptivity is similar to the value of emissivity.

Radiation of heat is responsible for heat transfer from objects in a room such as internal walls and furniture to the inner surface of the external wall. It is also responsible for part of the heat transfer across cavities and loss of heat from the external surfaces. Radiative transfers are reduced in buildings by reducing the emissivity of surfaces. Two examples of how this is achieved are the use of foil backed insulation boards and low emissivity coatings on the inner pane of double glazed units.

THERMAL TRANSMITTANCE (The U-value)

When designing low energy buildings we need to select constructional elements that minimise heat transfer and keep the heat inside the building. This can only be achieved if we have a method of comparing the heat transfer properties of different types of constructional elements. The method used is to compare their thermal transmittances. The thermal transmittance, also known as the U-value (figure IP2.2), is a measure of the speed with which heat is lost through one square metre of the element with 1K temperature difference across its faces. The units are W/m²K. The higher the U-value the greater is the rate of heat loss through that element. The building regulations recognise the importance of U-values by setting maximum U-values for different elements. For roof, walls, windows and floor these are 0.16, 0.35, 2.0 and 0.25 W/m²K respectively. For more details see chapter 3. The U-value incorporates the thermal characteristics of each layer in the element. The following sections describe these thermal characteristics and show how the U-value is calculated using a masonry cavity wall as an example.

Figure IP2.2 U-value

THERMAL CONDUCTIVITY

There are obvious differences between the heat conducting properties of a layer of brick and a layer of polystyrene. But when we are comparing two types of brick or a piece of polystyrene with a block of mineral wool, the similarity of the two types of material means we need more precise information to make a comparison. Because of this we use standard terminology to allow us to compare the heat conducting properties of different materials.

For the comparison to be fair we require a fixed set of conditions under which the assessment of materials is made. The most basic measurement made is that of a materials thermal conductivity. Thermal conductivity is a measure of the rate of heat conduction through one cubic metre of a material with 1K temperature difference across two opposite faces. This is illustrated in figure IP2.3

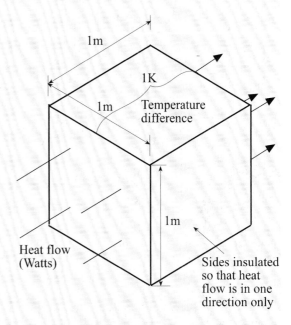

Figure IP2.3: Thermal conductivity

In reality measurements are carried out on small samples of material placed in a test cell. Four sides of the sample are insulated, one side of the material is heated and the rate of flow of heat through the sample to the opposite face is measured using thermometers. Some typical values of thermal conductivity are shown in table IP2.1 The larger the value of thermal conductivity the greater is the speed by which heat flows through the material. The table also shows that generally thermal conductivity increases with increasing density.

THERMAL RESISTANCE (R)

Thermal conductivity is essential for comparing different materials but is based on unit measurements. For actual construction thicknesses we use the term thermal resistance (m²K/W). This is a measure of the ability of an actual thickness of material to resist the passage of heat. It is based on the thermal conductivity and the thicknesss of the material used in the construction. This is illustrated in figure IP2.4.

Material	Density (kg/m3)	Thermal conductivity (W/mK)
slate	2700	1.9
sandstone	2100	1.3
brick engineering	2300	1.0
brick common	1790	0.72
plaster	1570	0.53
block (clinker)	1050	0.35
plaster board	960	0.16
pine	500	0.138
plaster lightweight	448	0.115
block aerated	400	0.08
carpet	186	0.06
glass fibre	12	0.04
mineral wool	150	0.04
expanded polystyrene	25	0.033

Table IP2.1 densities and thermal conductivities of common building materials.

Mathematically thermal resistance (R) is determined using the formula;

$$R = \frac{l}{k} \quad (m^2K/W)$$

Where:

l is the thickness of the material (m)
k is the thermal conductivity (W/mK)

For example the thermal resistance of 50mm (0.05m) of expanded polystyrene ($k = 0.033$ W/mK)

is $\quad \frac{0.05}{0.033} = \underline{1.5} \ m^2K/W$

To prevent heat loss from buildings the value of the thermal resistance should be as large as possible. From the above formula it can be seen that this is achieved by either increasing the thickness of the material or by

reducing the value of the thermal conductivity (k).

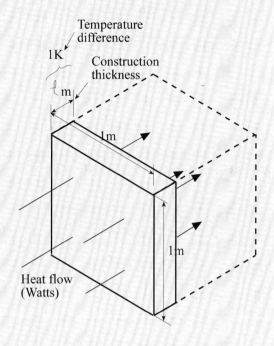

Figure IP2.4 Thermal resistance.

Material thermal resistances are used to calculate the U-value of the element along with airspace resistances which are discussed next.

CAVITY AND SURFACE RESISTANCE

Air gaps are present in many structural elements. In a masonry cavity wall the obvious air gap is the cavity itself. One of the main functions of the cavity is to prevent the passage of rain from the outer to inner leaves. It also offers a resistance to the movement of heat. The other resistances to heat flow are caused by still layers of air attached to the inner and outer surfaces of the element by friction, known as the inside surface resistance R_{si} and the outside surface resistance R_{so}. Heat transfer across air layers occurs due to convection and radiation. It follows that the size of the thermal resistance depends on the emissivity of the surface and the direction of heat flow (horizontal or vertical). Table IP2.2 shows how the thermal resistance of a cavity decreases when the emissivity of the surfaces changes from low to high as radiant heat exchange is facilitated. The outside surface resistance is created by still air attached to the outer surface of the wall and so is affected by the exposure category of the building as shown in table 2.3 in the main text.

Surface emissivity	Thermal Resistance (R_{cav}) m^{2}K/W
low	0.35
high	0.18

Table IP2.2 Values of R_{cav}

EXAMPLE CALCULATION OF A U-VALUE

Most methods of constructing the external envelope result in the creation of repeated thermal bridges through the layer. A thermal bridge is a high thermal conductivity pathway through an otherwise low thermal conductivity layer. Examples of this are mortar joints across a low density blockwork internal leaf and timber studs used to mount plasterboard spanning a layer of insulation applied to the internal surface of a wall. These thermal bridges can make up a substantial proportion of each square metre of the layer and so must be taken into account when calculating the U-value of the element.

The method used to calculate the U-value of elements with repeating thermal bridges is described in appendix B of part L1 of the Building Regulations. It involves the following steps;

1. Identify all heat flow paths through the element

2. Calculate the upper resistance limit (R_{upper}).

3. Calculate the lower resistance limit (R_{lower}).

4. Calculate the total resistance (R_T) of the wall from

$$R_T = \frac{R_{upper} + R_{lower}}{2}$$

5. Calculate the U-value of the wall using
$$U = \frac{1}{R_T} \quad (W/m^2K)$$

This is best illustrated by means of an example calculation of the U-value of a brick and block cavity wall with insulation within the cavity as shown in figure IP2.5.

Figure IP2.5 Heat flow paths through an insulated masonry cavity wall.

1. Identify all heat flow paths through the element

Figure IP2.5 indicates the two possible paths that heat can take whilst flowing through the element. Note that the thermal conductivity of the brick and mortar are similar and so can be considered to be a homogenous layer. The paths in terms of thermal resistance as determined in table IP2.3 are:

Route 1.... R_{si}, R_p, R_m, R_{ins}, R_{cav}, R_b, R_{so}
Route 2.... R_{si}, R_p, R_{bl}, R_{ins}, R_{cav}, R_b, R_{so}

Route 1 paths make up 10% and route 2 paths make up 90% of the overall wall area.

2. Calculate upper resistance limit

The upper resistance limit is calculated using:

$$R_{upper} = 1/(F_1/R_1 + F_2/R_2) \dots\dots\dots (1)$$

F_1 = Fractional area of route 1
F_2 = Fractional area of route 2
R_1 = Total thermal resistance of route 1
R_2 = Total thermal resistance of route 2
Determine the total thermal resistances of the two routes by summing individual thermal resistances along the

route.

$R_1 = 0.123 + 0.033 + 0.875 + 2.5 + 0.180 + 0.144 + 0.060$
$R_1 = 3.92 \ m^2K/W$

$R_2 = 0.123 + 0.033 + 0.553 + 2.5 + 0.180 + 0.144 + 0.060$
$R_2 = 3.59 \ m^2K/W$

Now calculate the upper resistance limit by substituting known values into equation 1 above.

$R_{upper} = 1/(0.1/3.92 + 0.9/3.59)$
$R_{upper} = 3.61 \ m^2K/W$

layer	Thickness (m)	Thermal conductivity (W/mK)	Thermal Resistance (m²K/W)
Surface Rsi	-	-	0.123
Plaster Rp	0.015	0.46	0.033
Mortar Rm (route 1)	0.105	0.12	0.875
Block Rbl (route 2)	0.105	0.19	0.553
Insulation Rins	0.075	0.03	
Cavity Rcav	-	-	0.180
Brick Rb	0.105	0.73	0.144
Surface Rso	-	-	0.060

Table IP2.3: Values of thermal resistance for each layer.

3. Calculate lower resistance limit

The lower resistance limit is calculated by adding the thermal resistance of each layer together. However the bridged layer is considered in terms of the fractional areas of each material. So for the black/mortar (bl/m) layer

$R_{bl/m} = 1/(F_{bl}/R_{bl} + F_m/R_m)$
$R_{bl/m} = 1/(0.9/0.553 + 0.1/0.875)$
$R_{bl/m} = 0.574 \ m^2W/K$

Now calculate lower resistance limit using the resistance of the block/mortar layer.

$R_{lower} = R_{si} + R_p + \mathbf{R_{bl/m}} + R_{ins} + R_{cav} + R_{br} + R_{so}$

$R_{lower} = 0.123 + 0.033 + \mathbf{0.574} + 2.5 + 0.180 + 0.144 + 0.060$
$R_{lower} = 3.61 \ m^2W/K$

4. Now calculate the U-value of the element.

The U-value is found using:

$U = 2/(R_{upper} + R_{lower})$

$U = 2/(3.61 + 3.61)$

$U = 0.28 \ W/m^2K$

If there are air gaps or metal ties penetrating the insulation layer that create more than a 3% increase in U-value, then further corrections to the U-value will be necessary to take this into account.

It can be seen in our calculation that the upper and lower resistance limits are the same. A much bigger effect will be noticed where there is substantial bridging of the insulation layer. One example is when structural members span the insulation in a concrete or steel framed wall.

REFERENCES

The method for calculating U-values is given in the following British Standards:

Walls and roof - BS EN ISO 6946:1997 Building components and building elements - Thermal resistance and thermal transmittance - Calculation method

Ground floor - BS EN ISO 13370:1998 Thermal performance of buildings - heat transfer via the ground - Calculation methods

Windows and doors - BS EN ISO 10077-1:2000 Thermal performance of windows, doors and shutters - Calculation of thermal transmittance - Part 1: Simplified methods, and prEN ISO 10077-2:2000 Thermal performance of windows, doors and shutters - Calculation of thermal transmittance - Part 2: Numerical methods for frames

IP3 - Steady State Heat Loss Rate

Heat is lost from a building through the envelope by conduction, convection and radiation and also by the escape of heated air from the building. These are known as fabric and ventilation heat losses respectively. Figure IP3.1 shows the equations used to calculate the speed with which heat is lost by these two mechanisms known as the fabric heat loss rate (Q_f) and the ventilation heat loss rate (Q_v).

$$Q_V = \frac{1}{3}.n.V.\Delta T$$

$$Q_f = \Sigma(U_x.A_x.)\Delta T$$

Figure IP3.1 Equations for fabric(Q_f) and ventilation(Q_v) heat loss rate

Where;

VENTILATION HEAT LOSS EQUATION

The size of ventilation heat losses depends on the temperature of the internal air compared to outside air (the warmer the air the greater its energy content) and the quantity of it leaving the building. As such the following variables are used in the equation;

n is the ventilation rate measured as the number of air changes per hour (ac/h). This is the number of times all of the air in the space is completely exchanged with fresh air in an hour. So for example if all of the warm air in a room were to be replaced by cool outside air in an hour then the ventilation rate would be 1.0 ac/h.

V is the volume of the space measured in cubic metres (m³). The amount of energy lost will depend on the volume of warm air leaving the building.

ΔT is the difference in temperature between the air inside the building and outside the building measured in degrees Kelvin (K). Note a change in temperature of 1K is the same as a change of 1 degree Centigrade (°C). We will use K here to be consistent with other texts. Temperatures in K are easily found by adding 273 to the temperature in Centigrade. For example, the room temperature at 21°C is equivalent to 294K.

FABRIC HEAT LOSS EQUATION

Fabric heat losses depend on the insulation value of the fabric and the area of envelope through which heat loss can take place. This changes for each individual element and so each element must be treated separately then added together. The one thing that is the same for each individual element is the temperature difference between inside and outside. As such the following variables appear in the fabric heat loss equation;

Σ. This is the symbol meaning 'add together'. It appears as the heat loss rate for each element must be calculated separately and then added together to give the heat loss rate for the entire envelope.

A_x is the area of element x (window, wall, floor, roof etc.) measured in square meters (m²).

U_x is the thermal transmittance of element x, also known as the U value, measured in W/m²K (see IP2). This is the heat loss rate in watts through 1 square metre of the element with 1K temperature difference across its faces.

ΔT is the inside - outside temperature difference as described above (K).

An example of how these equations are used to calculate the heat loss rate of a typical house is shown in IP3.1.

IP3.1 - Example Calculation

In this information panel the fabric and ventilation heat loss rates for the detached house shown in figure IP3.2. will be calculated

Figure IP3.2 Example house

Element	Area (m²)	U value (W/m²K)
Floor	56	0.25
Roof	56	0.16
Walls	115	0.35
Window/door	35	2.00

Table IP3.1 Example house data

FABRIC HEAT LOSS RATE

The U-value gives the heat loss rate through one square metre of a building element for 1K temperature difference across its internal and external faces. To determine the heat loss rate through the entire element we must multiply the U-value by the area of the element and the actual temperature difference across its faces. If the internal temperature is 21°C and the external temperature 0°C then the temperature difference, ΔT, is $21 - 0 = 21$°C.

For example the heat loss rate through the windows of the example house shown above is calculated from;

$$Q_{windows} = U_{windows} \times A_{windows} \times \Delta T ....(1)$$

where   Q   = heat loss rate (W)
U   = thermal transmittance (W/m²K)
A   = area of element (m²)
ΔT = temperature difference between inside and outside air temperatures (K)

Substituting the given values for the windows from table IP3.1 into equation 1 above we get

$$Q_{windows} = 2.0 \times 35.0 \times 21.0 \qquad (W)$$
$$Q_{windows} = \underline{1470}\ W$$

The heat loss rates for all of the elements are shown tabulated in table IP3.2. The final column shows the percentage contribution to the total fabric heat loss rate made by each element. Even though the windows have the smallest area they are responsible for over half of the fabric heat loss rate from the building.

Element	U	A	ΔT	Q	%
Walls	0.35	115	21	845.3	32
Floor	0.25	56	21	294.0	11
Roof	0.16	56	21	30.0	1
Window	2.00	35.0	21	1470.0	56
TOTAL				2639.3	100

Table IP3.2 Elemental heat loss rates.

VENTILATION HEAT LOSS RATE

The volume (V) of the building is 280m³. We will assume some attention has been paid to draughtproofing and the average whole house ventilation rate (n) is 0.75 ac/h. These values can be used in the equation for ventilation heat loss rate.

$$Q_v = \tfrac{1}{3} \times n \times V \times \Delta T$$

substituting the known values in gives,

$$Q_v = \tfrac{1}{3} \times 0.75 \times 280 \times 21$$
$$Q_v = \underline{1470}\ W$$

The total heat loss rate from the house is $Q_f + Q_v$
i.e $Q_{total} = 2639.3 + 1470$
$Q_{total} = \underline{4109.3}\ W$

threshold is known as the base temperature. The base temperature is 15.5°C and it is assumed that if the outside temperature is at or above this level then no heating is required in the building. If the outside air temperature falls below this threshold then space heating will be required.

Figure 2.1 Sea level dry bulb temperatures averaged over the heating season (October - April inclusive (data from CIBSE Guide A).

Location	Average External Temperature (°C)
Aberdeen	5.9
Manchester	7.4
Southampton	8.2

Table 2.1 Average external temperature at three locations measured over the heating season.

Degree days are calculated by summing the number of

24 hour periods over which the external temperature falls 1°C below the base temperature. For example if the external temperature is 13.5°C for 12 hours this is equivalent to 12 hours x 2°C below base line = 24 degree hours or one degree day. It follows therefore that the larger the number of degree days the more cold the climate and the greater the demand for space heating. Table 2.2 shows the total degree days for four regions measured over the heating season for the period 1984 - 1985. It can be seen that the south west of England has the lowest degree day total and the figures for the other locations increase the further north the location. Figure 2.2 shows isopleths of the 20 year average degree days for the UK. The darker the shading the higher the degree day total and greater the demand for space heating.

Location	Number of degree days
Cornwall	1800
London	2100
Manchester	2300
Central Scotland	2600

Table 2.2 Average degree day totals for four regions over the heating season.

This figure confirms the two principles governing outside temperatures described above. The further north in the country the higher the degree day totals, also the high lying parts of Devon and Cornwall show higher degree day totals as do the Pennines and the highlands of Scotland

As well as describing the severity of the climate, degree days can be used in energy management (chapter 11). One example is in the normalisation of energy consumption's in similar buildings in different parts of the UK. For example a business may have identical offices in Aberdeen and Southampton. The energy manager cannot compare the relative performance of these buildings directly as it is colder in Scotland therefore the building located there will naturally consume more energy. However this extra energy consumption could be masking additional energy consumption arising from a heating system fault. By dividing the energy consumption's of both buildings by the degree day totals in their respective locations the energy consumption per degree day is determined.

This eliminates the difference caused by the lower external temperatures and reveals any differences in energy consumption due to other factors.

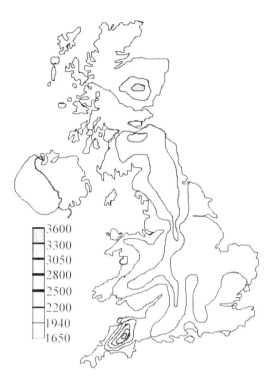

Figure 2.2 Degree day isopleths. Diagram from Fuel Efficiency Booklet 7: Degree Days. (1993) © Crown Copyright

LANDSCAPE AND SITE

The essential requirement for raising external temperatures is to allow good solar access to the site. For this to be achieved overshadowing by tall objects such as hills, trees or buildings to the south of the site must be avoided. On an existing site with obstructions to the south, the degree of overshadowing can be estimated using geometry and a knowledge of the suns angles of azimuth and altitude (see IP7), the height spacing and arrangement of buildings and obstructions.

Figure 2.3 shows the minimum shadow lengths created

by a house with a roof ridge 8m above the ground. Two shadows are shown, the first is for the worst case situation i.e. noon on the winter solstice, December 21st, when the sun reaches its lowest mid day position in the year this gives the maximum noon shadow length. The second line shows the position at noon on March 21st and September 21st i.e. around the beginning and end of the heating season. It can be seen that the second dwelling shown 24 metres to the south of the first will be overshadowed at noon during the depths of winter but will receive sunlight at the beginning and end of the heating season.

Figure 2.3 Shadow length at noon winter solstice and spring/autumn equinox.

Good solar access to a site can be achieved by;

* spacing out and staggering the buildings so that they do not overshadow each other (figure 2.4). This approach can create conflict with the economics of housing development that dictates that houses should be densely packed on the site to increase the number of units on the land.

* Roof pitches should be kept low, typically 40°, to reduce ridge height but greater than 10° to avoid wind suction (see table 2.4). This must be considered with due regard for minimum pitches specified for example when using slates.

* Where the site has a mixture of building heights keep low buildings to the south. This creates less over shadowing.

* Avoid placing minor buildings, such as a garage or store room to the south of the main building.

Sites on north facing slopes will be disadvantaged as shown in figure 2.5. It can be seen that in comparison to figure 2.3 when the site is sloping 5° to the north the overshadowing effect is increased. The effect of this reduced solar access is to increase the energy consumption. This was revealed in a mathematical study of the effect of site slope on the space heating energy consumption of domestic buildings[3]. The study found that in comparison to a flat site a 5° northerly slope increased the energy consumption of a typical house by 400kWh/year whereas a 5° southerly slope decreased the annual energy consumption by 150 kWh/year.

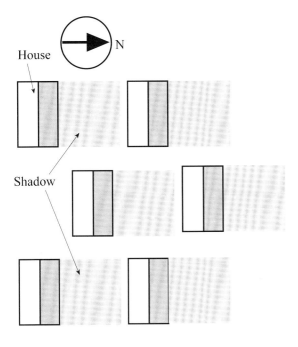

Figure 2.4 Housing layout for solar access.

The use of dark paved materials enhances the absorption of heat in the general vicinity of a building. Transfer of this heat to the surrounding air increases air temperatures. As a result, external air temperatures are elevated on the south side of buildings. It must be remembered however that dark paving materials, due to their reduced daylight reflectivities, may result in diminished daylight entry into the building.

The solar heating effect will be swept away if winds are allowed free access to the site. One way of trapping this pool of heated air is to form the building into a sun

trap arrangement (figure 2.6). The arms creating the sun trap should kept short to avoid an unacceptable degree of overshadowing at the early and latter parts of the day.

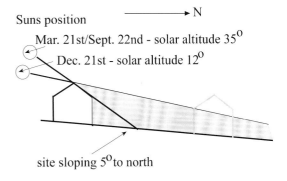

Figure 2.5 Effect of a sloping site on solar access.

The effect of solar absorption by building materials and protection from winds increases average temperatures. This leads to reduced heat losses and pre-heating of infiltration air. The gross effect is clearly demonstrated in cities which are typically 0.5°C warmer on average than the surrounding countryside. This is known as the heat island effect.

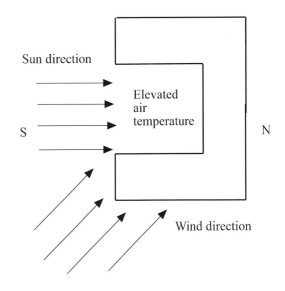

Figure 2.6 *Building form to create a sun trap.*

BUILDING ENHANCEMENT

If a proposed building is to be sited in an area with lower than average outside temperatures it will have a greater than average demand for space heating, resulting in higher costs. These higher fuel costs can be saved by applying additional insulation to the building. The cost of this insulation will be recouped from the value of energy savings made. Having returned the capital cost the savings will then continue for many years into the future.

Insulation is a passive and robust method of saving energy. Following installation it requires no monitoring or adjustments unlike devices such as electronic heating controls.

An example of the usefulness of additional insulation can be seen when comparing the heat losses through $1m^2$ of masonry wall constructed to a U-value of $0.35W/m^2K$ in both Southampton and Aberdeen. In Southampton 10.3 kWh of energy is required over a heating season to maintain $21^\circ C$ inside against the average outside temperature prevailing at that location. The same wall in Aberdeen would require 12.1 kWh of energy. An increase in energy requirement of 14% due to the lower outside temperatures.

The wall in Aberdeen would require additional insulation to reduce its U-value to $0.31W/m^2K$ to have the same heat loss as the wall in Southampton. This principle also applies to other external elements of the building such as roofs, floors and glazing.

2.3 Windspeed and Direction

There are two measurable aspects to the wind environment at a site. These are the windspeed measured in metres per second (m/s) and wind direction expressed in terms of the compass direction from which the wind is originating. Both aspects have an affect on ventilation heat loss rate and a small affect on fabric heat loss rate.

When wind hits a building it creates a pressure difference between the windward and leeward sides.

This drives cool air into the building and draws warm air out of the other side (figure 2.7). The energy used to heat the internal air is lost from the building. As the wind speed increases so does the pressure difference across the building. This in turn increases the ventilation rate. Figure 2.8 shows how the ventilation rate of a low energy building increases as the wind speed increases. In addition, it can be seen from the ventilation heat loss equation on page 23 that the ventilation heat loss rate increases in direct proportion to the increased ventilation rate. All of this means that increased wind speed increases the ventilation heat loss rate.

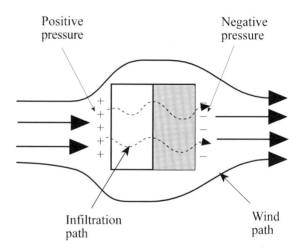

Figure 2.7 Wind induced infiltration.

The direction of the wind has two effects, firstly its direction dictates the temperature of the wind. Typically easterly and northerly winds are coldest whilst southerly and westerly winds tend to be warmer. Because of this the prevailing wind direction will have a strong influence on the temperature of infiltration air entering the building. Secondly, the wind direction determines which faces of the building the pressure difference acts across. If these faces contain openings such as doors, windows, cracks or service entries then infiltration will take place more easily. If the wind hits a well sealed facade such as a gable wall with no openings then it will be more difficult for infiltration to take place and the effect of the windspeed on heat loss will be less severe.

Figure 2.8 Increase in infiltration rate with increasing windspeed.

EFFECT OF WIND ON SURFACE RESISTANCE

There is a layer of air attached by friction to the surfaces of all building elements. This still layer of air adds to the thermal resistance of the wall. Inside the building it is known as the inside surface resistance (R_{si})outside, on the exterior surface, it is known as the outside surface resistance (R_{so}) (see page 20). The size of R_{si} depends on the orientation of the surface - whether vertical or horizontal as this affects convective movement of the layer, it also depends on the emissivity and absorptivity of the surface. These are the ability of the surface to emit and absorb thermal radiation respectively. R_{so} is affected by the same two factors but is also affected by external weather conditions. If the surface is exposed then the still layer of air will be swept away and the thermal resistance it adds to the element will be lost.

R_{so} only contributes a small percentage to the total thermal resistance of a well insulated wall. For example a wall of U-value 0.35 W/m^{2}K has only 1.75% of this provided by the outside surface resistance. But for elements with a large U value such as single glazing with a U-value of 5 W/m^{2}K, R_{so} contributes 20% of the total.

The effect of wind is seen when considering the variation of outside surface resistance and U-value of single glazing, in relation to changes in the exposure category of the glazing. From table 2.3 It can be seen that the heat loss rate through single glazing increases by 20% as the exposure category changes from sheltered to exposed.

	Exposure category		
	sheltered	normal	exposed
R_{so} (m^{2}K/W)	0.11	0.07	0.03
U value (W/m^{2}K)	5.00	5.60	6.00

Table 2.3 Effect of exposure on outside surface thermal resistance (R_{so}) and single glazing thermal transmittance(U-value).

UK WIND PROFILE

The UK is one of the windiest places in Europe. Figure 2.9shows average annual windspeeds for the UK that are exceeded for 10% of the time. High windspeeds are typically experienced at the top of hills, coastal regions and at the edges of smooth terrain such as lakes and fields.

The wind is slowed by friction when it passes over rough terrain. Because of this windspeeds tend to be lower over inland and urban sites. At any given location wind speed increases with altitude. It is known that on average windspeeds increase by 7% for every 100m increase in altitude[4]. Tall buildings may be sheltered on the ground floor but experience high wind speeds on the upper floors. The increase in windspeed with height will be more extreme on hilltops due to the way in which the airflow is forced upwards and over the top as shown in figure 2.10.

Other topography can also modify wind speeds. For example, the wind can be channelled through valleys or between tall buildings. In this situation the same volume of air is trying to pass through a small gap and so its speed must increase to maintain the same volume flow rate.

LANSDCAPING

Wind picks up speed when its travel is unhindered. Contact with any surface will create drag and slow the wind down. The more coarse the surface the greater the drag and slowing effect. One of the roughest natural landscapes is coarse vegetation. We can utilise this effect to reduce wind speed by planting rows of trees, in-filled with shrubs around the trunk, to reduce the wind speed. This reduces windspeeds up to the height of the trees.

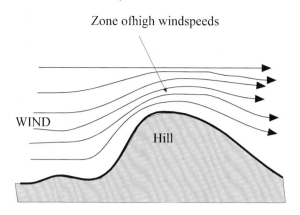

Figure 2.10 High windspeeds on hilltops.

Figure 2.9 Average annual windspeeds (m/s) exceeded for 10% of the time.

The effectiveness of a windbreak depends on its permeability. Permeability is a measure of how easily the air can pass through the windbreak. Values range from 0% to 100% where 100% is no obstruction to the wind such as that offered by an open field and 0% is an impermeable structure through which no wind can pass such as a brick wall or earth mound. Most planted and fence type wind barriers have a permeability within this range depending on the number of air gaps through it. Figure 2.11 shows the impact of barriers with zero and 50% permeability on windspeeds.

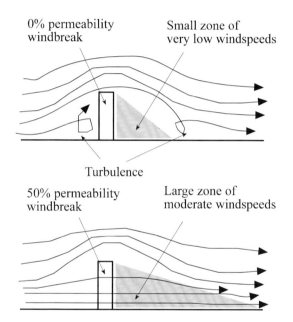

Figure 2.11 Effect of barrier permeability on airflow

The impermeable windbreak creates a small zone of still air close to the rear of the structure. This is useful if a small highly protected zone is required such as a small yard or building entrance. Glazed walls are often used to protect outdoor swimming pools in this way. However turbulence created by the wind being forced up and over the wall creates eddies. This rapid, random air movement causes discomfort to people outside of the still zone and encourages leaf and litter collection in the turbulent wind vortices before and after the wind barrier. A windbreak with a permeability of 40-50% allows some wind through its structure making the airflow pattern less turbulent. The overall effect does not completely eradicate the wind but does create a larger zone of moderate wind speeds.

Care must be taken to site any trees with sufficient separation from the building to avoid overshadowing it from the effects of solar gain. As a rough guide a minimum gap of 4 -5 times the height of the trees is recommended between the building and windbreak. By choosing trees that lose their leaves in winter solar access can be maintained even when the sun is at a low altitude. However the effectiveness of the windbreak will be diminished when out of leaf.

A tree belt, unless planted with mature trees and shrubs, will take a number of years to grow sufficiently high to be effective. The cost of land set aside for landscaping and the cost of the trees themselves will need to be recouped from the value of saved heating energy. However there are non-energy advantages to shelter belts these are; the enhanced aesthetics of sites planted with trees; the creation of habitats for wildlife, the sequestration of carbon dioxide and the increased comfort of persons using the outside spaces due to reduced wind speeds.

If a site wide windbreak cannot be accommodated consideration should be made to planting at the corners of buildings where windspeeds are particularly high as the air makes its way around the building.

BUILDING ENHANCEMENT

Fabric improvements can be made that reduce the infiltration rate at all wind speeds. These techniques are discussed more fully in chapter 5. The general principles are;

- seal the building envelope to remove any infiltration routes into and out of the building.

- carefully position openings to avoid the predominant wind direction.

- the main entrance doors should not be on opposite faces of the building as this would allow infiltration air to pass easily through the building from high to low pressure zones.

- entrances should not be positioned at the corners of buildings as windspeeds will be greatest here as it moves around the building.

The form of individual buildings and the arrangement of groups of buildings and can be designed to reduce their interaction with the wind. Generally this involves avoiding direct obstruction of the wind which would cause it to create large pressure differences across the building. In effect it is advantageous to make the building more streamlined so the air flows past it rather than set up pressure differences. In addition the grouping of buildings should aim to slow windspeeds across the site rather than offer long channels through which the wind can build up speed.

Table 2.4 lists the ideas used to reduce the sensitivity of individual buildings to the wind. Table 2.5[5] lists the suggestions for avoiding wind channelling around groups of buildings.

Individual Buildings - Low Wind Impact
Avoid 'flat' roofs with a pitch less than 10° - wind passing over these roofs causes an upward suction which can draw air vertically out of the building
Step back successive storeys on high rise buildings - The pyramid effect helps smooth wind flow around the building
Use hipped roofs with pitches of 30 - 45° on housing - this encourages smooth airflow
Avoid long walls - the shorter the extra path length the wind must travel to circumnavigate a wall the slower it will travel

Table 2.4 Reducing the impact of the wind on individual buildings.

2.4 Driving Rain

In the UK rain is a common occurrence and buildings are adequately served with rainwater drainage systems to deal with rain falling on the roof. However, when the rain combines with wind it can produce driving rain. Driving rain is rain that falls at an angle to the vertical and so can wet masonry walls.

The thermal conductivity of masonry materials depends on the density of the material . Table IP2.1 on page 20 shows how the thermal conductivity of brick varies with density. The lower the density the less heat is conducted out of the building. Low densities are achieved by voids in the material that are filled with air. In driving rain the masonry becomes wet and the voids are filled with water. Water conducts heat better than air ans as a consequence the thermal conductivity of a wet material increases. The thermal conductivity of brickwork with a density of $1700kg/m^3$ for 1% and 5% moisture content are 0.62 and 0.84W/mK respectively, an increase in thermal conductivity of 35%.[6] A masonry cavity wall constructed to have a U-value of 0.35 W/m^2K at 1% moisture content will have a U-value of 0.36 W/m^2K at 5% moisture content an increase in heat loss rate of 3%.

Groups of Buildings - Low Wind Impact
Stagger buildings on the site instead of using regular rows - this removes clear pathways through which the wind could be channelled or pick up speed. If a long row is unavoidable limit its length to under 24m.
Keep buildings heights similar - the wind passing over a building may then encounter a higher building this could reverse the direction of wind flow causing turbulence.
Arrange buildings into courtyards - this creates a central sheltered zone. It is more useful if solar gains are also encouraged in the space.
Avoid patterns that look like a funnel on plan - wind will be channelled through funnel shaped arrangements. If there is a possibility of wind being collected leave gaps in the rows (>3m) to allow the wind to percolate out.

Table 2.5 Reducing the impact of the wind on groups of buildings.

UK DRIVING RAIN PROFILE

Figure 2.12 is a map of the UK showing areas affected by driving rain as indicated by the exposure category of the area. It can be seen that the west coast is particularly exposed and therefore susceptible to driving rain. This is because south west and westerly winds tend to be warm but, having travelled over the oceans, carry a great deal of moisture which falls out as rain over land. By the time the wind reaches the east coast its speed has been reduced by friction over land and the rain has already fallen. This generally makes the east coast an area of lower exposure and driving rain index.

Figure 2.12 UK exposure category map. (GPG95) © Crown Copyright

BUILDING ENHANCEMENT

Traditional buildings found in wet areas such as the Pennines utilised masonry methods which helped shed water from the masonry surface (figure 2.13). In new buildings masonry materials should be water resistant or treated with water repellent coatings to prevent them becoming saturated. Any coatings should be permeable to water vapour to allow moisture within the masonry to escape. Reducing the U-value of a masonry wall using additional insulation reduces the significance of the contribution made by the external masonry layer and so the effect of moisture content is less of a concern.

LANDSCAPE

The landscaping methods mentioned previously under wind effects will offer some protection against driving rain. If the horizontal component of the windspeed can be reduced then the rain is less likely to impinge upon the vertical masonry surfaces.

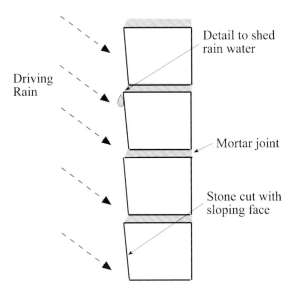

Figure 2.13 Traditional stone detail designed to clear rainwater from face of the wall.

2.5 Solar Radiation

The two thermal effects of solar radiation that are important in reducing energy consumption are the warming effect on the external air (section 2.2) and also the contribution it makes to space heating when it enters the building. The other important component of solar radiation is daylight which, when introduced into buildings, can offset the need for electric lighting. Passive solar design is considered more fully in chapter 8 and daylighting design in chapter 6. This section will consider the availability of solar energy.

UK SOLAR PROFILE

Figure 2.14 shows the average solar irradiation (MJ/m^2) for the UK. It can be seen that the daily solar energy available on the north coast of Scotland is 8MJ/m^2 compared to 11 MJ/m^2 on the south coast of England.

Figure 2.14 UK average solar irradiation map.

LANDSCAPE

Solar access requires the avoidance of overshadowing caused by tall trees and buildings situated to the south of the site.

The majority of UK trees are beginning to come into leaf by mid April. By mid May they are in full leaf, with single trees typically allowing through only 18% of the solar radiation incident upon them. By mid September the majority of trees are beginning to lose their leaves this process is complete by mid October. When out of leaf the trees typically allow through 65% of the solar radiation incident upon them[7].

Buildings block out direct solar radiation and so their spacing and roof ridge height should be planned to allow good solar access to buildings to the north. One way of doing this is to keep roof pitches at a shallow angle. Some degree of overshadowing is inevitable in all but the most open sites in mid winter when the solar altitude is at its lowest.

2.6 Passive Ventilation and Cooling

Since comfort cooling was developed early in the last century, sealed and air conditioned office buildings have been seen by property consultants as the most desirable and easiest to let. However, the energy used for air conditioning and the damage caused to the ozone layer by leaking refrigerants has seen a shift towards naturally ventilated and cooled buildings (chapter 10).

A central requirement of this natural strategy is the presence of ventilation paths such as opening windows. One barrier to this is external air and noise pollution as this would enter along with the ventilation air. As a result, designers of passively ventilated buildings should ensure the site is not near sources of environmental pollution such as factories or major roads. If the site is affected by these problems then adjustment of the orientation and location of the building is needed to ensure openings are away from sources of pollution.

Natural ventilation is driven by the wind and stack effects, exposing the building to the wind by avoiding obstructions such as trees will encourage single sided and cross ventilation in narrow plan buildings. The building should be well sealed so that the natural ventilation can be used when wanted by opening and closing purpose built openings such as windows.

PASSIVE COOLING

Just as we try to raise external temperatures to reduce space heating energy consumption, depression of external temperatures will reduce cooling energy consumption. The two strands to this strategy involve shading external spaces from the influence of the sun and the introduction of evaporative cooling. Both of these functions can be provided by trees. Leaves on trees require sunlight and so have evolved to intercept the sun. This shades the spaces below. The movement of nutrients from root to branch occurs as a result of transpiration which involves the evaporation of water from the leaves. For water to evaporate it must absorb

latent energy. In doing so it cools the surrounding air. Fountains and water features can also reduce ambient temperatures through evaporation. They also add an important psychological element causing occupants to 'feel' cooler because of the sight and sound of the water feature.

2.7 Transport

Buildings do not just consume energy for space conditioning. Figure 2.15 shows the energy inputs to a building throughout its life. These can be generally categorised as energy for production of materials and delivery to site, the construction process, energy in use, energy used in conveying the workforce to the building and finally energy to demolish and recycle or dispose of materials.

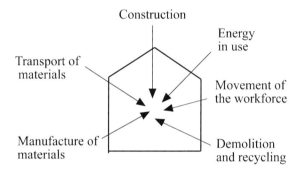

Figure 2.15 Building lifetime energy flows.

By far the greatest proportion of energy consumed occurs whilst the building is in use i.e. energy to run building services and also to deliver staff and materials to and from the workplace.

In many cases the daily petrol energy used in cars during the journey to work can be of a similar size to the energy used by the building services. This has been illustrated in an energy usage survey of the offices of the Cheltenham and Gloucester building society where the commuting energy usage was $334 \text{kWh/m}^2/\text{y}$. This compares with a gas and electricity consumption of 135 and $369 \text{kWh/m}^2/\text{y}$ respectively. It can be seen that the annual car fuel consumption is almost two and a half times that of the gas energy use and of a similar size to the electricity energy use[8].

Private cars use more fuel per passenger mile than public transport. To reduce transportation energy usage building planners can assess the closeness of their chosen site to suitable public transport systems. As with other energy issues a balance is required between this and other factors that determine the location of a building. Examples are the closeness to markets for goods, closeness to motorway links and proximity to the community using the services the building provides.

2.8 Conclusion

The preceding sections have illustrated that the climate of a site can have a strong influence on the energy consumption of a building constructed on it. This influence can be positive as in the case of solar access for passive solar space heating or detrimental as in the case of uncontrolled infiltration due to exposure to the wind. In both cases careful consideration of the climate, landscape and building fabric can reduce the worst effects of the climate on a buildings energy consumption.

One point of note is that the climate as described may be subject to change due to global warming. The climatic effects of global warming are still being debated. Any change in the UK climate will require a change in the ways that buildings respond to it. Some of the predictions of climate change are;

Increased incidence of high windspeeds and greater intensity and frequency of storms - This will not only increase the wind induced heat losses described in section 2.3 but will require greater consideration of wind loading factors in structural design.

Hotter summers - Most UK buildings do not require air conditioning for comfort since the summer cooling period is short. However, prolonged periods of high temperatures especially when temperatures do not fall significantly at night, can disrupt passive cooling strategies based on exposed mass and night time ventilation (see chapter 10).

Colder winters - Average temperatures encountered during the heating season may fall. Some predictions suggest that melting ice caps could reverse the gulf stream that keeps the UK warmer than comparable coun-

tries at the same latitude. This would result in a mini ice age. The resulting low temperatures would require a drastic increase in insulation levels to maintain comfort and minimise energy consumption levels.

Increased rainfall - Predictions suggest rainfall rates could fall in southern European countries leading to drought. In the UK rainfall rates could increase leading to greater incidences of driving rain and flooding.

REFERENCES

1. Building Research Establishment. BRE digest 350 Climate and Site Development Part 2: General Climate of the UK. p3. HMSO 1990

2. Energy Efficiency Office. Fuel Efficiency Booklet 7: Degree Days. HMSO 1993

3. Project Summary 045 Estate Layout for Passive Solar Housing Design. Ref ETSU S 1126 (1990)

4. Building Research Establishment. BRE digest 350 Climate and Site Development Part 1 : General Climate of the UK. p3. HMSO 1990

5. Building Research Establishment. BRE digest 350 Climate and Site Development Part 3: Improving Microclimate Through Design. p7. HMSO 1990

6. CIBSE Guide A Thermal Properties of Building Structures, pA3-5 CIBSE Publications 1980

7. Building Research Establishment. BRE digest 350 Climate and Site Development Part 3: Improving Microclimate Through Design. p6. HMSO 1990

8. Standeven, M., Cohen R. and Bordass W. PROBE 3 C&G Chief Office. pp 31-34. Building Services Journal, February 1996

03 F O R M

In this chapter we will find that;

- Increasing the external surface area of a building increases the fabric heat loss rate.

- Fabric heat losses can be reduced by adding additional insulation.

- Increasing the size of a building reduces its surface area to volume ratio.

- Increasing the surface area by adopting a narrow floor plan allows the building to take advantage of passive solar gains, daylight and natural ventilation.

- One method of assessing the balance between heat loss and passive energy gains for alternative floor plans is the LT method of design.

- Increasing the volume of a building increases the ventilation heat loss rate.

- Ventilation heat losses can be optimised by increasing the floor area to volume ratio.

- Ventilation heat losses can be reduced by sealing the external fabric of the building.

- The internal planning of spaces to match external thermal and lighting conditions can lead to energy savings.

- Grouping dwellings together reduces the number of external walls through which heat loss can occur and therefore reduces energy usage.

- Cooling energy consumption can be reduced by increasing the volume of rooms.

3.0 Introduction

There are many factors that have an influence on the form of a building. Cost is a major factor, simple cubical buildings are less expensive to construct than complex forms. Planning and design considerations may require the design of a building to be influenced by the form of its neighbours. Functional requirements and aesthetics also have an important role in deciding the form of a building. For example some functions can only take place in a large volumes such as cinemas and certain manufacturing processes.

The internal and external form of a building has a significant impact on its energy consumption. Some of these impacts have already been discussed in chapter 2 where methods were presented for reducing the impact of the wind on individual buildings by creating more streamlined forms (Table 2.4). There are also some aspects of form which will be discussed in subsequent chapters, one example of this is in chapter 10 where the use of towers and sloping ceilings are described as a means of encouraging natural stack ventilation.

In this chapter we will discover that changing the form of a building can reduce energy consumption in one area but increase it in another. Specifically these are that increased surface area increases fabric heat loss rates but also allows the capture of free energy flows. Secondly, increasing the volume of a building increases ventilation heat loss rates but also reduces ventilation and cooling energy consumption. Often a compromise has to be made to obtain an overall reduction in energy consumption. This compromise must be informed by the energy flows in the building as described in chapter 1. For example, in domestic buildings there is a high demand for space heating and a low demand for ventilation and space cooling. As a consequence domestic room volumes should be kept small. In commercial buildings it is desirable to avoid air conditioning, one method of doing this is to increase room volumes.

The following chapter describes the effect that modifying the internal and external form has on building energy consumption.

3.1 Surface Area and Fabric Heat Loss

The formula for the steady state heat loss rate through the fabric of a particular building element has been given previously in figure IP3.1 in information panel 3. The equation shows that the fabric heat loss rate (Q_f) is directly proportional to the area of the element. Therefore, any changes to the form that increase the surface area will result in an increased heat loss rate.

This can be investigated further by comparing the surface areas of four detached buildings with the same volume but different floor plans leading to different surface areas. Room heights, window area and total floor area are the same in all four shapes. The only difference is in surface area (figure 3.1). The shapes are:

- Square, when combined with its height this form represents the smallest practical surface area for a given volume. The actual smallest surface area to volume ratio is obtained by a sphere but this form is not often used in practice.

- Elongated, the square plan is stretched into a rectangle. The width of the building is reduced and the length is extended. This has resulted in slight increases to the wall area in comparison to the square as shown in table 3.0

- Cross, this form is highly convoluted and results in a large increase in wall area

- Bungalow, this is a single storey building. This form results in a reduction in wall area in a manner similar to a semi-detached house. This eliminates external walls. The floor and roof on the other hand have doubled in size.

Table 3.1 shows the total surface area of each shape and compares them to the square plan building that is taken as the standard. It can be seen from table 3.1 that

the elongated, cross and bungalow plan forms have 4, 20 and 29% more surface area respectively than the square plan.

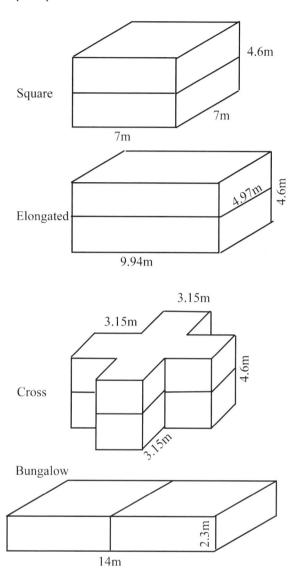

Figure 3.1 Buildings with different plan shapes

However, the increase in surface area does not represent the increase in heat loss rate since different surfaces have different thermal transmittance values (U-values) (see IP3). This means that the increase in heat loss rate will be greatest when a surface of high U-value increases in area. To take this into account we must weight each surface in terms of its heat loss rate, by multiplying the area of each element by a weighting factor. The weighting factors we will use are the U-values as shown in table 3.2. The outcome of this exercise is shown in table 3.3.

Plan shape	Area of element (m²)		
	Wall	**Floor**	**Roof**
Square	129	49	49
Elongated	137	49	49
Cross	174	49	49
Bungalow	97	98	98

Table 3.0 Areas of building elements for various plan shapes

Plan shape	Total surface area (m²)	Area relative to square
Square	227	1.00
Elongated	236	1.04
Cross	272	1.20
Bungalow	295	1.29

Table 3.1 : Surface areas of the four building shapes relative to the square plan form

Element	Weighting Factor
Walls	0.35
Roof	0.16
Windows	2.00
Floor	0.25

Table 3.2 : Weighting factors for each element of the building

Plan shape	Weighted surface area (W/K)	Weighted area relative to square
Square	128	1.00
Elongated	131	1.03
Cross	148	1.16
Bungalow	148	1.23

Table 3.3 : Heat loss factors for various shapes of building

By comparing the relative surface areas (table 3.1) and weighted surface area (table 3.3) it can be seen that the actual heat losses are lower than suggested simply by looking at total surface area increases. In particular the bungalow has seen a considerable improvement between total area increase and increases in heat loss. This is because the element with the largest increase in area is the roof and this has the lowest thermal transmittance of all the elements.

The conclusion is that any deviation from a square plan and cubical form will result in increased fabric heat losses. However the size of these losses can be reduced by adding additional insulation to the elements that have increased in area.

As well as adopting a cubical form a number of other techniques can be used that result in a reduced surface area. These are;

- Use insulated ceilings rather than insulated exposed pitched roofs

- Avoid projections and extensions causing deviation from a cubical form

- Make external porches unheated or, if heated, make them internal halls

- Attach unheated spaces such as a garage or conservatory to external walls to buffer it from the external elements.

- Use flat glazing systems as opposed to bay windows

SURFACE AREA TO VOLUME RATIO

As stated in Chapter 1 there is a difference in energy usage between housing and commercial buildings. In housing space heating energy use dominates. In larger commercial buildings space heating still exists but lighting, ventilation and possibly air conditioning take on an increased importance. This is in part due to the different activities in the two types of buildings but is also due to the lower surface area to volume ratio found as buildings increase in size.

This is illustrated in figure 3.2 where our square plan

building has been increased in size by 2, 3 and 4 times. It can be seen that the surface area to volume ratio has fallen from 1.01 in the original domestic scale building to 0.25 in the larger commercial scale building. What this means in practice is that the internal space in the small building will be in greater contact with the outside world via the external surfaces. As such the spaces will experience fabric heat loss but will also be able to take advantage of solar gains, natural light and ventilation. In the large building less of the interior space is in contact with the outside world through the external walls. The core areas of the space will experience less heat loss but will, at the same time, be poorly supplied with daylight, ventilation and passive solar gains.

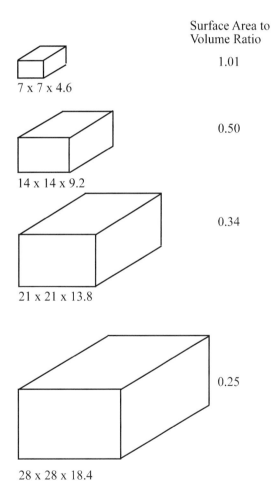

Surface Area to Volume Ratio

1.01

7 x 7 x 4.6

0.50

14 x 14 x 9.2

0.34

21 x 21 x 13.8

0.25

28 x 28 x 18.4

Figure 3.2 Surface are to volume ratio with increasing building dimensions

Since solar gains, natural ventilation and daylight are forms of free energy. Deep plan buildings will be disadvantaged. The implications of this is pursued further in the following sections.

3.1.1 Surface Area and Natural Energy

The dependence of a building on fossil fuels can be reduced by taking advantage of natural forms of energy. These are;

• Daylight - used to replace the need for artificial lighting.

• Natural ventilation - used to replace the need for mechanical ventilation driven by fans.

• Solar heat gains - used to replace energy consumption by the space heating system.

Examination of this list shows that each form of natural energy is obtained through the external skin of the building. It follows therefore that increasing the surface area will increase the possibility of taking advantage of these natural energy flows.

SOLAR GAINS

Considering the building forms shown in figure 3.1 it can be seen that if the elongated form were to be oriented with its main axis in an east-west direction then one of its large faces would face south. The building would, therefore, be able to collect a greater amount of solar energy than the cube. The amount of solar energy gained depends on the solar intensity on the vertical face, the ability with which this energy can enter the building (transmission coefficient) and the area of the glazing. Beyond optimum orientation of the building and exposing the site to sunlight we have little influence on the solar intensity. Similarly the transmission coefficient of the glazing is a factor of the glazing system, so to increase solar gains the area of glazing on the south facade must be increased. It is essential that this is achieved whilst reducing the glazed area on the north facade so that the overall glazed area does not increase.

Various studies have estimated that careful passive solar design can provide up to 10% of the space heating energy needs of a domestic building. The net reduction in space heating energy use is less than this since fabric heat losses would increase as the surface area increases following extension of the southern facade. Continuing our consideration of the elongated plan shape, table 3.3 indicates an increase in fabric heat loss rate of 3% giving a net reduction in space heating energy use of 7% as a result of elongating a cubical domestic building along its east/west axis.

DAYLIGHT

So far we have considered the various forms in terms of domestic space heating. In terms of lighting most rooms in houses are sufficiently shallow in depth to be adequately served with daylight from appropriately sized vertical windows. However, if the building forms were used for large-scale commercial buildings then square floor plans would result in deep spaces. The inner areas of which would then be distant from the windows resulting in poor daylighting and the consequential use of artificial lights. As a rule of thumb useful daylight penetration is considered to be available up to a depth of 2½ times the window head height from the windows into the room (approximately 5m).

In chapter 1 it was pointed out that electricity is expensive and highly polluting relative to other fuels. For this reason its use should be avoided. One way of doing this is to use narrow building forms such as the elongated shape or the cross-shape indicated in figure 3.1. Taking the cross plan as an example, the increased surface area results in 16% more fabric heat losses than a simple square plan. However, the plan depth will be reduced so that natural light can be used in preference to artificial light. Since electricity is almost five times as expensive as gas, any savings in lighting electricity will have approximately five times the value of space heating energy increases. A similar situation applies to carbon dioxide output arising from the use of the two types of fuel.

Single storey buildings can have deep plans as they can be illuminated with daylight using roof lights.

NATURAL VENTILATION

As with daylighting single sided natural ventilation of spaces is considered possible up to a depth of 5 to 6m from outside walls and for cross ventilation across a plan depth of 15m between two outside walls (chapter 5). It can be seen then that both the elongated and cross forms will reduce the plan depth allowing natural ventilation to take place. This will avoid the energy consumption by fans used to drive ventilation air through ductwork to the core of the building. In this way energy savings of approximately 20kWh/m²/year can be made which is a typical ventilation fan energy consumption.

APPLICATION IN PRACTICE

Much emphasis is now being placed on natural ventilation in office design by incorporating narrow plan depths as is illustrated in the Building Research Establishment Environmental Office of the Future which has a plan depth of 13.5m[1]. This technique has also been applied to low energy hospital designs which have wards arranged in a cruciform shape around a central nurses' station[2].

LOSS VS GAINS ENERGY BALANCE

By optimising the above natural energy flows we are trying to obtain a net improvement in the energy consumption of the building. To be successful we need to achieve the following balance;

solar gains + reductions in artificial lighting + reductions in mechanical ventilation > increase in fabric heat losses

As the size of the building increases and its energy flows become more complex it becomes more difficult to make sure that we are achieving the required balance. This can be determined by modelling the energy flows in the building using computer techniques. This gives results with a resonable accuracy dependant on the limitations of the data and model. The disadvantage is that it is time consuming to set up the model in the first instance. A simpler method that uses graphical techniques is the Lighting and Thermal (LT) method of design.

3.1.2 The Lighting and Thermal (LT) Method of Design

The LT method of design[3] is a technique that is used to make comparisons between the energy consumption of alternative floor plans. This is illustrated in the following example.

In office buildings we wish to reduce the energy consumption by encouraging the use of daylight, passive solar gains and natural ventilation. This can be achieved by reducing the depth of the floor plan. To investigate this further we will consider the energy consumption of two alternative floor plans for a 2304m² mid floor of an office building. The two alternative floor plans are square (figure 3.3) and L shape (figure 3.4)

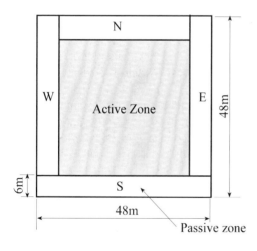

Figure 3.3 Square floor plan.

The following assumptions are made about each floor;

- Assume a glazing ratio of 50%. This is the percentage of the total external wall which is glazed.

- Assume a transmission factor of 0.35. Within the LT method are three transmission factors which describe the degree of over shadowing of the building. These are 1.0 no shading, 0.7 light

shading and 0.35 heavy shading.

The first stage in the method involves dividing the building plan into passive and active zones. Passive zones are those which benefit from natural light, solar gains and ventilation. They are considered to extend from the perimeter to a depth of 6m. The passive zones are further distinguished by orientation. Note that the technique only uses four orientations (north, south, east and west) so a zone orientated 10° east of south would be considered to have a southerly orientation. Small deviations such as this are considered to have little effect on the energy consumption. Active zones make up the remainder of the floor plan and are those areas requiring mechanical ventilation and artificial lighting. Figures 3.3 and 3.4 show the active zone shaded and the passive zones unshaded and further identified by orientation.

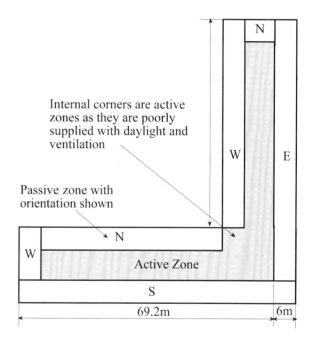

Table 3.4 L shaped floor plan.

The first analysis is to compare the areas of active and passive zones in the building. As shown in table 3.4 The square plan shape has 48% more active zone area than the L shaped building. Since the active zones require the greater use of mechanical services this indicates that the square shaped building will use more energy to provide comfort conditions than the L shaped floor plan.

Plan shape	Area of passive zones (m^2)	Area of active zones (m^2)
Square	1008	1296
L shape	1442.4	861.6

Table 3.4 Areas of active and passive zones for two floor plans

To put numerical values on to this, an analysis must be made of the energy consumption of each zone using the LT method. The method is described in IP4 on page 44 and the outcome is shown in table 3.5. It can be seen that the energy consumption of the square plan building is 10.3% more than the L shaped building.

Plan shape	Zone energy consumption (MWh)		
	Active	Passive	Total
Square	294.19	131.98	426.17
L shape	198.17	188.37	386.54

Table 3.5 Predicted annual energy consumptions for two plan shapes

Table IP4.1 gives a breakdown of the total energy consumptions for each plan shape in terms of lighting, heating and air conditioning. The savings in the L shaped building arise from reductions in lighting and heating loads. It could be anticipated that the narrow plan form would have a higher space heating requirement due to its larger surface area. However this is offset by additional solar gains through the extended south face of the building. The largest energy consumption reductions occur in the lighting energy usage. The technique assumes full use of photoelectric lighting controls, turning lights off in response to the entry of natural light.

The technique is not intended to give an accurate value for the energy consumption of a proposed building. This is because it uses simplifications and assumptions which may not accurately reflect all buildings to which it is being applied[4] However, its strength lies in its simplicity in allowing comparisons to be made between the energy consumptions of alternative plan forms at the design stage.

GENERAL OUTCOME

From the discussions above it can be deduced that buildings in which space heating is the predominant energy flow, such as housing and small commercial buildings should aim for a cubical form. Buildings having a high demand for lighting, ventilation and cooling such as hospitals or offices should adopt a narrow plan form.

The 10.3% savings in energy described in the above example represent a significant quantity of energy. However, it must be remembered that these savings are not free. Construction costs will be higher for a narrow plan building and a larger area of building land will be needed to accommodate the same floor area.

3.2 Volume and Ventilation Heat Loss

Inspection of the equation for steady state ventilation heat loss rate (page 23) reveals that ventilation heat losses are directly proportional to the volume of the building. Reducing the volume of heated spaces would therefore reduce the heat loss rate from the building.

Ventilation heat losses are not the only problem. Tall spaces experience stratification due to the ascent of warm air towards the ceiling. This creates a temperature gradient that increases between the floor and ceiling. The temperature at low level (up to 2m from the floor) may be in the range of 18-21°C. This is the occupied zone. Temperatures may increase to 28-30°C at heights over 4m (figure 3.5). This effect causes additional energy consumption in two ways. Firstly, energy has been used to create high air temperatures in a space which is unoccupied. Secondly, the temperature difference across the roof structure is increased. This increases the rate of heat loss through the building fabric. The first step towards minimising the problem is to reduce ceiling heights where possible. The second is to use radiant heaters as these rely less on warm air for creating comfort. The third is to use destratification fans[5]. These are fans installed at high level within a space. They have an in-built thermostat which allows the fan to operate when temperatures at high level go over a certain threshold, say 28ºC. The fan will drive

IP4 - LT Method of Design

The annual energy consumption for the two floor plan shapes described in the main text (section 3.1.2) can be determined using charts of energy consumption against perimeter glazed ratio. These charts are provided in copies of the LT method of design. The charts give annual energy consumption in terms of megawatt hours per square metre (MWh/m²) broken down into lighting, heating and ventilation/cooling energy use. Charts exists for the four orientations of passive zone in different building types for example, residential, office and retail. Two sets of charts are available one for warm regions (zone 2) and another for cooler regions (zone 1). An example of a chart for a south facing passive zone for an office situated in climatic zone 1 is shown in figure IP4.1.

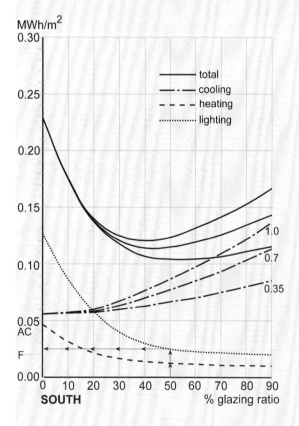

Figure IP4.1 LT curve for a south facing office passive zone in climatic zone 1, assuming an illuminance of 300lx and a cooling load of 15W/m²

The following features can be seen on the graph

- Heating curve - dashed line. As the glazing ratio increases solar gains increase and so the demand for space heating falls. Eventually at about 60% glazing ratio the space becomes saturated with solar gains. The space heating can only be reduced until it is off. Once this is achieved no further reduction in space heating energy consumption is obtained by increasing glazed area.

- Cooling curves - dot/dash line. As the glazing ratio increases the solar gains increase and so the air conditioning system is activated increasing the cooling energy consumption. Three curves are shown identified by different transmission coefficients 1.0, 0.7 and 0.35 these represent no overshadowing, moderate overshadowing and heavy overshadowing respectively. The greater the over shadowing the smaller the transmission coefficient and so less the gains.

- Lighting curve - dotted line. As the glazing ratio increases the energy used for lighting reduces as the lighting control system responds to the available daylight and modulates the artificial light output downwards. At 60% glazed ratio the passive zone is saturated with daylight and no further savings are made. This causes the curve to flatten out.

- Total energy curve - solid line. This set of curves is the total energy consumption against glazing ratio. It has a U shape indicating that initially energy consumption falls as use is made of natural lighting and solar gains. However when these benefits plateau out and energy used for cooling increases the curve rises once more. This curve therefore shows a distinct minimum total energy consumption at 40-55% glazing ratio depending on transmission coefficient.

In the example described in the main text the building is assumed to have a 50% glazing ratio. Starting from this point on the x-axis the energy consumption for each

Page 44

square metre of the passive zone for lighting, heating and ventilation and cooling can be determined. The arrowed line in figure IP3.1 shows how the lighting energy consumption is determined to be 0.025MWh/m^2. Since the area of the south facing passive zone is 288m^2 the lighting energy consumption for all of the south facing passive zone is 288m^2 x 0.025MWh/m^2 = 7.2MWh.

This process is then repeated for heating and ventilation/cooling. Following this the energy consumption of the other orientations of passive zones is determined using other charts of appropriate orientation. The energy consumption of the active zone is determined by considering it to have zero glazing ratio. i.e. values of energy consumption per square metre for heating, lighting and ventilation/cooling energy use are taken from the y axis. As can be seen from figure IP4.1 these values are 0.129, 0.045 and 0.056 MWh/m^2 respectively. Once again the energy consumption of the full area of active zone is found by multiplying the area of the active zone by the sum of the heating, lighting and ventilation/cooling values. Finally, the energy consumption of the entire floor is determined by summing the energy consumptions for all of the passive zones and the active zone together. These values are shown in table 3.4 in the main text for both the square and L shaped floor plans broken down into active and passive zone consumptions. Table IP4.1 shows these energy consumptions broken down into the component parts.

	Energy consumption (MWh)	
	square	L shape
Lighting	204.62	164.45
Heating	84.53	81.82
Vent. and cool.	137.02	140.22
Total	426.17	386.54

Table IP4.1 Breakdown of energy consumptions predicted by the LT method of design

The method includes factors for converting the energy consumptions into output of carbon dioxide. The conversion factors for heating, lighting and ventilation/cooling are 0.22, 0.19 and 0.22 respectively. Multiplying the values in table IP4.1 by the appropriate conversion factor gives the annual carbon dioxide emissions in tonnes for each component. The figures for carbon emissions for each plan form are shown in table IP4.2. It can be seen that the square plan form emits more carbon dioxide than the L shaped plan and that the biggest difference occurs in CO_2 output due to lighting.

	Carbon dioxide output (t)	
Energy use	square	L shape
Lighting	45.0	36.2
Heating	16.1	15.6
Vent. and cool.	30.1	30.9
Total	91.1	82.7

Table IP4.2 Carbon dioxide emissions.

the warm air at high level down to the occupied space.

If it is assumed that the plan size of a building has been fixed using functional criteria then the deciding factor on room volume is the ceiling height. The Building Regulations specify a minimum ceiling height of 2.3m for domestic properties. For larger spaces this ceiling height would create an oppressive 'feel' to the room. As horizontal dimensions increase vertical dimensions must also increase in proportion to avoid this perception.

No destratification

With destratification

Figure 3.5 Stratification of warm air in a tall space and destratification using a high level fan.

Various ratio relationships between horizontal and vertical distances in rooms have been considered but there is no definitive guidance on optimum room heights for a given plan area. This is possibly because psychology has an important role here where perceived room heights are dependent on shade and colour of finishes, presence of windows and 'ceiling indicators' such as lines in the structure or finishes running

horizontally around the room below the ceiling height. Currently architects call upon their experience to determine appropriate room heights. However, for simple spaces this would be a useful area for further research the outcome of which would produce useful design guidance.

FLOOR AREA TO VOLUME RATIO

One way of determining if the space inside a building is under-used is to calculate a floor area to volume ratio. The larger the value of this ratio, the better utilised is the space. There are a number of ways in which this ratio might be increased. They are:

- Make use of loft spaces in domestic buildings

- Use mezzanine floors in large buildings

- When renovating old buildings suspended ceilings can be used to reduce the ceiling height and hence heated volume. However this remedial work is often criticised for its damaging effect on the aesthetics of the space.

3.2.1 Volume and Cooling

In the previous section we discovered that increasing the volume of a building increases ventilation heat loss rates. However in this section we will find that increasing the volume of rooms that are prone to overheating can reduce temperatures in the occupied zone and so avoid the need for cooling energy use.

The cause of high temperatures in buildings is the heat gained by the internal air from sources other than the heating system. These sources are, in order of size, the sun, lighting, people and appliances (computers etc.).

In addition to the high air temperatures further discomfort is caused by the presence of radiant heat sources within the room. The main source is the ceiling warmed by hot air rising to the top of the room. The human body is very sensitive to thermal radiation and will be affected by the radiation from the ceiling, especially about the head.

The higher air temperatures caused by these heat gains results in thermal discomfort. If the space temperature rises above 28°C for prolonged periods air conditioning is considered necessary as a means of removing heat from the air and reducing temperatures. However the need for air conditioning can be avoided or the length of time over which it operates can be reduced by increasing the volume of the room. This is achieved by increasing the ceiling height.

Three effects come in to play as illustrated in figure 3.6, firstly the increased head room allows warm air to rise upwards and out of the occupied space; secondly, the radiant effect of the ceiling is lessened due to its increased distance from the occupants. Thirdly the high ceilings allow the inclusion of high level openable windows within the room. This means that high level ventilation paths can be created which sweep the warm air out of the building without impinging on the occupants in the occupied zone. Low level ventilation routes directly affect the occupants causing draughts or movement of papers and so where provided should be under occupant control.

Strong radiant heat

Low ceiling

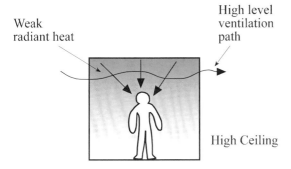

Weak radiant heat

High level ventilation path

High Ceiling

3.6 Increased room height as a means of improving thermal comfort

It has been reported[6] that an increase in ceiling height from 2.5m to 3.5m in a medium weight office can reduce peak temperatures by 1.5°C. This reduction can mean the difference between needing and not needing air conditioning.

A balance must be made between increased ventilation heat losses and reductions in cooling energy use. As a general rule, room heights and hence volume should be kept low in dwellings and small commercial buildings where space heating is the dominant energy flow and ceilings should be raised in medium to large commercial buildings where it is desirable to avoid air conditioning. (see chapter 10).

One problem with raised ceiling heights is that it increases the distance between ceiling mounted light fittings and the tasks to be illuminated. This increase in distance will reduce the light levels on the task. To counteract the reduction more light fittings would be required which in turn would increase the electrical consumption of the lighting system and add to the cooling load. To avoid this problem and reduce the number of luminaires required, pendant light fittings or task lamps should be used to illuminate rooms with high ceilings. This topic is discussed more fully in chapter 7.

3.3 Internal Planning

So far we have considered the shell of the building and the size of spaces contained within. However energy consumption reductions can also be achieved by considering the planning and arrangement of the internal spaces of a building.

There are two issues involved;

- *Orientation.* External conditions differ on the north and south faces of a building. The availability of daylight and solar energy is higher on the south face of a building than the north. On average outside temperatures are higher on the south face of a building.

- *Cellular spaces.* Different spaces in a building require different comfort and working conditions. To maintain optimal conditions in all spaces they should be isolated using partitions so that the heating, cooling and lighting systems can be controlled on a room by room basis to maintain desired conditions.

ORIENTATION

Since solar gains are achieved on the south face of a building it is wise to place those spaces requiring the highest comfort temperatures on the south side of the building. Spaces requiring lower comfort temperatures such as circulation routes, those in which physical activity is taking place such as workshops and heat generating spaces such as kitchens should be placed on the north side of the building. There are exceptions to the above rules for example offices in which computers are being used require comfortable temperatures but would not benefit from south facing solar gains. This is because the computer equipment itself will be adding heat to the space. The addition of solar gains could cause the space to require air conditioning. Computer suites should be considered as heat generating spaces and should be situated on the north side of the building.

Figure 3.7 shows floor plans for a low energy house. It can be seen that the main living spaces are on the south side of the building and kitchen, bathroom, toilets and circulation are on the north side of the building. The rooms to the north act as a transition or buffer zone between the warmer south facing rooms and the cooler/darker conditions to the north.

Figure 3.7 floor plans of a low energy house

The following planning considerations should also be considered;

- Cold zones in the centre of heated spaces should be avoided. One example is where unheated stairwells are placed in the centre of a block of flats. If they are placed on outside walls they can act as a buffer to the external environment.

- In housing, garages should be attached rather than detached as they can act as a buffer between the occupied space and the external environment.

CELLULAR SPACES

Cellular spaces generally use less energy per square metre than open plan spaces. This is because a greater degree of control can be exercised over cellular spaces. Partitions should be placed between spaces requiring different conditions. For example, circulation routes only require 18°C comfort temperature compared to 21°C for working spaces. If the two spaces were combined together then the entire volume would have to be heated to 21°C. In addition, the recommended task illuminances will be different. For circulation spaces we need a task illuminance of 150 lx, for a work space 400 lx is required. On this occasion some difference can be maintained between the two spaces even if combined into a single open space by installing fewer luminaires in the circulation route. However, the difference cannot be too great or a noticeable contrast will exist between the circulation and office spaces causing the circulation route to appear dark.

The effect of separating spaces is illustrated by comparing the energy consumption of a naturally ventilated open plan office and a naturally ventilated cellular office[7]. The energy consumption breakdown is shown tabulated in table 3.6 and graphically in figure 3.8.

It can be seen that the total energy consumption of the open plan office is 18% greater than the cellular office. Table 3.5 reveals that the biggest increases in consumption in the open plan office compared with the cellular office is for Lighting and Office equipment. The extra lighting energy consumption is due to the fact that the lighting cannot be turned off in unoccupied spaces as easily as it can in individual offices. This may be due to the lack of individual switches or the gloomy effect created by switching off the lights in a section of a large open plan office.

The two internal arrangements have the same heating and hot water energy consumption. However it could be anticipated that the space heating energy consumption in the cellular office could be reduced by individual temperature control of rooms. For example thermostatic radiator valves can be fitted to south facing rooms. Occupancy sensors or manual switches can be used to modulate down the heating in unoccupied rooms.

Energy Usage	Cellular	Open Plan
Heating and hot water	79	79
Lighting	14	22
Office equipment	12	20
Catering and other electricity	5	7
Fans, pumps, controls	2	4
Cooling	0	1
TOTAL	112	133

Table 3.6 Energy consumption of naturally ventilated cellular and open plan offices.

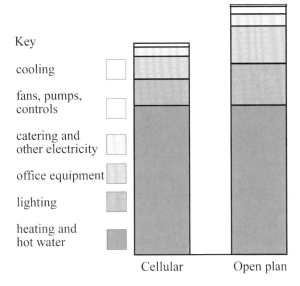

Key

cooling

fans, pumps, controls

catering and other electricity

office equipment

lighting

heating and hot water

Cellular   Open plan

Figure 3.8 Energy consumption of naturally ventilated cellular and open plan offices.

3.4 Grouping of Buildings

A detached building of cubical form has six surfaces through which heat can be lost. By grouping buildings together the number of external surfaces can be reduced. This is illustrated by considering the heat loss rate from a detached house, a semi-detached house (one less external wall per dwelling), a mid-terraced house (two less external walls per dwelling) and a flat in the middle of a block of flats (4 less external surfaces per dwelling).

Table 3.7 shows the fabric heat loss rate for these types of housing and the fabric heat loss rate relative to the detached house. From this table it can be seen that the mid-flat, mid-terrace and semi-detached house have a fabric heat loss rate which is 43%, 22% and 12% lower than an equivalent sized detached house.

House type	Fabric heat loss rate (W)	heat loss relative to detached (%)
detached	2551	100
semi-detached	2267	88
terrace	1984	78
mid flat	1455	57

Table 3.7 : Fabric heat loss rate for various house styles (all have same window area)

The figures will differ for an end of terrace house and top or ground floor flats which have more external walls than a property that is more shelterd by other dwellings in the group.

REFERENCES

1. Bunn, R. Building Analysis: Environmental Office of the Future. Building Services Journal, pp18-23. March 1997.

2. Corcoran, M. Building Analysis : Wansbeck Hospital. Building Services Journal, pp19-22, June 1993

3. Baker, N. V. and Steemers K. The L.T. Method 2.0: An

Energy Design Tool for Non-Domestic Buildings. Cambridge Architectural Research Ltd. 1993

4. Burberry, P. LT Method of Energy Assessment. Architects' Journal, pp27-28, March 1994

5. Iles, P J, Destratification of Air in Industrial Buildings, BRE IP 9/95, HMSO, May 1995

6. BRECSU. General Information Report 31 Avoiding or Minimising the Use of Air Conditioning : A Research Report from the EnREI Programme, p19, HMSO, 1995.

7. BRECSU. Energy Consumption Guide 19: Energy use in offices. HMSO February 1998

04 F A B R I C

In this chapter we will find that;

- Fabric heat losses are reduced by selecting or constructing building elements with low U-values.

- Successive revisions of the building regulations have reduced maximum allowable U-values.

- The rate of heat loss through a building element is determined by multiplying its area by its U-value and the temperature difference across it.

- The carbon index (CI) is a method of rating a domestic buildings energy performance in terms of the pollution output arising from its energy consumption.

- Heat is lost through all the elements of a building but the glazing loses heat at the fastest rate.

- Multiple glazing incorporating low emissivity coatings and cavity gas fillings reduce glazing U-values.

- The U-value of a glazing system depends on the glazed area and the frame material/construction.

- Where no views are required, but daylight is, glazing can be replaced by transparent insulation materials (TIM).

- Much of the heat loss through floors in contact with the ground occurs at the perimeter.

- Buildings can be super-insulated so that they require little or no space heating.

- There are four potential problems with highly insulated buildings; thermal bridging, outer leaf damage, rain penetration, freezing of loft pipework and thermal discomfort.

- As U-values are reduced small elements such as

mortar joints become more important and so are included in U-value calculations.

- As U-values are reduced the quality of workmanship used to construct elements becomes critical.

4.0 Introduction

Heat is lost from a building by two routes. Conduction, convection and radiation across the building fabric known as fabric heat losses and by infiltration, known as ventilation heat losses. This chapter will concentrate on fabric heat losses. Ventilation heat losses will be considered in the next chapter.

To reduce fabric heat losses from a building the shell must be well insulated. A well insulated element has a low thermal transmittance (U-value). The thermal performance of the envelope is best when all of the elements of the building have similar U-values. However, it can be seen from figure 4.1 that in practice some elements are better insulated than others. The reason for this is that some elements are easier to insulate than others.

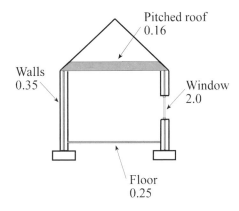

Figure 4.1 Maximum U-values (W/m²K).

For example, pitched roofs have traditionally been well insulated. This is because it is relatively simple to install and accommodate large thickness of insulation in the loft space. Masonry cavity walls on the other hand are usually insulated by filling part or all of the cavity with insulation so a well insulated wall would require a wide cavity filled with insulation. However, cavity width is typically limited to 150mm, greater widths are difficult to achieve due to the limited length of wall ties and width of standard lintols. Glazing stands out as being poorly insulated, having a U-value that is eleven times bigger than that of the roof. Windows are extremely useful multi-function devices giving views, ventilation, passive solar gains and daylight. Unfortunately the high U-values of glazing systems is difficult to reduce and so windows remain the main source of heat loss from buildings.

This chapter will look at all of the elements making up the shell of a building but will give special consideration to glazing due to its thermal weakness. Finally it will consider the advantages and disadvantages of super insulation of domestic buildings.

4.1 Building Regulations

The building regulations list the requirements that buildings must achieve to ensure that they do not fail, are not a risk to people and do not damage the environment. Enforcement of the building regulation requirements is the role of local authority building control officers. They inspect plans, calculations and other information submitted to them by the builder or architect and also carry out site inspections.

The section of the regulations that applies to energy is Part L : Conservation of Fuel and power[1]. It is concerned with the prevention of carbon emissions from buildings arising from the use of fossil fuels. Part L1 is concerned with domestic buildings and Part L2 with non-domestic buildings.

For both domestic and non-domestic buildings to comply with the regulations it must be demonstrated that resonable provision has been made to:

- Limit the heat loss through the fabric and from heating system distribution pipes and ducts and

also hot water tanks.

- Provide energy efficient heating systems (see chapter 9)

- Provide lighting systems with energy efficient lamps and controls (see chapter 7)

- Provide documentation on the commissioning and operation of the building and its services so that the owner can operate the building efficiently.

In addition non-domestic buildings should:

- Limit heat gains through the building fabric.

- Ensure that mechanical ventilation and air conditioning systems do not consume more energy than is reasonable (on installations serving areas >200m²).

- Insulating pipes and ducts so that heat gains by chilled water and air running through themare limited.

The following sections will consider the general requirements for domestic and non-domestic buildings. It should be rememberd that the Building Regulations specify minimum standards. For low energy designs it will be necessary to design buildings with an energy performance that exceeds some of these standards.

4.1.1 Domestic Buildings

There are three methods of demonstrating that a proposed domestic buildings complies with the building regulations.

- The elemental method

- The target U-value method

- The carbon index (CI) method.

There are three methods as each give differing opportunities for design flexibility which is important if low energy houses are to be aesthetically pleasing as well as energy efficient.

ELEMENTAL METHOD

The elemental method is the simplest method of demonstrating compliance with the Building Regulations. Unfortunately, it also provides the least design flexibility. The method concentrates on fabric standards and so certain minimum heating system standards must also be in place. This involves having minimum central heating efficiencies as specified in table 4.1(see section 9.2).

Central heating fuel	SEDBUK (%)
Mains natural gas	78
LPG	80
Oil	85

Table 4.1 Minimum SEDBUK efficiencies to enable the elemental and target U-value methods to be used.

Compliance is achieved using this method if the building is constructed with elements having U-values equal to or lower than those listed in table 4.2. Because of the high heat losses experienced through windows their area is limited in this method. The area of openings, including windows doors and rooflights, should not exceed 25% of the total floor area of the building. A smaller opening area can be used but it is not recommended to go below 17% of the total floor area so that adequate daylighting can be maintained.

The elemental U-value method allows some flexibility by allowing some elements to have higher U-values if the effect of them is offset by having lower U-values elswhere. There are limits to this and the U-value of the roof should not exceed 0.35 and that of the walls/floor not exceed 0.7W/m²K.

TARGET U-VALUE METHOD

This method of compliance involves calculating an overall target U-value (U_T) for the building. The average U-value of the proposed design is then calculated. If the average U-value is at or below the target then the building complies with the building regulations.

The target U-value is obtained from the following equation:

$$U_T = [0.35 - 0.19(A_R/A_T) - 0.10(A_{GF}/A_T) + 0.413(A_F/A_T)]$$

where:

U_T = Target U-value (W/m²K)
A_R = Exposed roof area (m²)
A_{GF} = Ground floor area (m²)
A_F = Total floor area (m²)
A_T = Total area of the building shell (incl. floor) (m²)

This method is intended to give flexibility to designs so that elements can be used with high U-values which would then be offset by areas of low U-values elswhere. The method also gives allowance for improved boiler efficiency and solar gains as detailed below.

Exposed element	U-value
Pitched roof with insulation between rafters	0.20
Pitched roof with integral insulation	0.25
Pitched roof with insulation between joists	0.16
Flat roof	0.25
Walls, including basement walls	0.35
Floors including ground floors and basement floors	0.25
Windows, doors and rooflights (area weighted average) in metal frames	2.2
Windows, doors and rooflights (area weighted average) in wood or PVC frames	2.0

Table 4.2 Maximum elemental U-values (W/m²K)

Boiler efficiency. When the proposed heating system has an efficiency which is different to that described in table 4.1 the target U-value must be changed. This is done by multiplying the target U-value by a factor f_e where:

$$f_e = \frac{\text{proposed boiler SEDBUK (\%)}}{\text{reference boiler SEDBUK (\%)}}$$

This means that lower boiler efficiencies will result in the need for lower U-values and increased efficiency will result in the option to have higher U-values.

Solar gains. If solar energy can enter the building then it can offset the need for fossil fuel heating. The target U-value method recognises this and varies the target U-value depending on changes in solar access. The first example is when metal window frames are used instead of PVC or timber. In this case the target U-value is increased by 3% to take into account the fact that the frame is smaller and so the solar aperture is bigger and therefore the potential for solar gains is greater. The second variation is based on the fact that the basic target U-value method assumes an equal distribution of glazing on the north ($^+/_-$ 30°) and south ($^+/_-$ 30°) sides of the building. If more glazing is placed on the south side and the area reduced on the north then the target U-value is modified by multiplying it by a factor ΔS where:

$$\Delta S = 0.04 \times [(A_S - A_N)/A_{TG}]$$

where:

A_S = Area of glazing facing South ($^+/_-$ 30°) (m²)
A_N = Area of glazing facing North ($^+/_-$ 30°) (m²)
A_{TG} = Total area of glazing (m²)

CARBON INDEX METHOD

The carbon index method aims to give an energy performance comparable to the elemental method whilst also allowing a great deal of design flexibility. The method involves calculating the energy performance of the building using a standard assessment procedure (SAP) and then converting this figure into a carbon index.

The standard assessment procedure (SAP) for the energy rating of dwellings is a calculation method which is used to determine the energy used in, and cost of, heating a house over a year. Data on the thermal properties of the fabric, ventilation system, space heating system, controls, water heating system and heat gains to the building are entered into a pro-forma (included as an appendix in part L of the Building regulations) or SAP calculation programme. The final outcome is a SAP rating which sits on the scale between 0 and 100. The higher the rating the better the energy efficiency of the building. It is considerd that an energy efficient building would have a SAP rating of 80 or more.

The carbon index is found by first converting the energy consumption of the building calculated in the SAP procedure to a CO_2 emission expressed in tonnes per year (tonnes/y). This figure is then divided by the total floor area of the building to give a carbon factor (kg/m²) that is independent of building size. The following formula is used to convert the carbon factor into the carbon index.

$$CI = 17.7 - 9.0 Log_{10}(CF)$$

CI = carbon index
CF = carbon factor (kg/m²)

The carbon index gives a better indication of the impact that the building energy consumption has on the environment. For example if two buildings had the same space heating energy requirement but one was heated using electric heaters and the other using gas heaters, the electrically heated house would emit the most carbon dioxide due to the use of electricity. The requirements of the building regulations would be met if the carbon index for the dwelling is greater than 8.0.

4.1.2 Other Buildings

For buildings other than housing there are three methods for demonstrating compliance with the building regulations. These are;

- The elemental method

- The whole building method

- The carbon emissions calculation method

ELEMENTAL METHOD

This method works in the same way as the elemental method for housing. Each element must not exceed the U-values given in table 4.2. There are however two additional elemental U-values, these are that large doors such as vehicle access doors should have a U-value no greater than 0.7W/m²K and roof light U-values should not exceed 2.2W/m²K.

Commercial buildings tend to have more complex window arrangements than domestic buildings and so the maximum window area requirement is more complex. Doors and vertical windows are based on exposed wall area. Rooflights are considered separately and their allowable area is based on a percentage of total roof area. The actual percentages vary depending on building type as shown in table 4.3. Note that shop windows have no size limit.

Building type	Windows and doors as a % of the exposed wall area	Rooflights as % of area of roof
Residential	30	20
Places of assembly, offices and shops	40	20
Industrial and storage buildings	15	20
Vehicle access doors and display glazing	As required	

Table 4.3 Maximum allowable areas of glazing in commercial buildings

This method allows the trade-offs for design flexibility as described in section 4.1.1.

The elemental method is based on fabric standards but there are also parallel requirements to ensure that the whole building performs well. These are:

- The building should conform to airtightness standards as demonstrated by air-permeability testing (see section 5.3)

- The building should avoid overheating (see section 10.1.1)

- The heating plant should be energy efficient as demonstrated using heating plant with acceptable carbon intensities (see section 9.2).

- The hot water system should be energy efficient (see section 9.6)

- The electric lighting system should be energy efficient (see section 7.4)

WHOLE-BUILDING METHOD

The whole-building method is intended to give more design flexibility than the elemental method. There are methods for offices, schools and hospitals. For schools the building must conform with the Department for Education guidance note (DfEE, Guidelines for environmental design in schools, Building Bulletin 87, TSO, 1997). Hospitals must conform to NHS estate guides (NHS Estates: Achieving energy efficiency in new hospitals, TSO, 1994).

For offices it is necessary to calculate the carbon performance rating (CPR) of the building, taking into account air-conditioning and mechanical ventilation (ACMV), space heating and lighting. The method is described more fully in BRE Digest 457: The carbon performance rating for offices. Compliance is demonstrated if the whole-office CPR is no greater than the figures shown in table 4.4 and the envelope meets the thermal and air-tightness standards specified in the Building Regulations.

Building type	Maximum allowable CPR ($kgC/m^2/year$)	
	New office	Refurbished office
Naturally ventilated	7.1	7.8
Mechanically ventilated	10.0	11.0
Air-conditioned	18.5	20.4

Table 4.4 Maximum whole office carbon performance ratings.

CARBON-EMISSIONS CALCULATION METHOD

Unlike the whole-building method this method can be applied to all building types and requires a calculation of the annual carbon emissions of the proposed building to be made. The value obtained must not exceed the carbon emissions calculated for a notional building of similar type and size that meets the compliance criteria of the elemental method.

4.2 Windows and Heat Loss

Windows, which are made up of two components, the glazing and the frame, are weak elements when it comes to keeping heat in the building.

The main component glass, is a thin high thermal conductivity material. The only additional insulating properties are added by the inside and outside surface and cavity thermal resistances. However, the thermal performance of the glazing can be improved by;

- Increasing the number of sheets of glass

- Increasing the size of the cavity between the sheets of glass

- Replacing the air in the cavity with argon gas

- Applying a low emissivity layer to the inner pane of glass

The other element in the window system is the frame. The performance of the frame can be improved by;

- Using low thermal conductivity frame materials

- Creating thermal breaks in the frame

Each of these methods of improving performance are discussed in more detail below.

SHEETS OF GLASS

As the number of sheets of glass increase the U-value decreases. The U-values for single, double and triple glazing set in a timber frame are 4.8, 2.8 and 2.1 W/m²K respectively. More than three sheets of glass can be used but the system starts to become impractical due to the increased cost, weight and dimensions of the unit. Similar performance to multiple glazing can be achieved using special coatings (See below) for example double glazing with a low emissivity coating has a similar U-value to triple glazing with no coatings.

The U-values for the multiple glazing given above are for sealed units with a 12mm air gap between. The air in the cavity is dried to avoid condensation forming on the outer sheet of glass. The dried air is kept in the unit and the separation between the panes maintained using an edge seal (figure 4.2). This edge seal forms a cold bridge between the panes and so heat losses are greatest around the perimeter. The U-value of the double glazed unit excluding frame can be given as a centre of pane value or an overall value taking into account the greater heat loss at the edges.

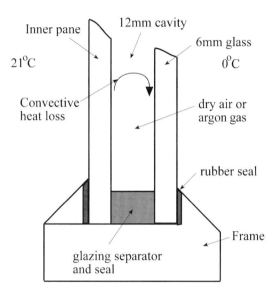

Figure 4.2 Sealed double glazed unit.

CAVITY WIDTH

Increasing the width of the cavity between the sheets of glass reduces the U-value. This is demonstrated in figure 4.3 which shows the centre pane U-value of double glazing decreasing as cavity width increases. It can be seen that beyond 16mm cavity width no further reductions occur. This is because the insulating effect of an increased layer of air is offset by increased convective heat transfer which can take place more easily across a wider air gap. The U-values of double glazed units with 6, 12 and 16mm air gaps set in a timber frame are 3.1, 2.8 and 2.7 W/m²K respectively.

Figure 4.3 Graph of U-value against cavity width for double glazing (4mm air 4mm, no coatings).

CAVITY GAS

Reductions in the U-value of double glazed units can be obtained by replacing the dry air in the cavity with gases such as argon. Argon has a lower thermal conductivity than air (162 and 241 W/mK respectively) which will reduce conductive exchanges across the cavity. Argon is also more dense than air (1.784 and 1.293 kg/m³   respectively) which will make convection currents more sluggish. The U-value of a double glazed unit with a 12mm cavity width and with air and argon fillings are 2.8 and 2.7 W/m²K.

With time the argon gas may escape from the glazing as the edge seals degrade however this will be replaced by moisture carrying air and so will be revealed as a failed unit containing condensation that would require replacement.

LOW EMISSIVITY COATINGS

All objects above room temperature emit energy in the form of thermal radiation. The thermal radiation is an electromagnetic wave and this exists in many different wavelengths making up a continuous spectrum. However, for an object at a particular temperature there will be one wavelength of radiation that is emitted more strongly than the others. Radiation from hot objects such as the sun with a surface temperature of 4000°C has a peak emission at the short wavelength end of the spectrum. As the temperature of the radiating object is reduced the wavelength of the radiation peak increases. Radiation from objects at room temperatures emit

mainly long wavelength thermal radiation.

The ability of an object to radiate energy is known as its emissivity. A perfect radiator has an emissivity of 1 and an object that radiates no heat has an emissivity of 0. Most building materials have an emissivity of 0.8 - 0.9. Light coloured and smooth objects have a lower emissivity. Polished aluminium foil for example has an emissivity of 0.5. Clear float glass has an emissivity of 0.9. However, by coating this glass during manufacture with a fine layer of metal oxide the emissivity of the glass surface is reduced. Two types of 'low E' coating are available known as 'hard' and 'soft'. Hard coatings have emissivities in the range 0.15 to 0.2 and soft in the range 0.05 to 0.1. Coating the outer surface of the inner pane of a double glazed unit with a low E coating reduces the radiant transfer of heat from inside to outside (figure 4.4).

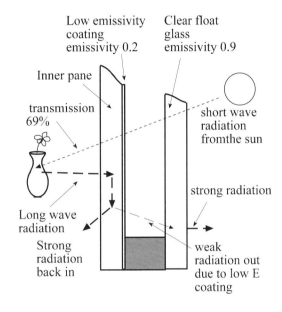

Figure 4.4 Low emissivity double glazing.

The low emissivity coating has minimal effect on the transmission of solar radiation from outside the building to inside. Total transmission of solar radiation for standard double glazing and low emissivity double glazing is 72% and 69% respectively. This short wave energy is absorbed by objects in the room and is re-emitted as long wave radiation. This is absorbed by the inner pane of glazing causing its temperature to rise. The heat contained in the inner pane is in turn re-radiated both into and out of the building. Radiation outwards is reduced because of the low emissivity coating. However, radiation back into the room occurs as normal. It is as if the inner pane is reflecting the long wave radiation from objects in the room back into the room. The effect of this is to reduce heat transfer through the glazing system. The U-value of 12mm double glazing in a timber frame for standard double glazing and low E (emissivity = 0.2)double glazing are 2.8 and 2.3 W/m²K respectively.

FRAME MATERIALS

Materials have different thermal conductivities depending on their density. The frame, made up of these materials, can form as much as 15% of the window opening. The thermal characteristics of the frame will therefore have a strong influence on the overall U-value. The thermal conductivity of the four most common framing materials are shown in table 4.5. uPVC, hardwood and softwood have similar thermal conductivities, but softwood has the lowest value of the three. Aluminium on the other hand has a high thermal conductivity and if used would considerably reduce the overall U-value of the glazing system. This is illustrated by the variation in indicative U-values of 12mm air gap double glazing system for various frame materials shown in table 4.6.

Material	Thermal conductivity (W/mK)
Softwood	0.13
Hardwood	0.15
Aluminium	160
uPVC	0.17

Table 4.5 Thermal conductivities of different window frame materials.

One way of improving the thermal performance of all window frames, regardless of material, is to incorporate a thermal break into their construction. This is a barrier of low thermal conductivity material separating the inner layer of the frame from the outer. An example of a thermal break is shown in figure 4.5. The U-values shown in table 4.6 show that the U-value of a metal framed double glazed unit is reduced by incorporating

a 4mm thermal breakfrom 3.7 to 3.4 W/m²K.

Frame material	U value (W/m²K)
Wood	2.8
Metal	3.7
Metal (4mm thermal break)	3.4
Metal (12mm thermal break)	3.2
uPVC	3.0

Table 4.6 Indicative U-values of double glazing with different frame materials.

Figure 4.5 Cross section of a window frame showing position of the thermal break.

Lowest U-values are achieved by incorporating all of the above ideas for example, triple glazing with a soft (E = 0.05) low-E coating with 16mm air gaps ina timber or uPVC frame has a U-value of 1.3 W/m²K

NOVEL GLAZING

One idea for reducing the thermal transmittance of double glazing is to remove the conduction/convection path from between the outer and inner panes of glass . This involves removing the air in the cavity to create a vacuum[2]. Radiant heat exchanges would still occur but could be reduced by a low emissivity coating on the outer surface of the inner pane as described above. The problem with vacuum glazing is that the air pressure on the outer and inner panes is not counteracted by internal air pressure and so would crush the glazing at mid pane and cause it to break. To overcome this the cavity is reduced to 1mm and small support pegs are moulded into the glass throughout its area as shown in figure 4.6. This will create small thermal bridges but the cross sectional area of the supports are kept small to minimise this. Close inspection of the glazing would also allow the supports to be seen. Vacuum glazing is not widely available. It has a centre pane U-value of $0.8W/m^2K$.

Figure 4.6 Section through vacuum glazing.

4.3 Transparent Insulation Materials (TIM)

Windows are multi-functional elements letting in solar gains, daylight and ventilation whilst allowing views out and contact with the outside world. If a view is not required clear glazing can be replaced by transparent insulation material (TIM). TIMs have a low U-value and are actually translucent rather than transparent. This means light can get through them but it is diffused and so provides no view of the outside world. Limited contact with the outside world is retained by allowing changes in external daylight level to be perceived.

Locations where TIM can be used are rooflights and glazing panels above or below eye level. There are a number of different types of transparent insulation material including; multi-layer polycarbonate sheets,

aerogel and fibre glass panels.

GLASS REINFORCED PLASTIC

Glass reinforced plastic is a polymer sheet material that is reinforced using glass fibres. The sheets are 2mm thick and corrugated to give structural strength when spanning openings. Three sheets can be used to form a multi layer rooflight as shown in double layer form in figure 4.7. The light transmission of this is 50% and the U-value is $2.0 \ W/m^2K$. This system is widely used in factory unit rooflights. The system can also be constructed using polycarbonate and PVC sheets giving a choice of thermal and light transmission properties.

Figure 4.7 Rooflight composed of a double layer of corrugated GRP sheeting.

GLASS FIBRE

In this system translucent glass fibres are used to fill the void between translucent glass or plastic sheets as shown in figure 4.8. The glass fibre layer acts as an insulator but still allows light to pass through. Increasing the thickness of the layer of insulation reduces the U-value but results in a reduced light transmission as indicated in table 4.7.

AEROGEL

The low thermal conductivity of most insulating materials arises due to the presence of air filled voids within the material. Aerogel is silicon dioxide (the main constituent of glass) that has been formed into tiny beads 2-6mm in diameter containing microscopic pores. Because of the numerous air filled voids the material has a low thermal conductivity[3]. The product gets its name because it is formed by drying a gel of silicon dioxide. When it sets the porous structure is formed. Unfortunately contact with moisture after drying will destroy the porous and therefore insulating properties of the material. The framing/enclosure system in which it is used must protect it from contact with moisture.

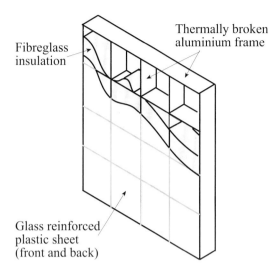

Figure 4.8 Structure of a translucent insulation panel.

Light Transmission (%)	U value (W/m^{2}K)
20	2.74
15	1.25
10	0.99
8	0.78
5	0.56

Table 4.7 Light transmission and U-values for glass fibre translucent insulation panels.

The material is held in place within a sealed sandwich of glass sheets. The U-value of a 16mm double glazed unit with an infill of aerogel is 1.0 W/m^{2}K. Light transmission is approximately 50%. One concern with this substance is its tendency to settle within the glazing. This is due to movement caused by cycles of expansion and contraction due to intermittent solar heating.

4.4 Other Elements

DOORS

Doors have traditionally been constructed out of solid timber with single glazed panels to allow light into hallways. Because of this they have a similar U-value to glazing and are, therefore, included with glazing in the determination of maximum glazed areas in the Building Regulations. New developments in doors has seen the introduction of insulated uPVC doors with low emissivity double glazed panels having an overall U-value of 1.0W/m^{2}K.

FLOORS

Ground floors can be either timber boards supported on floor joists with a cavity beneath or concrete in contact with the ground. Suspended timber floors are insulated between the joists. The insulation must be supported in place using thin ply wood sheets or plastic mesh (figure 4.9). Suspended floors are ventilated on the underside to prevent moisture build up and decay. The joists themselves should be hung from the inner leaf masonry using brackets so that they do not penetrate the inner leaf blockwork and create an air infiltration path (see chapter 5). In addition to this an air tight barrier must be included in the floor to prevent draughts entering the room from the ventilated sub floor space.

Figure 4.9 Suspended timber floor.

Heat losses through all parts of a suspended timber floor are uniform since conditions either side of the floor at all locations across it are similar. However, with solid floors in contact with the ground heat losses will be greatest along the edges adjoining the external wall (figure 4.10). This is because the ground underneath the centre of the floor will, over time, heat up reducing the temperature difference that causes heat loss. At the edge of the building the ground will be cooler because it loses heat to the outside and so more heat will be lost through the floor at the perimeter. Vertical edge insulation helps prevent perimeter heat losses (figure 4.11).

Figure 4.10 Heat loss is greatest at the perimeter of a solid floor.

Figure 4.11 Floor insulation being laid against edge insulation on a solid floor. Photo from GPG 94 Energy efficiency in new housing -ground floors (1993) © Crown Copyright

As a consequence of the different patterns of heat loss at the perimeter and centre of a large floor, the centre of it will have a small U-value and the edge will have a high U-value. The average U-value of the entire floor will depend on the relative sizes of perimeter and core floor areas. In large dimension floors, such as in commercial buildings, the core area will dominate and

so the average floor U-value will be low. In small floors such as in housing the perimeter areas will dominate and so the average U-value will be high. The amount of insulation needed in a solid floor in contact with the ground to achieve maximum U-values therefore depends on the perimeter (P) to area (A) ratio. This ratio is found by dividing the perimeter measured in metres by the floor area measured in square metres. With small floors the size of the perimeter is comparable to the area and so the the P/A ratio is large. Here a greater thickness of insulation is required. On large floors the size of the floor area is larger than the size of the perimeter and so the P/A ratio is small. Here a smaller thickness of insulation is needed to achieve a given U value. This is illustrated in table 4.8 which shows that the thickness of insulation (thermal conductivity $0.03W/mK$) needed to achieve a U value of $0.25W/m^2K$ decreases as the P/A ratio decreases.

P/A Ratio	Insulation thickness (mm)
1.0	91
0.9	90
0.8	88
0.7	85
0.6	82
0.5	77
0.4	70
0.3	59
0.2	39

Table 4.8 Thickness of insulation required in a solid floor in contact with the ground to achieve a U-value of $0.25W/m^2K$.

EXTERNAL WALLS

The type of construction used to form vertical elements of the outer shell varies depending on whether it is a domestic or commercial building. The basic requirements are however the same. The wall must be structurally sound, must have a low U-value and must prevent the ingress of wind and rain.

The majority of house walls in the UK are masonry cavity walls (figure 4.12). A smaller number of houses in the UK are made using timber frame construction. Timber frames have historically been used in the UK where the gaps between the frame was filled with masonry and mortar. This produced a wall prone to rain penetration and suffering from high heat losses. Modern timber frame walls have the gaps between the frame filled with insulation (figure 4.13). A large thickness is accommodated and so timber frame walls can have U-values as low as 0.15 W/m²K. Brick is often used as an external cladding material held away from the frame on brackets creating a cavity to prevent rain penetration. A breathable water resistant barrier is also incorporated into the construction for this purpose.

Figure 4.12 Insulation batts in a masonry wall. (GPG 95) © Crown Copyright

Small commercial buildings can use masonry and timber frame walls but taller buildings use steel or concrete frames. Again, as with timber framed buildings, brick can be used as cladding with insulation behind or, as is the case with shed type industrial and out of town retail units, insulated cladding panels are used composed of insulation sandwiched between thin metal sheets.

NOVEL WALL SYSTEMS

There are a number of experimental domestic wall systems currently being tried out. These include straw bale housing where the walls are constructed from straw bales used as construction blocks. The bales are rendered on the outer skin to provide protection from the rain and plastered on the inside. Openings are framed by timber. This type of wall gives low U-values and is considered as a sustainable material since CO_2

is absorbed by the material as it grows and little energy is used to construct the walls. A second system uses hollow polystyrene blocks in the same way that the straw bales are used.

Figure 4.13 Timber framed wall.

4.5 Super Insulation

It is possible to insulate buildings to such an extent that no heating system is required to maintain comfort conditions. A recent report from BRECSU[4] identified three categories of super insulated housing. The basic category is the **zero heating house**. The house is so highly insulated and draught proofed that the space heating requirement is met from casual gains from the sun, occupants bodies, lighting, appliances and cooking. An electrical supply is needed for appliances and a minimal heating system is installed for severe winters, reduced occupancy or for sensitive occupants such as the young, ill or elderly. The U-values required for a zero heating house are low as shown in table 4.9.

This type of house can be upgraded into a **zero CO_2 house** if the electricity and water heating were to be supplied from renewable sources. To be a zero CO_2 house it must create no net emissions of carbon dioxide over the course of a year. It can do this in two ways. Firstly it can utilise green electricity tariffs, as described in chapter 1, which are derived from renewable sources. Secondly, it can consume fuels and release CO_2 in the winter months but must pay this back by exporting the same amount of energy (based on CO_2 output) from renewable energy produced on site during other times in the year.

Element	U value (W/m²K)	How achieved
Roof	0.08	500mm celulose fibre
Floor	0.10	300mm expanded polystyrene
Walls	0.14	250mm full fill cavity
Windows /doors	1.7	Triple glazing with low E coating

Table 4.9 Elemental U-values for a zero heating house.

The next category is the **autonomous house** which satisfies the requirements of the above two standards but must be entirely separated from mains services. This includes electricity, gas, water and sewage. A grid connection to the electricity system is permissible but the building must generate its own electricity and over the course of a year be a net exporter. Rain and grey water must be collected, stored, filtered and sterilised on site for the water supply and sewage must be treated on site.

4.5.1 Risks of Super Insulation

Super insulation can eliminate the need for a space heating system however there are a number of technical risks associated with achieving this. These are:

- Thermal bridging

- Outer leaf damage

- Rain penetration

- Freezing of loft pipework

- Thermal discomfort.

Each of these is discussed in more detail below.

THERMAL BRIDGING

Ideally a super insulated house will have a continuous coating of insulation applied to its entire outer skin. In practice this is difficult to achieve since dense, high thermal conductivity elements are needed provide the structure of the building. These can create a thermal bridge between the inside and outside of the building. One example of this is shown in figure 4.14[5] which shows a thermal bridge created at the junction between the wall and ground floor. The high thermal conductivity masonry must be continuous as it has to transmit the loads it carries to the ground via the foundations. You could not link up the floor and wall insulation as the weight of the internal leaf would crush it. Figure 4.15 shows how cold bridging is minimised by overlapping the insulation. This is achieved by taking the wall insulation down below the floor slab and bringing the floor insulation up at the edge of the floor slab. There is a continuous thermal path but it has been made less effective by using low thermal conductivity blockwork. The insulation also makes the path narrow and tortuous.

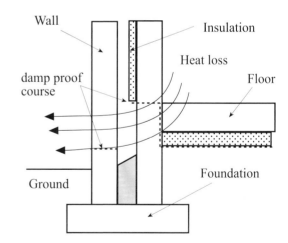

Figure 4.14 Thermal bridge between ground floor and wall.

Thermal bridging is also likely to occur at cavity closers, joins between intermediate floors and cavity walls and across lintels above windows and doors. The Building Research Establishment has produced a report[6] which describes thermal bridging in detail and the methods by which it can be avoided.

Low thermal conductivity blocks

Path for heat loss made more difficult

Figure 4.15 Elimination of thermal bridge.

OUTER LEAF DAMAGE

Figure 4.16 shows the fall in temperature through a wall of U-value 0.35 W/m^{2}K from 21°C inside to -4°C outside. It can be seen that the temperature of the outer leaf is below freezing temperature (0°C). This is because one of the effects of highly insulated walls is to raise internal surface temperatures as heat is kept in the building whilst at the same time reducing external fabric temperatures. This temperature will freeze any water in the masonry causing expansion and damage to the brickwork. It is essential that good quality outer leaf brickwork is used with sufficient water resistance and strength to avoid frost damage occurring.

RAIN PENETRATION

Achieving very low U-values in traditional cavity masonry wall construction requires that the entire cavity is filled with insulation. Table 4.2 shows that a super insulated house wall has a fully filled 250mm cavity. The main function of the cavity is to avoid the penetration of rain from the outer leaf to the inner leaf. Complete fills can introduce pathways for the rain to cross the cavity, wet the inner leaf, and damage finishes in the living spaces. There are three methods of avoiding this problem. The first is to maintain a cavity in areas that are at most risk from rain penetration. These are sites exposed to driving rain, as described below. The

second is to apply impervious but breathable cladding to the outer leaf. The third is to use insulation materials which do not have continuous horizontal pathways throughout their structure running between the outer and inner leaves along which water can run. An example of this are mineral wool batts which are woven so that the layers of material run vertically down the insulation layer rather than across it.

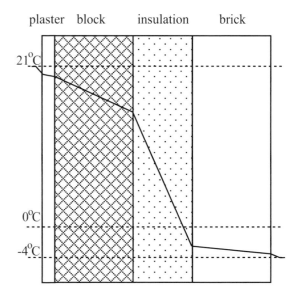

plaster   block   insulation   brick

Figure 4.16 Temperature profile through a highly insulated wall.

In section 2.4 the concept of driving rain was introduced and figure 2.12 showed a map of the UK indicating the six driving rain exposure categories ranging from very sheltered to very severely exposed[6]. The categories are for walls facing the prevailing wind direction on an open site. The actual exposure can vary depending on building height and topography. Higher floors and peaks of gable ends may be more exposed and buildings surrounded by trees may be in an exposure category one below those indicated in figure 2.14.

FREEZING OF LOFT PIPEWORK

The high insulation levels in first floor ceilings reduces the roof U-value but can lead to freezing temperatures occurring in the loft space. The effects of this are two fold. Firstly, warm moist air travels upwards throughout the building and may enter the loft space through unsealed loft hatches. When in the loft the water vapour will condense back to liquid water due to the low temperatures. The liquid water can soak into and degrade insulation materials and encourage decay of structural timbers. The problem can be overcome by ventilating the loft space at the eaves and ridge so that any moisture laden air is swept out of the loft space. It is also advisable to seal the loft hatch.

The second concern of low loft temperatures is the possibility that water tanks and pipework situated in the loft could freeze. This is avoided by insulating pipes and tanks individually or detailing the insulation to cover pipes and tanks rather than go under them (figure 4.17). This keeps the water systems within the heated space.

Figure 4.17 Loft Insulation to maintain ventilation and prevent pipework freezing.

THERMAL DISCOMFORT

In a building that has a degree of heat loss through its fabric, space heating is required to maintain comfort. If extra casual gains occur, such as solar heating, then the heat output from the heating system can be reduced to maintain a constant total heat input. With super insulated housing that does not have a mechanical heating system there is no capacity for reducing heat input if the building gets too warm. Heat input is provided solely by casual gains. So modification of

internal temperatures must be achieved my varying the size of the casual gains or by increasing heat losses. It must be assumed that heat gains from lighting, appliances and people are constant since it would be unacceptable to turn off lights and appliances or eject people if the building were to get too warm. Solar gains can however be reduced by lowering or adjusting blinds. This works but can cause the use of additional lighting and requires a high level of user interaction. The use of exposed mass within the building can help to even out temperatures. The mass absorbs excess heat when room temperatures are high and releases it when room temperatures fall again. Finally free cooling can be used. If the outside air temperature is lower than inside then additional ventilation will bring in cool fresh air and exhaust excess heat out of the building. This is particularly important in rooms such as the kitchen where cooking can account for short duration heat input of a few kilowatts. Heat inputs would greatly exceed heat losses unless the heat released from cooking were to be extracted at source.

4.6 Workmanship

To achieve low U-values a high standard of workmanship and site supervision is required. For example, insulation products need to be installed as per manufacturers guidelines so that there are no gaps present and making sure mortar is not dropped on the top of insulation batts creating gaps and cold bridges. Additional instructions and working drawings may be needed where detail is important or installation procedures are complex.

On completion, the insulation and cold bridging of the external envelope can be checked using thermography[9]. Thermography is an imaging technique similar to photography except that the camera is sensitive to infra red radiation (heat) as opposed to visible light. A thermographic image of a wall would be made up of different shades or colours. The lighter the shade or colour the greater the heat loss.

REFERENCES

1. The building regulations Part L conservation of fuel and power. 2002

2. Roche L. and Collins R. Smart Glass. Building Services Journal.pp 27-29 August 1997

3. Field A. Super insulation from Sand. Building Services Journal pp45-46. October 1994.

4. General Information Report 53. Building a Sustainable Future: Homes for an Autonomous Community.HMSO October 1998

5. Good Practice Guide 93. Energy Efficiency in New Housing: Detailing for designers and building professionals: Key detailing principles. HMSO. November 1993

6. Building Research Establishment. BRE Report 242. Thermal Insulation Avoiding the Risks. 2002

7. BS8104 Code of practice for assessing exposure of walls to wind driven rain. HMSO

8. Good Practice Guides. 99 to 110. Energy Efficiency in New Housing: Site Practice for Tradesmen. HMSO 1993.

9. Building Research Establishment. BRE Report 176. A practical guide to infra-red thermography for building surveys, 1991

05 VENTILATION

In this chapter we will find that;

- In a domestic building constructed to current insulation standards the ventilation heat loss rate can be greater than the fabric heat loss rate.

- Ventilation heat losses occur when warm air leaves the building and is replaced by cold outside air.

- For infiltration to occur gaps through and a pressure difference across the fabric are required.

- The rate of heat loss depends on the volume of the space, the temperature difference between inside and outside and the ventilation rate.

- Draught proofing by sealing cracks and gaps in the building envelope can reduce the infiltration rate to 0.5 ac/h.

- Fabric sealing techniques can reduce the infiltration rate to 0.2 ac/h.

- At infiltration rates less than 0.5 ac/h purpose built ventilation systems are required to maintain air quality.

- The amount of energy used by a fan depends on its efficiency, the rate of air movement and the resistance of the distribution system to air movement.

- The efficiency of an air movement system is described using the term "Specific fan power". An efficient system will have a value less than 1.5 kWh/m^3

- The duration of operation of a mechanical ventilation system must be limited by controls.

- Air to air heat recovery can be used in well sealed and mechanically ventilated buildings.

- In some commercial buildings natural ventilation can be used to replace mechanical ventilation

5.0 Introduction

A source of fresh air is a vital requirement for all buildings. It provides oxygen for breathing, dilutes and displaces pollutants such as body odours and metabolic carbon dioxide, avoids condensation by removing moisture, keeps buildings cool by removing excess heat and allows combustion appliances to operate safely. Unfortunately, ventilation also removes warm air, representing a loss of heat from the building.

Two terms are used to describe the movement of air in to and out of a building; infiltration and ventilation. **Infiltration** is the natural movement of air through cracks, gaps and porous elements of the building envelope. The air movement is driven by pressure differences created by the wind and the buoyancy of warm air. **Ventilation** can be either "natural" when it is the movement of air through purpose built openings in the fabric by naturally occurring pressure differences or "mechanical" when driven by fans through ducted openings. All of these processes are often simply referred to as "ventilation". Heat lost by both infiltration and ventilation is known as ventilation heat loss.

The speed with which air enters and leaves a building is known as the ventilation rate. This can be measured in litres of fresh air per second (l/s) or for particular rooms as a number of air changes per hour (ac/h). This is the number of times the air in a room is completely replaced by fresh air each hour.

In the past buildings were draughty places exacerbated by the presence of open fires which drew air from the room and up out of the chimney. Many existing buildings remain draughty. New building that are fitted with central heating and room sealed appliances that do not require flues are less draughty. In a house with no special attention paid to draught proofing the ventilation rate will be approximately 1.5 ac/h. If this was applied to the example house shown in figure IP3.2 it would give a ventilation heat loss rate of 2.9kW which is greater than the fabric heat loss rate as shown in figure 5.1. The figure also shows the benefits of further reductions in ventilation rate. At 0.5 ac/h the ventilation heat loss rate is just over one third that of the fabric heat loss rate.

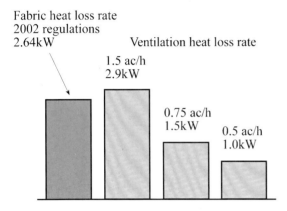

Fabric heat loss rate
2002 regulations
2.64kW

Ventilation heat loss rate

1.5 ac/h
2.9kW

0.75 ac/h
1.5kW

0.5 ac/h
1.0kW

Figure 5.1 Fabric and ventilation heat loss rates.

NON ENERGY ISSUES

Reducing the infiltration rate can have many advantages beyond reducing heat losses these are;

- Avoiding thermal discomfort arising from draughts

- Preventing dust and pollution ingress on polluted sites

- Ensures insulation, especially in cavities, is not short circuited

- Allowing correct operation of mechanical ventilation systems

- In hot climates, preventing overheating

- Reducing the capacity and hence cost of the heating and cooling system

THE ROLE OF OCCUPANTS

One major factor that has an influence on ventilation rate is the role of occupants. Door and window opening can greatly increase ventilation rates. This is outside the control of the building designer. However, it may be possible to provide sensors on windows which, in conjunction with an energy management system, can turn off the heating or air conditioning system when windows are opened.

This chapter will concentrate on the methods by which the air tightness of buildings can be improved, adequate ventilation maintained, heat recovered from exhaust air and natural ventilation provided in commercial buildings.

5.1 Infiltration

The routes by which air enters and leaves a building are as follows;

- Porous building materials.

- Cracks around service entries.

- Cracks in the join between window/door frame and the wall.

- Door and window opening.

- Suspended timber ground floors.

- Ventilated cavity - floor to wall connections.

- Ventilated cavity - dry lining plasterboard.

- Loft hatch.

- Open flues and chimneys.

- Openings for fans through walls.

- Steel and concrete framed commercial buildings are prone to leakiness around curtain walling elements.

The air movement is driven by pressure differences built up by the wind and temperature variations between inside and outside the building. Wind induced ventilation was described in section 2.3. Ventilation caused by temperature differences is called stack ventilation because a height difference is also required. This is illustrated in figure 5.2.

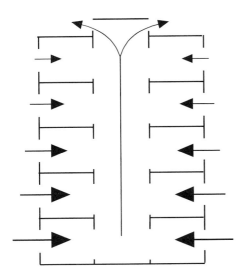

Figure 5.2 Stack ventilation.

Air inside buildings is generally warmer than the air outside due to heat gains from the heating system or casual sources. Warm air is less dense than cold air, so the air inside the building is less dense than that outside. Air inside the building will tend to rise and as it does so it creates a low air pressure relative to outside. As the warm air leaves the building at high level the low internal pressure draws fresh cold air in to the building through openings in the fabric. The pressure differences set up by this mechanism increase as temperature differences between inside and outside increase and also as the height difference between exhaust and intake points increases. So if the outside and inside temperatures are constant there will be a larger pressure difference between outside and inside on the ground floor than on the top floor. The pressure difference decreasing with each successive floor from ground level. In tall buildings this can mean that air movements on the ground floor are excessive and air movement on the uppermost floor is sluggish. Where stack ventilation is being used to replace the use of fans (section 5.6) the system can be balanced by varying the size of a damper opening between the room being ventilated and the stack. If air movement is excessive they can be closed, when sluggish they can be opened. The height of the stack must be carried

above the height of the building to maintain a height difference between the top of the stack and the topmost floor. Ventilation towers rising above the building is a necessary aesthetic of passively ventilated buildings driven by stack ventilation

In commercial buildings there are many routes that air can take in moving vertically up and out of the building these include lift shafts, stairwells and vertical service ducts. Air movement in these routes needs to be controlled to ensure the effective operation of purpose built vertical ventilation ducts.

5.1.2 Retaining Heated Air

There are two ways in which warm air can be retained in a building. These are ensuring internal air does not escape during door opening and draught proofing the external shell of the building.

DOOR OPENING

Warm air can escape as people and goods enter and leave buildings. In domestic and commercial buildings the amount of warm air that escapes when entering the building can be reduced by creating a draught lobby (figure 5.3). This is a zone at the entrance to the building having two doors. The first is the external door. Entering this will allow the air within the lobby to escape but the air beyond the second doors is retained in the building. The external door should be closed before progressing through the internal draught lobby door.

Figure 5.3 Draught lobby

Draught lobbies at the entrance to commercial buildings can restrict the flow of people. If this is a concern the draught lobby doors can be replaced by automatic doors which are normally closed but open when a person approaches them. When the flow of people is at its peak, such as at lunch time, it is possible that the automatic doors will be permanently open. To avoid this situation, revolving doors can be used. The nature of revolving doors means they form a permanent seal across the opening at all times whilst still allowing people to make their way in to and out of the building.

In factories and warehouses the main movement in to and out of the building is by raw materials inwards and goods outwards. These are often bulky requiring fork lift trucks to move them as a result factory doors are large. The concerns with large doors are their size and that they take a long time to open and close. This combination allows large volumes of warm air to escape during the door opening and closing process. A number of techniques are used to avoid this. The first is to replace the door with a flexible barrier. One example of this is the use of overlapping plastic strips hung vertically within the opening. When no movement is taking place the weight of the plastic strips causes them to hang together and seal the door. People and vehicles can push their way through the plastic strips creating an opening which is only as wide as is needed. After passing the plastic strips fall back in to place to form a complete barrier. The plastic strips are not ideal as strong winds can force them to open causing draughts.

An alternative draughtproof door are fast acting doors (figure 5.4). These are reinforced plastic sheets covering the door opening. The plastic sheet is attached to a motorised roller. When a vehicle approaches the door it is detected using sensors such as photocells or ultrasound, the motor is activated and this rapidly rolls up the barrier for the vehicle to pass. Once passed the barrier rapidly descends to cover the doorway again. The speed of opening and closing is up to 3m/s so a 6m high door will be opened in two seconds. The door is designed to prevent air loss and by the nature of its construction is not highly insulated. More highly insulated doors are available composed of hinged horizontal panels. The U-value of these doors is 0.4W/m²K. So heat is retained better than the fast, lightweight door when it is closed. However their speed of

operation is reduced to 1.5m/s

Figure 5.4 Fast acting door. photo fromGPCS 294 Energy efficient refurbishment of industrial buildings (1995). © Crown Copyright

The loading of goods on vehicles can take a long time with the loading bay doors open throughout the process. There are a number of ways heat loss through these doors can be avoided;

- Design the loading bay door dimensions and threshold heights so that when vehicles back up to the opening a seal is created between the trailer and pads around the loading bay door. This system also saves energy when frozen foods are being loaded into a refrigerated vehicle (figure 5.5).

- Partition the space behind the loading dock so that the space where goods are stored and people work for most of the time is heated but the loading bay area forms a separate zone and is unheated

- Use a heating system that is not based on warm air. Radiant heaters (chapter 9) should be used as these heat people rather than the air.

- Use sensors to turn the heating system off when doors are opened.

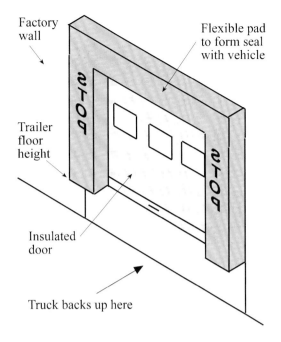

Figure 5.5 Loading door/vehicle seal

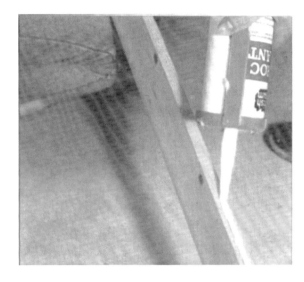

Figure 5.6Flexible silicon sealant being applied to a skirting board. photo fromGPG 93.2 Energy efficiency in new housing - detailing for designers and building professionals (1993) © Crown Copyright

DRAUGHT PROOFING

Draught proofing involves increasing the air tightness of the external envelope by closing air paths through it. These air paths were identified in section 5.1. The way in which they can be closed are:

Porous building materials. Construction materials have differing permeability's to air. Materials should be chosen with a low air permeability or the envelope should be sealed as described in section 5.1.2 below.

Service entries, masonry structure, joins between frames and walls The air movement routes around and through these are cracks and gaps. Gaps appear when two materials are butted together. Cracks are formed when a rigid material is trying to move, for example due to settlement or shrinkage, but is prevented from doing so by being held in position by the rest of the structure. The stresses that build up in the material cause it to crack. These cracks should not be filled using rigid fillers since further movement will crack the filler material. Instead the filler must be flexible. In this way further movement can be accommodated and the seal created by the filler retained. Silicon rubber extruded from a tube is an example of this type of material (figure

Door window openings, loft hatches. Sometimes the gap to be sealed is one that needs to be opened and closed. In this case a permanent sealant adhering to the two opposite surfaces is inappropriate. A flexible material must be used attached to one surface that will create a seal with the opposite surface. Rubber strips in the form of tubes and short nylon brushes are two examples of the materials that can be used. Rubber strips are usually held in position using self adhesive strips. The brush type seals require a more secure fixing and are usually screwed into place.

Floor wall joints/dry lining. There are no clear air movement paths through continuous materials such as in-situ concrete. However when two materials join or one material penetrates another an interface is created through which air can travel. Within buildings there are numerous interfaces like this. One example is where floor joists are supported at their ends by penetrating the inner leaf blockwork. A second is where plasterboard terminates at the floor (figure 5.7). The method for dealing with these infiltration routes firstly involves identifying them then creating detailed design drawings and site instructions to eliminate or seal them. In the case of our two examples joists can be hung from the inner leaf using brackets rather than penetrating it and silicon sealant can be used along the top and bottom edges of the skirting board to seal the infiltration route through the lower edge of the plasterboard (figure 5.8).

Figure 5.7 Infiltration routes.

Figure 5.8 Infiltration routes closed using 'robust details'.

Open flues and chimneys. Flues are designed to remove dangerous gases from the combustion appliance and deposit them safely outdoors. This is achieved by the natural buoyancy of hot combustion gases rising up out of the flue. Fresh air for combustion is drawn from the room in which the appliance is situated. If the appliance is powerful then much air will be drawn from the room and purpose built ventilation openings are required in the room wall or suspended floor to allow air to enter the room to make up for the combustion air removed from it. This process naturally removes warm air from the room to be lost up the flue. Ventilation rates in a typical house with and without an open fire are 4.0 and 1.5 ac/h respectively. However, the presence of open flues is an essential safety feature and flues should never be restricted or combustion gases will spill into the room and asphyxiate the occupants. To avoid this source of ventilation the combustion appliances should be room sealed. This means they do not take combustion air from the room. Instead they have a small section of ducting alongside the flue which brings combustion air into the appliance from outside the building (figure 5.9).

Draught proofing techniques as described above can reduce the ventilation rate of a domestic buildings to 0.5 ac/h. If the ventilation rate is reduced below this level problems may occur with poor air quality and condensation.

Figure 5.9 Room heater with balanced flue

5.1.2 Envelope Sealing

In some very cold countries such as Canada there is a requirement to treat the external envelope of the building as an air tight barrier. This means that as well as draught proofing to seal up cracks and gaps, the porous masonry materials must also be sealed. This involves building a continuous air tight membrane covering the entire outer skin of the building including walls, floor and upper floor ceiling. Good seals must be made between windows and doors and around service entries. As well as being continuous the barrier must be durable so that any movement in the building will not create tears.

The type of materials used include plastic sheeting such as polythene. Great care must be taken with sealing joins between sheets. Liquid compounds can also be used which are sprayed on to the masonry and which set to form a flexible airtight membrane. Finally, foamed plastic can be injected into the cavity between the leaves in masonry walls. This sets to create an airtight barrier and also offers thermal insulation. A thermographic study may be required to ensure the plastic foam is continuous.

Using sealing techniques as described above can reduce the ventilation rate of a domestic building to a value as low as 0.2 ac/h. This low ventilation rate would produce unacceptable air quality and condensation problems within the building. To avoid these problems purpose built and therefore controllable infiltration openings must be created in the building envelope. This form of ventilation must be used in conjunction with mechanical ventilation to remove heat, moisture and odours whenever they appear in high quantities. A strategy for the adequate ventilation of air tight buildings is described in section 5.3.

5.2 Air-tightness Testing

It is assumed that if a building is constructed using details which are known to give good air-tightness performance then the envelope leakage will be low. However, the only way to confirm this is to test the air tightness of the envelope. This is usually carried out by pressurising the building using fans[1]. For domestic buildings the front door is replaced by a panel containing a fan. The fan is run at a known speed until a constant internal pressure is achieved inside the building, usually 50 Pa above atmospheric pressure. (Pressure is measured in Pascals (Pa), normal atmospheric pressure is 101Pa but this is not noticed due to a balance between internal and external atmospheric pressures). At constant pressure the volume of air being moved into the building by the fan equals the volume of air escaping from the building through leakage routes. 50Pa is not a large pressurisation. This is useful as it means the building is performing close to normal pressures whilst masking temperature induced pressure variations. However wind pressures can greatly exceed 50Pa and so pressure testing should not be carried out on windy days.

The value obtained from this test is known as the Air Permeability of the building, measured in cubic metres of air per hour per square metre of envelope area (m^3/h/m^2). The air movement is divided by envelope area so that buildings of different sizes can be compared. The value represents the volume of air lost each hour through 1m^2 of the building envelope. Table 5.1 below shows good and best practice values of air permeability obtained by pressurisation testing in commercial buildings[2]. Some buildings when tested have extremely poor air permeability's with values as high as 34.0 m^3/h/m^2.

Building Type	Air permeability (m^3/h/m^2)	
	Good Practice	Best Practice
Office, air conditioned	5.0	3.0
Supermarket	5.0	3.0
Office naturally ventilated	10.0	7.5
Industrial buildings	15.0	10.0

Table 5.1 Good and best practice air permeabilities

The value obtained for air permeabilities is fine for comparing the air tightness of different buildings but to calculate the ventilation heat loss rate the ventilation rate measured in air changes per hour (ac/h) is required. This can be measured by pressurising the building and carrying out a tracer gas test as described below. However, the ventilation rate at pressure is greater than under normal atmospheric conditions. Experience has shown that by dividing the ventilation rate at 50Pa by 20 an approximation of the ventilation rate at normal atmospheric pressures can be determined.

Measurements of air change rate at standard room temperatures and pressures can be carried out using tracer gas measurements. Here a known volume of tracer gas is injected into the room. When first released the mixture of tracer gas and room air will result in a maximum concentration. This concentration is measured using a gas analyser. As ventilation of the space takes place some of the tracer gas will leave the building and be replaced by fresh air. As time progresses the concentration of tracer gas will slowly fall. The rate of fall in concentration indicates the ventilation rate. Ambient conditions such as internal/external temperatures and external wind speeds should be measured at the time of the tracer gas tests.

The specific route by which air is escaping from the building can only be determined by visualisation techniques. Visualisation involves releasing fine dust or smoke into moving airstreams. The movement of the dust/smoke reveals the movement of air streams. Outside the building smoke may be seen escaping through various cracks and gaps in the envelope. A second technique involves thermal imaging. The air inside the building is heated. Thermography outside the building would reveal escaping warm air as a bright plume on the thermographic image.

5.3 Building Regulations

Ventilation is considered in the building regulations. The aim is to provide adequate ventilation in buildings to avoid problems with poor air quality whilst reducing energy losses. Adequate ventilation is considered in part F of the regulations, energy losses are considered in part L.

AIR QUALITY REQUIREMENTS

There is a general acceptance that infiltration rates should be minimised as this is uncontrollable and that infiltration should be replaced by a three stranded strategy[3]. The approach is based on the principle of "build tight and ventilate right";

- Provide purpose built natural ventilation paths into the building which can be controlled.

- Provide openable windows for higher levels of short term ventilation.

- Extract moisture and odours at source using extract fans or passive stack ventilators.

Purpose built openings are often known as trickle ventilators they are sleeved ducts running from outside to inside the building through the building fabric often through the head of a window frame (figure 5.10). A rain and insect proof terminal is attached to the outside. On the inside is a terminal which incorporates an adjustable damper. This allows adjustment of the unit to provide the correct level of infiltration through the device. Sometimes this damper is automatic. For example it could be a flap within the duct which is normally in the fully open position. As wind speed increases air movement through the duct increases. This rapid air movement would cause draughts and excessive heat loss but the air movement lifts the damper which partially close the duct, restricting the air movement. When the wind speed drops the damper falls back to the open position. Table 5.2 shows the recommended open area of trickle ventilator for various locations. In commercial buildings it is recommended to have 400mm² of openable area for each square metre of floor area[4].

Openable windows are used on occasions when trickle ventilation is inadequate. Examples of this are in summer when the room is warm and ventilation is required to remove heat. A second example is when odours such as cooking smells or paint fumes have entered a room and require clearance. The building regulations requirement is for an openable window area of at least 5% of the floor area for habitable rooms and the toilet. Kitchens and bathrooms have no minimum openable window size as the window ventilation is backed up by mechanical extract. Windows should be closed when the ventilation problem has cleared.

Extract fans are used where the source of moisture or odours is known such as in kitchens, toilets and bathrooms. Fans consume electricity and remove heated air so they should only be operated when moisture or odours require removal. Activation of the fan may be manual by switch or automatic by linking to the bathroom light switch. Switching off the fan can again be manual, requiring the occupant to remember to switch the fan off, or it can be timed so that the fan runs on for a sufficient period of time to clear the residual moisture and odours. Another method is to use sensors such as humidity sensors that detect the moisture content of the bathroom air when the moisture content rises the fan switches on. When the moisture content returns to normal the fan switches off. Table 5.2 lists the extract rates specified for domestic buildings in the building regulations. Note, the kitchen extract rate can be reduced to 30 l/s if the extractor is fitted within 300mm of the hob. This usually means an over the hob extract hood.

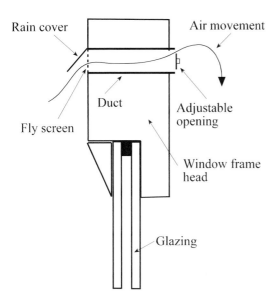

Figure 5.10 Trickle ventilator.

Room	Ventilation requirements		
	window	trickle	extract
Kitchen	opening	4000	60 l/s
Habitable Room	5% floor	8000	-
Bathroom	opening	4000	30 l/s
Toilet	5% floor	4000	6 l/s

Table 5.2 Ventilation requirements for various rooms.

In well heated, well managed dwellings controlled use of fans for moisture clearance is the most energy efficient method[5]. In less well heated homes passive stack ventilation (PSV) can be used (figure 5.11). This is a continuous background ventilation system comprising of a vertical duct running between the room requiring ventilation and the outside. The duct terminal should terminate at or above the apex of the roof to avoid wind induced down draughts. Air is extracted from the room by natural buoyancy up the stack. Recommended duct sizes are; kitchen 125mm, bathroom 100mm and toilet 80mm[6].

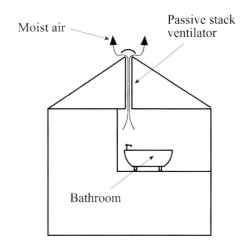

Figure 5.11 Passive stack ventilator.

In winter the temperature difference between inside and outside the building is at its greatest and so buoyancy in the stack will be increased. At this time a damper may be required in the stack to limit air movement.

The use of a PSV removes the need for extract fans that typically consume electricity at a rate of 90 Watts when extracting at 60 l/s and 35W at 30 l/s. However, it must be remembered that so long as the temperature is higher inside the building than outside warm air will be lost from the building via the PSV.

PART L REQUIREMENTS

A domestic buildings can demonstrate compliance with the energy conservation aspects of the Building Regulations by the incorporation of "robust details" that are known to reduce a buildings air permeability. One example of this is the use of joist hangers attached to the inner surface of the blockwork leaf of a cavity wall instead of running joists though the blockwork wall into the cavity. Air-tightness testing is mandatory in buildings over 1000m² floor area. The requirement is for the air permeability to be less than 10m³/h/m². The long term aim is to reduce this threshold to 5m³/h/m² by 2008.

5.4 Mechanical Ventilation

Mechanical ventilation involves the use of electrically driven fans to move air. The use of fans means that the amount of air delivered to or removed from a space can be closely managed. The energy consumption of a mechanical ventilation system arises due to;

- The electricity consumed by the fans. This depends on the efficiency of the electric motor, type of fan and the design of the air movement system as a whole.

- The heat lost from the building in the extract air. In some circumstances a proportion of this heat can be recovered using air to air heat recovery devices.

Both of these forms of energy consumption are discussed in more detail below.

5.4.1 Fan Energy Consumption

The electricity consumed by fans is a substantial proportion of the total amount of energy consumed in a mechanically ventilated and air conditioned building. This is illustrated in figure 5.12 which shows the breakdown in energy consumption of a best practice air conditioned building. It can be seen that fans, pumps and controls together consume 17% of the total energy consumption, equivalent to that used for lighting and over twice as much as that used in refrigeration.

A fan consumes electrical energy in order to move air from one location to another. To do this the fan must be sufficiently powerful to overcome the resistance

that the ductwork system offers to the flow of air. Figure 5.13 illustrates some of the elements that are involved in determining how much energy is consumed in a ventilation system. They are:

- **The type of impeller**. The type of impeller has important implications for system efficiency. The most efficient types are backward curved centrifugal fans, followed by aerofoil section propeller bladed fans. Uniform cross section propeller fans are the least efficient.

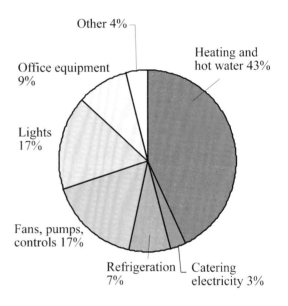

Figure 5.12 Breakdown of the energy consumption of a good practice air conditioned office.

- **The efficiency of the motor**. The electric motor in a fan is a machine for converting electricity to rotational movement. Unfortunately, some of the electrical energy is converted to heat by friction in the bearings, magnetic induction in the metal and resistance in the windings of the motor. As a result the motor is not 100% efficient at doing its task. The waste appearing as heat may also need to be removed by an air conditioning system so adding to the cooling load. The efficiency of a typical 3kW motor is 81%. More expensive but higher efficiency motors are available with improved bearings and low loss windings which have an efficiency of 85%.

- **Speed of the fan.** The greater the volume of air required the faster the fan must rotate. Increased speed increases the electrical consumption of the fan and vice versa. Maximum volumes of air are not always required by spaces. For example, a lecture theatre may require maximum volumes when fully occupied but require less fresh air when there are fewer people in the audience. An air quality sensor can be used to detect the level of occupancy based on carbon dioxide (CO_2) concentrations breathed out by the occupants. When fully occupied the concentration of CO_2 will be high, When unoccupied the CO_2 concentration will be low. A controller can use this information to instruct a variable speed drive to adjust the speed of the fan to deliver the required volume of air to reduce CO_2 levels to normal levels.

Diameter of duct
(flow rate of air)

Efficiency of fan

Presence of restrictive elements

Controls

Electrical supply

Volume of air moved

Figure 5.13 Factors involved in ventilation system energy consumption.

Larger section ducting allows air speeds to be reduced from typical values of 4 to 10m/s to 1 to 2m/s. This is because the larger cross sectional area encloses a larger volume of air for each metre of air movement. Finally, consideration should be made to separating the heating and cooling process from the ventilation process. Air has a low energy carrying capacity and so much larger volumes are needed to heat or cool a room than is needed for ventilation only. The energy consumed by a combined heating/cooling and ventilation system is much more than a ventilation only system. When a ventilation only system is being used heating or cooling can be provided by room based heating/cooling units.

- **System resistance.** The fan can only move air if it can generate a sufficiently large pressure differential to overcome the resistance to movement caused by friction in the system. The least friction is offered by straight lengths of ducting. Other components offer additional resistance as illustrated in table 5.3. The resistance factors shown relate to the resistance to airflow created by a straight 1m length of ducting. To reduce system resistance ducting should be; as short as possible, as straight as possible (where bends are used they should be gradual rather than abrupt) and the number of components used should be kept to a minimum. Finally, the system should be maintained regularly for example removing dust build up and replacing blocked air filters.

Component	resistance factor
90° bend (round)	0.65
90° bend (square)	1.25
branch	0.9
abrupt reducer	0.3
smooth reducer	0.04
open damper	0.3
diffuser	0.6

Table 5.3 Resistance factors (relative to 1m of duct) of some common ductwork components.

- **Controls.** The use of fans should be restricted to when ventilation is needed. Various control systems are available that restrict the operation of the fan. At its simplest this may involve a time switch that only allows the fan to operate during the hours of building occupancy. Better systems also monitor the requirement for ventilation. So if the ventilation is to remove moisture, provide ventilation for people or remove heat then relative humidity, air quality or temperature sensors should be used respectively. These sensors provide the information for a controller to switch off the fan when acceptable air quality conditions have been achieved.

SYSTEM POWER CONSUMPTION

The method of specifying system power consumption uses the value of specific fan power, measured in kWh/m^3. This is the rate of energy consumption by the fan (kW) divided by the rate of air flow (m^3/h). Table 5.4 lists values of specific fan powers against the system efficiency they represent. High efficiency systems should aim for specific fan powers less than 1.5kWh/m^3 with a best practice goal of 1.0 kWh/m^3.

System efficiency	Specific fan power (kWh/m^3)
High	< 1.5
Medium	1.5 to 4.0
Low	> 4.0

Table 5.4 Efficiency rating of specific fan powers.

DISPLACEMENT VENTILATION

Displacement ventilation is a method of ventilating a space that incorporates many of the low energy features described previously. The energy savings arise from the fact that air is input to the room at a very slow speed, considerably reducing fan energy consumption in comparison to traditional high level ventilation systems (figure 5.14).

With this system air is input to the room at very low velocity using raised floor terminals or low level wall terminals. The incoming air is usually tempered down to 18°C which is a relatively high temperature when compared to all air cooling systems. The low airspeed and high temperature are necessary to avoid discomfort since the air is input directly into the occupied zone.

The supply air is cooler than the existing room air and so it pools in a layer along the floor. The presence of any sources of heat such as occupants bodies, office electronic equipment or pools of sunlight on the office floor will heat this pool of air causing an upward convection current to develop at the site of the source of heat. As a result, fresh cool air is automatically brought

to the heat source. Heat sources usually coincide with a source of pollution. Occupants for example give out heat, metabolic CO_2 and odours. The rising warm stale air from these sources is extracted at high level.

Because of the relatively high input air temperature displacement ventilation cannot satisfy very high cooling loads and so it is often used in conjunction with a chilled ceiling or chilled beam cooling system (see section 10.6).

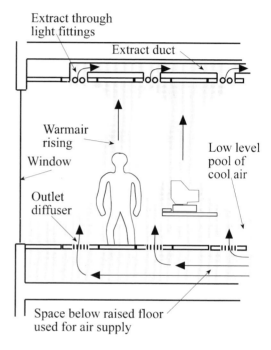

Figure 5.14 Displacement ventilation and chilled ceiling system.

5.5 Heat Recovery

When air is extracted from a building it is carrying energy with it either in the form of heat or coolth. If possible some of this energy should be recovered and used to pre-heat or pre-cool the fresh incoming air. The way in which this is achieved depends upon the type of mechanical ventilation system being utilised.

The three main types of mechanical ventilation system are;

- **Supply ventilation**. Here a fan is used to supply air to a space. Air is lost from the space via cracks and gaps in the building envelope. This system does not allow heat recovery.

- **Extract ventilation**. Here a fan is sited close to a source of pollution. The fan removes polluted air from the building. Supply air enters the building through cracks and gaps in the envelope. This system does not allow heat recovery.

- **Balanced ventilation**. This system uses two fans. One to supply air to the space and one to extract air from it. This system can allow heat recovery to take place.

5.5.1 Domestic Systems

When ventilating single rooms such as a kitchen, a small through the wall ventilation with heat recovery unit can be used (figure 5.15). The unit has two fans and two sets of ducting making it a small balanced ventilation system rather than an extract ventilation system. The fans cause incoming cool fresh air and out going warm stale air to pass through an air to air plate heat exchanger. The two air flows are separated by the thin metal or plastic sheets that make up the heat exchanger (figure 5.16).

The temperature difference between the warm exhaust air and the cool supply air causes heat to flow to the incoming air stream raising its temperature. Figure 5.17 shows the heat recovery efficiency of the unit against rate of air flow. As the extraction rate increases the efficiency falls off. This is because the air moves through the unit much quicker and so there is less time for heat exchange to take place.

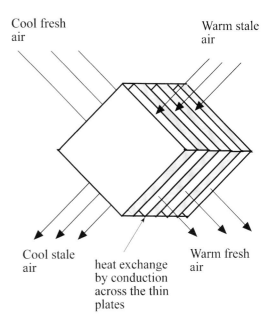

Figure 5.16 Air to air plate heat exchanger.

Figure 5.15 Through the wall ventilation unit with heat recovery.

Figure 5.17 Graph of efficiency against extract rate for an air to air plate heat exchanger.

TEMPERATURE EFFICIENCY

The efficiency of air to air heat exchangers is usually expressed as a temperature efficiency. Figure 5.18 shows the parameters used in calculating the temperature efficiency (TE)

$$TE = \frac{T_4 - T_3}{T_1 - T_3} \times 100$$

where;

T_1 = Extract inlet temperature to heat exchanger (°C)
T_2 = Extract leaving temperature (°C)
T_3 = Supply inlet temperature to heat exchanger (°C)
T_4 = Supply leaving temperature (°C)

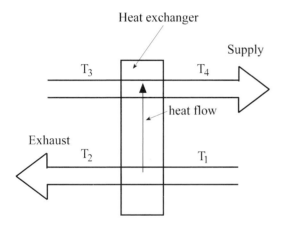

Figure 5.18 Temperature efficiency parameters.

MECHANICAL VENTILATION WITH HEAT RECOVERY

In highly sealed domestic buildings all rooms require mechanical ventilation to provide good air quality. To supply this a whole house mechanical ventilation with heat recovery (MVHR) unit is required. Such a system is shown in figure 5.19. The heat recovery unit is shown installed in the loft space however an alternative location is within a cupboard above the cooker extract hood (figure 5.20). Heat recovery is carried out using an air to air plate heat exchanger as described previously.

The MVHR system can only operate effectively if the house is well sealed[7]. In this way heat is recovered from all of the extracted air. If the house were leaky then air could enter and leave the building without passing through the heat exchanger.

Figure 5.19 Whole house mechanical ventilation with heat recovery.

Figure 5.20 Bahco heat recovery unit showing installation and finished appearance. © Crown Copyright

Page 80

5.5.2 Commercial Systems

When ventilation is combined with air conditioning the simplest form of heat recovery is to recycle a large proportion of the extracted air, say 80%, back in to the room (figure 5.21). In this way 80% of the energy in the air extracted from the room is recovered. A small proportion of fresh air, 20%, is added to the recirculated air to maintain air quality.

Figure 5.21 Recirculation of conditioned air.

When the air quality is poor, contaminated with either odours or moisture, then 100% exhaust and 100% fresh air should be used. An indoor air quality sensor can be used to determine the proportion of recirculated air varying from 80% to 0% as the room air quality changes from good to bad respectively.

In some rooms such as in a public house where smoking is taking place the air quality is always poor and so 100% fresh air should be used. In this circumstance air to air heat recovery should be employed.

PLATE HEAT EXCHANGERS

Air to air plate heat exchangers as described in the previous section for housing are also used for commercial heat recovery. Their location in an air con-

ditioning system is shown in figure 5.22.

Plate heat exchangers have a number of advantageous features;

• They have no moving parts that require maintenance.

• They keep the air streams separate so that no cross contamination can occur.

• No energy is required for their operation although fan power may need to be increased to overcome air resistance through the unit.

Figure 5.22 Location of air to air plate heat exchanger.

THERMAL WHEELS

Thermal wheels (efficiency 85%) are composed of a circular matrix of tubes through which air can flow (figure 5.23). The wheel is positioned across the inlet and exhaust ducting so that supply air passes through the upper half of the wheel and exhaust air passes through the lower half. As the exhaust air passes through the wheel the matrix is warmed. The wheel rotates slowly bringing this heated section into the path of the incoming air stream. The incoming air stream is heated by contact with the warmed thermal wheel matrix.

The thermal wheel requires an electric motor to rotate it and so the energy consumption of this needs to be considered in assessing the heat recovery efficiency.

Thermal wheels should not be used in areas where cross contamination of air flows would be a problem such as hospital operating theatres. This is because it is not possible to fully isolate the exhaust air from the supply air.

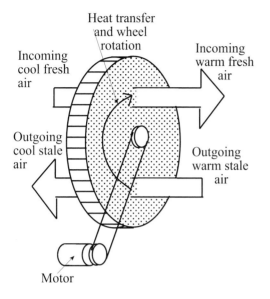

Figure 5.23 Thermal wheel.

RUN AROUND COILS

Run around coils (efficiency 55%) are heat recovery devices that can be used when supply and exhaust ducts are not run alongside each other. A finned coil is situated in the path of the exhaust air (figure 5.23). Air passing through the coil heats up a water and antifreeze mixture circulating in the pipe work. A pump circulates this heated solution to a similar coil installed in the supply duct. The supply air becomes heated by passing through this coil. Topping up, electrical consumption and maintenance of the system will need to be considered in the economic analysis of this device.

HEAT PUMPS

Heat pumps are similar to run around coils in that they can exchange heat between ducts that are separated by distance. They differ from run around coils in that they are filled with a refrigerant which evaporates in the coil situated in the exhaust duct. As the refrigerant

evaporates it absorbs heat. The refrigerant vapour then flows to the coil in the supply duct where it condenses and in doing so releases the heat it has absorbed. The pipe work is fitted with a compressor and pressure reducing valve that enable movement of the refrigerant and the evaporation and condensation of the refrigerant to take place.

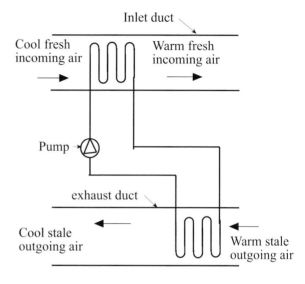

Figure 5.24 Run around coil.

BY-PASSING THE HEAT EXCHANGER

In summer it is desirable to cool a building by bringing in fresh cool ventilation air. This is known as free cooling. However, if this ventilation air has to pass over a heat recovery device it will be pre-heated before entering the building. It is necessary at times therefore for incoming air to be able to by-pass the heat recovery unit. This requires some extra ducting and dampers to re-route the airstream. An additional benefit to by-passing the heat exchanger is the fact that it avoids the pressure drop in the system caused by the heat recovery unit. The pressure drop for example in a run around coil is approximately 60Pa, through a thermal wheel it is 120Pa. A pressure sensor and variable speed control unit are required for the system to detect that the heat exchanger has been by passed indicating that the fans do not need to work as hard to push air through the ducting.

ECONOMICS OF HEAT RECOVERY

Heat recovery devices represent a capital cost that must be recovered in the value of energy savings made. For heat recovery devices to be economical;

- The capital and installation costs should be low

- The running costs should be low

- The amount and therefore value of energy recovered should be high

There are a number of factors that affect the size of costs and savings;

Initial costs involve the capital and installation costs of the heat recovery device. However, some of this may be offset by savings arising from reductions in the size of boiler or cooling plant, made possible by the availability of recovered energy.

Running costs involve a debit in terms of electricity used by fans, pumps and motors and also maintenance costs. The credit is in the value of recovered energy. Running costs and credits are strongly dependent on the hours run by the system and availability of energy for recovery and the efficiency with which it is recovered. For example cost effectiveness will be greatest in winter when differences between inside and outside temperatures are at their largest. Similarly the cumulative value of energy savings will increase in buildings where the ventilation system runs for a large number of hours each day.

5.6 Natural Ventilation in Commercial Buildings

Since the operation of fans consumes energy it is desirable to avoid their use whenever possible. This is difficult in buildings with deep floor plans as more of the floor space will be away from the perimeter where natural ventilation is available. One of the ways of reducing the need for mechanical ventilation is to keep floor plans narrow as described previously in section 3.1.1. Single sided natural ventilation, which arises due to wind turbulence is illustrated in figure 5.25.

The rule of thumb for single sided ventilation is that it is available up to a depth of 6m from the facade. Cross ventilation (figure 5.25) is driven by pressure differences across the building due to the wind. The rule of thumb for cross ventilation is that it is effective across a plan depth of 13m. This is assuming there are no partitions across the space which would close the ventilation pathway.

With both single sided and cross ventilation it is desirable to have high level ventilation openings as these can clear pollutants without the air stream impinging on the occupants and creating draughts.

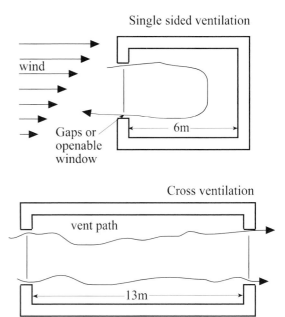

Figure 5.25 Single sided and cross ventilation.

A number of designers are achieving deeper floor plans than described above by providing ventilation stacks within the building. An internal stack shortens the distance over which the air must travel to reach an escape point so cutting down on the resistance to movement. The stacks may be purpose built vertical ducts or an internal atrium. A good example of a duct/ lightwell system is the passively ventilated library at Coventry University[8]. This building has a 50m square plan shape. Air enters each floor via four corner lightwells. It is then drawn to either perimeter ventilation stacks or a central lightwell/ventilation stack. This creates a radial air distribution pattern which gives good air distribution across the space Figure 5.26.

Plan

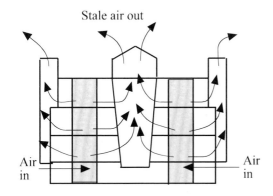

Schematic section

Figure 5.26 Stack ventilation at Coventry University library.

REFERENCES

1. CIBSE Technical Memorandum TM23 Testing Buildings for Air Leakage. CIBSE Publications 2000

2. Bordass, W. Envelope Airtightness. The Architects Journal. pp 48-51 13th April 2000.

3. The Building Regulations Part F: Ventilation HMSO 1995

4. Building Research Establishment. Digest 399: Natural Ventilation in Non-domestic Buildings. HMSO October 1994.

5. Wolliscroft, M. The Passive Approach Does it Stack Up? Building services, pp 28 -30. September 1994.

6. Building Research Establishment Information Paper 13/94. Passive Stack Ventilation. HMSO 1994

7. Stephen, R K. Domestic Mechanical Ventilation: Guidelines for Designers and Installers. BRE IP/18/88. HMSO 1988.

8. Field, J.Building Analysis: Coventry University Library. Building Services Journal pp18-22. December 2000.

FURTHER READING

Good Practice Case Study 10: Llanerchydol Park, Welshpool. January 1990

General Information Leaflet 9: Domestic Ventilation. February 1993

Good Practice Guide 224: Improving Air Tightness in Existing Homes. 1994

06 DAYLIGHT

In this chapter we will find that;

- Daylight can be used to remove or reduce the need for electric lighting.

- The percentage of daylight that reaches a point in a room is known as the daylight factor.

- Most daylighting is provided by vertical glazing. The height and width of glazing affects daylight penetration and spread respectively.

- Daylight distribution within a room is improved by light reflective surfaces.

- Increasing window size to increase the entry of daylight can lead to problems of excess heat loss and glare in winter and overheating in summer.

- Daylight tends to be concentrated near the window. Penetration of daylight deep into rooms is poor.

- Various techniques can be used to improve the spread of daylight in a room. These include; light shelves, louvres, prismatic glazing and prismatic films.

- Roof lights are an effective method of improving daylight penetration in single storey buildings or top floors of multi storey buildings.

- Light pipes direct light along guides to internal spaces.

- Atria and lightwells can improve daylighting in deep plan buildings but their design needs to be considered carefully.

- Daylight can be assessed at the design stage using graphical techniques such as daylight factor protractors, physical modelling using an artificial sky or computer modelling.

6.0 Introduction

Daylight is the preferred form of illumination in buildings. The human eye has evolved using it and therefore it delivers the best colour rendering properties of any light source. It also gives building occupants contact with the outside world. Weather variations, and the passage of the day are revealed in changing patterns of daylight. Of most importance to this subject is the fact that unlike electric lighting, it does not require electricity to create it. However, daylight is not entirely free. It is provided through glazing systems which are thermally poor and so there is a cost in terms of additional space heating energy consumption. This energy consumption is not solely due to the provision of daylighting but is also associated with the other functions of windows which are the provision of views and ventilation.

Daylight can only reduce the buildings energy consumption if electric lighting is turned down or switched off in response to daylight entry.

An effective daylight strategy therefore requires;

- Fenestration, plan shape and internal finishes and layout design for optimum daylight entry and distribution.

- Reduction of heat losses through the glazed areas.

- Avoidance of glare.

- Avoidance of unwanted solar gains.

- Design and control of electric lighting in response to available daylight (see chapter 7).

The potential for energy savings from daylight are large. In figure 1.3 it was shown that electric lighting accounts for 20% of the energy consumption of a typical naturally ventilated office. Table 6.1 shows the percentage of the total energy consumed by lighting in a range of building types. It also shows estimated potential savings arising from the adoption of a daylighting strategy[1]. The greatest savings occur when;

- The electric lighting system has been wired into zones that can be controlled separately in response to daylight availability.

- Where there is a well motivated workforce or central control system switching off lights in response to daylight entry

- In spaces where illumination with daylight is preferable to artificial illumination

Building Type	Proportion of total primary energy used for lighting (%)	Estimated saving from the uptake of a daylight strategy (%)
multi residential	45	small
offices	30-50	20-40
shops	90	small
education	22	10-30
health	20-30	10-20
factories	15	10-20

Table 6.1 energy consumption by electric lighting and potential savings from daylighting

Following these rules it can be seen from table 6.1 that the greatest potential for savings from daylight is in offices. This is because daylight is valued and wiring and control systems can be installed to make use of it. In shops the potential saving from daylight is small. This is because traders value electric lighting as a means of displaying goods to their best advantage. Multi residential buildings have a small savings potential since each room is under individual occupant control.

This chapter will look at how these savings can be realised beginning with a study of how daylight enters a building. This knowledge will enable us to optimise certain elements such as glazing and internal finishes to improve daylight entry. The chapter will then investigate the problems associated with daylighting

including poor distribution in rooms, heat losses, glare and summertime overheating. The chapter will end by considering how daylighting in buildings is assessed. Note, within the text daylighting is sometimes referred to as natural lighting and electric lighting is also known as artificial lighting.

6.1 Daylight

The sun is a large nuclear fusion reactor. Hydrogen and deuterium combine within the suns outer layers to produce helium and large quantities of energy. This energy is radiated away from the sun as electromagnetic (EM) radiation. Electromagnetic radiation is emitted as a waveform. The EM radiation from the sun is not comprised of a single wavelength but has many wavelengths making up a range or spectrum of values. Each different wavelength has different properties (figure 6.1). The shorter the wavelength the more energy is contained within the radiation. The very short and therefore most energetic wavelengths are cosmic rays, x- rays and gamma rays. The next group is the ultraviolet (UV) radiation.

Daylight is the band of wavelengths between 400 and 760nm that are visible to the eye. This band can be sub divided into individual wavelengths which the eye detects and the brain interprets as different colours. All of these wavelengths combined together to give white light. It is this mixed light which makes up daylight. The actual spectral distribution in daylight varies depending on weather conditions and time of day. An extreme example is the dominance of red wavelengths late in the day as the sun sets.

Daylight is comprised of two components, sunlight and skylight.

Sunlight is light from the sun that passes through a clear sky. It is directional which means it can create distinct pools of bright light within rooms and causes objects to cast shadows. It also carries with it a large amount of infra red radiation (heat). This can be useful in winter for solar heat gains or problematic in summer by causing overheating. Overheating is a particular concern in commercial buildings as they already suffer from heat gains given out by equipment and high occupant densities. Where sunlight can enter a room some form of adjustable sun screening is usually required so that glare and energy deposition can be controlled.

Figure 6.1 The electromagnetic spectrum

Skylight is sunlight which has been scattered and diffused by moisture and particulates in the atmosphere. The more heavily overcast the sky the more scattered and therefore less directional the light is. Skylight provides less light and much less heat than sunlight. Even so, the amount of light provided by even a heavily overcast sky would easily satisfy most visual requirements if it were able to enter a building.

STANDARD SKIES

The quantity of daylight is very variable depending on the time of day, atmospheric pollution and weather conditions. To help in daylighting design a number of fixed standard sky models have been proposed so that people working on daylight designs can do so to a common standard.

Clear blue sky - This sky model is used for sunlighting design. As the name implies it is for summers in the UK or countries with hot climates where sunlight predominates. In the UK daylighting design is carried out using overcast sky models as this is the most common situation encountered here.

Uniform overcast sky - This sky model represents a heavily overcast sky. It is considered to have uniform luminance. That is to say it is equally bright regardless of which direction you look in. It can be described graphically as a band whose uniform thickness represents the constant luminance in all directions (figure 6.2). Uniform overcast skies are not often used for design purposes.

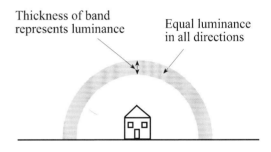

Figure 6.2 Luminance distribution of a uniform overcast sky

Commission International de Eclarage (CIE) standard overcast sky - This sky model is intended to give an indication of the variation in the brightness of a less overcast sky than the uniform overcast sky. It has a defined luminance distribution that is considered to be three times brighter when looking directly overhead than when looking at the horizon. There is a gradual variation between maximum and minimum luminances as the angle of view increases from the horizon to the zenith(figure 6.3). This sky model is the one that is used most frequently for UK daylighting design.

The illuminance provided by a sky varies depending on how overcast it is and the time of day. For design purposes it is assumed that standard overcast skies produce an illuminance of 5000 lux on the ground. This is a conservative figure since there is usually more daylight than this and so 5000 lux is exceeded for 85% of the working day (09.00 - 17.00 hours) by the actual sky throughout the year.

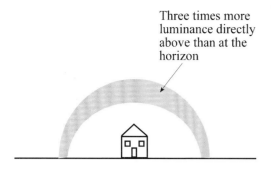

Three times more luminance directly above than at the horizon

Figure 6.3 Luminance distribution of a CIE sky

The luminance distribution of these standard skies are built into various daylighting design methods which are described in more detail in section 6.7.

6.2 Daylight Factors

Because of the variability of daylight it is difficult to be specific about absolute quantities entering a room. Instead the amount of daylight at a particular point in a room is described by the daylight factor. The daylight factor is the proportion of the unobstructed external daylight illuminance that reaches a point inside the room. If the building were to be removed, the point of interest would receive all of the available daylight and so the daylight factor would be 100%. If the room had no windows the daylight factor would be 0%. The amount of daylight entering a typical domestic room is small and so the typical average daylight factor across a room can be as low as 3%. The daylight factor at any point in the room remains the same on both bright and dull days even though the illuminance provided by natural light will be greater on a bright day than a dull day.

The daylight factor at a particular point in a room can be determined from the formula;

$$DF = \frac{E_i}{E_o} \times 100 \qquad (\%)$$

where   DF = daylight factor (%)
E_i = Illuminance at the reference point (lux)
E_o = External Illuminance (lux)

For example if the external illuminance E_o due to a

standard overcast sky is 5000 lx and the average illuminance on a work surface near a window was 300 lx then the average daylight factor over the surface would be;

$$DF = \frac{300}{5000} \times 100 \ = 6\%$$

Points of similar daylight factor within a room can be joined together to give a contour map of daylight distribution as shown in figure 6.4. Measurements are usually taken at a certain level above the floor within the room called the working plane height. This height is that at which the important visual task is taking place. It could be floor level in the case of circulation routes but in workplaces it is an imaginary plane passing through the top surface of the desks - approximately 0.85m above the floor.

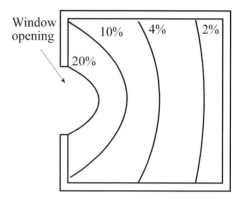

Figure 6.4 Plan of a room at working plane height showing daylight factor contours.

Figures 6.4 and 6.5 show the daylight factor contours in a domestic living room. It can be seen that the daylight factor is relatively high near the windows but this rapidly falls off towards the back of the room. This reduction in daylight with distance away from the windows is one of the issues that requires attention in daylighting design.

COMPONENTS OF THE DAYLIGHT FACTOR

The daylight reaching a point in a room is considered to be made up of three components (figure 6.6). The sky component (SC) which is daylight directly from the sky, the externally reflected component (ERC) which is daylight reflected from external objects and

IP5 - Lighting Terminology

This information panel gives a description of some of the terminology used in natural and artificial lighting studies.

luminous intensity (I) is the power of a light source when viewed from a particular direction. It is measured in units of candela (cd). This is a modern unit but is named after the old practice of comparing the luminous intensity of light sources against a standard candle.

Luminance (L) is a measure of the luminous intensity of light emitted or reflected in a given direction divided by the area of the surface. Luminance is therefore measured in candela per square metre cd/m^2. It can be considered to be the brightness of a surface, although strictly speaking brightness is the human appreciation of the luminous intensity. There are two types of luminous surfaces, the first are self luminant surfaces such as the sun and light bulbs. The second are surfaces that reflect light and therefore appear to be light sources themselves. Room surfaces do this as does the moon which appears lit but is in fact reflecting sunlight from the other side of the earth.

The luminance of self luminant surfaces depends on the power of the light source i.e. its ability to emit light and its surface area. So for example if the power of the source is fixed a small surface area light source would appear brighter than a larger surface area with the same power. For example if a light bulb and a fluorescent tube had the same power the tungsten bulb would appear brighter than the fluorescent tube because its light emitting power is concentrated into a smaller surface area.

The luminance of reflective surfaces depends on how much light is falling on the surface (see illuminance below) and how much of this is then reflected back into the observers eye. This latter factor depends on the reflectance of the surface. A perfectly reflecting surface would have a reflectance of 100%. A surface which absorbed all of the light falling on it would have a reflectance of 0%. Table IP5.1 shows the reflectances of various surfaces. The two physical aspects of the surface that affect its reflectance are surface colour and texture. The reflectance of white painted plaster is greater than that of white painted concrete. This is because, for a given colour, the more coarse its texture the lower the reflectance. The reflectance of raw concrete is lower than that of white painted concrete. Here the texture is the same but the raw concrete has a darker surface and therefore absorbs more light.

Surface	Reflectance (%)
Raw concrete (grey)	40
White painted concrete	60
White painted plaster	80
Brown carpet	10
Light plywood	35
Brick	30
Gloss white paint	85

Table IP5.1 Reflectances of various surfaces.

With a given amount of light falling on the surface the higher the reflectance the higher the luminance of the surface.

Illuminance (E) is a term which describes how much light energy is falling on to a surface. The amount of light energy flowing through a particular volume of space is called the **luminous flux** (F) measured in lumen (lm). If this flux falls on an area (A) m^2 then the illuminance, E will be;

$$E = \frac{F}{A} \quad (lux)$$

Illuminance is the value given in lighting design guides to recommend the amount of light needed so that tasks can be carried out efficiently, safely and in comfort. Table IP5.2 lists some recommended values of illuminance for various tasks. Generally the more complex the task the more light that is needed and so a greater illuminance is required. When lighting is provided by an array of electric lights the illuminance will vary across the working plane. There will be a peak illuminance directly beneath the luminaires and a minimum in between the rows of luminaires.

Illuminance uniformity is a term based on the ratio between minimum and average illuminance that is used to describe the variation of illuminance across the working plane. Maintained illuminance is the minimum acceptable illuminance for a given task. This will be reached because the light output of lamps diminishes with age. At this stage the tubes must be replaced to raise the illuminance above the maintained illuminance level.

Task	Recommended Illuminance (lux)
Circulation (stairs)	150
Classroom desk	300
Office desk	500
Laboratory bench	500
Electronics assembly	1000
Operating theatre	2000

Table IP5.2 Recommended Illuminances for various spaces

COLOUR RENDERING

The ability to see individual colours on an object depends on the spectral composition of the light source. This is because in order to see a particular colour on a surface, that colour of light must be present in the light hitting the surface. Good colour rendering is illustrated in figure IP5.1. Good quality light such as daylight or a full spectrum electric light source is used to illuminate a blue surface. Blue wavelength light is reflected from the surface and enters the eye hence the surface appears blue. The other wavelengths are absorbed. Since the illuminating source contains all wavelengths this light would allow the colour of all surfaces to be distinguished. However, figure IP5.2 illustrates a case of poor colour rendering. The surface is illuminated by a tungsten bulb which is strong in light output towards the red part of the spectrum but poor in light output in the blue part of the spectrum. Since there is little blue light to be reflected the surface appears black. It is for this reason that it is difficult to distinguish between navy blue and black garments under tungsten lighting.

Surfaces that are white under full spectrum light apper to have a yellow tint under tungsten light as they are relecting the wavelengths that are are hitting the surface. The human eye sees this as a 'warm' white light. The effect is exagerated when taking photographs indoors without a flash. The photograps when developed have a strong yellow tint.

The ability of different sources of light to reveal the colour of surfaces is specified using the **colour rendering index (Ra)**. The colour rendering index is a number. A value above 80 is good and above 100 excellent. In spaces where colour rendering is important such as graphic design studios lamps should be chosen with a colour rendering index above 90.

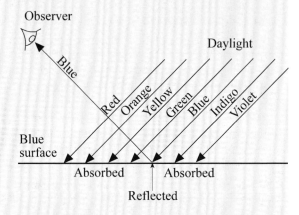

Figure IP5.1 Full spectrum light source gives good colour rendering

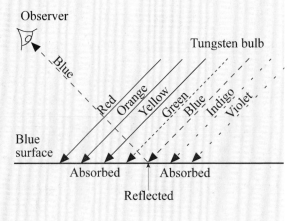

Figure IP5.2 Limited spectrum light source gives poor colour rendering.

finally the internally reflected component (IRC) which is daylight reaching the point of interest having been reflected from internal surfaces. All of the components are described as a percentage of the available daylight that reaches a point within the room by the path taken. Summing all of the components together gives the daylight factor i.e. DF = SC + IRC + ERC. An understanding of the factors affecting the size of these components can reveal how daylight entry to rooms can be improved.

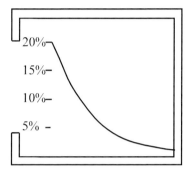

Figure 6.5 Section of a room with overlaid graph of daylight factor against distance in to the room.

Figure 6.6 Components of the daylight factor

Sky component The size of this component depends on;

- Brightness (Luminance) of that part of the sky which is visible from the reference point. This depends on how overcast the sky is.

- The size and location of the piece of sky seen from the point of interest. This depends on the window dimensions. If we assume the sky is a CIE sky, a tall window will allow the reference point to see a larger and brighter area of the sky than a short window as shown in figure 6.7.

- Obstruction of the sky by external objects such as trees or other buildings.

- The daylight transmission factor of the glazing system. Glazing bars reduce the size of the window opening and glazing does not have perfect light transmission. Single glazing transmits 87% of the available daylight falling upon it whilst double glazing has a transmission factor of approximately 77%. Window films or dirt build up reduces light transmission further.

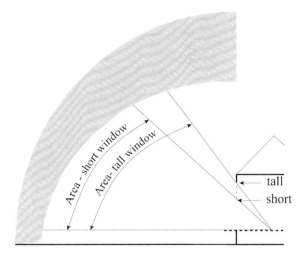

Figure 6.7 Area of sky seen by the reference point through tall and short windows.

Of the three components, the sky component is the most important since it is not degraded by reflections. However, its importance diminishes as the point of interest moves away from the window. This is illustrated in figure 6.8 which shows that a point away from the window sees a smaller, and on average lower luminance, area of sky than a point near the window.

Internally reflected component. The size of this component depends on all of the factors described above for the sky component with the addition of:

- The reflectance of the internal surfaces. Typical reflectances of walls and ceilings are in the range 60 - 80%. These are high values because the surfaces are usually painted light colours. Floors on the other hand have reflection factors in the range 20 - 30% this is low because floors are often dark or carpeted to hide marks made by shoes.

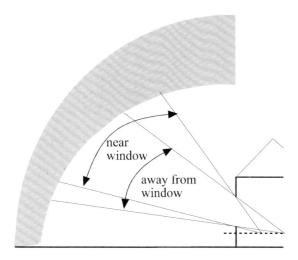

Figure 6.8 Area of sky seen by reference points near to and away from the window

The internally reflected component is less significant than the sky component near the window but becomes more important at the back of the room away from the window. This is because most of the daylight reaching the rear of the room has been reflected there from internal surfaces.

Externally reflected component. The size of this component depends on all of the factors described above for the sky component with the addition of;

- The size of the external object

- The reflectance of the external object. Most external objects have a low reflectances as illustrated in table 6.2 . This is because they often have dark rough surfaces such as trees, masonry or concrete.

Because of the low reflectancess of external objects the externally reflected component is usually the smallest of the three components contributing to the daylight factor. If there are no vertical external surfaces near to the window the ground may contribute an external component, however this is unlikely to reach the working plane without being internally reflected also.

Surface	Reflectance (%)
grass	12
soil	15
tarmac	10
paving	40
brick	30
concrete	42

Table 6.2 Reflectances of some common external surfaces.

6.2.1 Improving Daylight Entry

From a knowledge of how daylight enters a room, derived from looking at the components of the daylight factor, we can make some recommendations for improving daylight entry. These are;

- Avoid the obstruction of windows by external objects such as trees, climbing plants and buildings. Remove obstructions or maintain as much separation between windows and external structures as is possible

- Make external surfaces opposite or beneath windows light coloured. Light coloured paving will reflect daylight upwards into the building.

- Tall windows increase the depth of daylight penetration in to the room

- Wide windows increase the spread of daylight across the room

- Use splayed reveals to increase the area of sky 'seen' by points within the room.

- Use alternatives to reflective or absorbent glazing as a method for reducing solar gains. These methods reduce daylight entry too. Consider using adjustable solar control such as venetian blinds which can be retracted on dull days to maximise daylight entry.

- Select glazing systems with the minimum of glazing bars.

- Keep internal surfaces light to improve internal reflections and distribution of light.

- Keep the interior space open to daylight flow. For example use glazed or spindle balustrades. Allow deeper spaces such as corridors to borrow some daylight through glass panels within or above doors.

- When the building is occupied avoid placing obstructions such as furniture or plants etc. behind windows. There is a particular problem in schools where the windows are wrongly used as an additional display board with childrens work obstructing the entry of daylight.

6.3 Daylighting Problems

Increasing the height and width of windows increases the depth and spread of daylight. It also results in larger windows. Large windows create problems with increased heat loss, glare and solar overheating. Daylighting strategies are only successful if the three problems are considered and eliminated at the design stage.

INCREASED HEAT LOSS

The most effective method of reducing the amount of heat lost through glazing is to reduce its area. A compromise must be made between reasonable levels of daylight and acceptable heat losses. As window sizes increase there comes a point when the room is supplied with enough daylight for the activities being carried out in that space. Further increases in window area will not bring in any more useful light. This has been illustrated previously in figure IP4.1 on page 44 where increasing the glazed ratio beyond 40% in a south facing office begins to increase energy consumption rather than reduce it.

The second method of reducing glazing heat losses was discussed in chapter 4. This involved reducing the U-value of the glazing using multiple glazing, low emissivity coatings and cavity fill gases. Where a view is not required but daylight is, transparent insulation materials can be used. Movable insulation such as insulated shutters, blinds or curtains can be used to reduce heat loss through glazing during the hours of darkness. This also eliminates the unsightly 'black hole' effect that occurs when looking at windows in a lit room at night. If the internal surface of the movable insulation is light coloured it will also reduce the loss of electric light by reflecting it back into the room.

Reducing heat losses through glazing removes the associated problem of cold down draughts from the glazing and reduced surface temperatures, both of which can cause thermal discomfort.

GLARE

Glare is the discomfort or interference with vision caused by a bright object appearing in the field of view. Glare occurs as a result of how the eye adapts to its visual environment. The eye can adapt to a very wide range of ambient light conditions from a 0.1 lux moonlit night to 100,000 lux bright sunlit day. It does this by adaptation and adjusting the size of the pupil. On bright days the pupil is small, restricting the entry of light in to the eye. On dull days the pupil is large facilitating the entry of light into the eye. However the eye does not accommodate all of this range at the same time. Instead it adapts to a small band of luminances within the large range as illustrated in figure 6.9

As the eye adapts to differing light conditions the adaptation zone slides up and down the full range of adaptation. The eye adapts to light changes relatively slowly. What this means is that if we assume the situation in figure 6.8 represents adaptation to typical room luminances then as the eye falls upon a large, bright window it will see luminances near to the bright day end of the scale. Too much light will enter the eye and discomfort or silhouetting of objects of interest will occur.

Moonlit night   Range of   Bright day
                    adaptation

Figure 6.9 Adaptation of the eye to differing lumi-nance levels showing the limited range at any par-ticular time.

Glare can be reduced in two ways. Firstly by reducing the contrast between surfaces in the room and the window and secondly by ensuring that windows are not placed in important fields of view. Reduction in the contrast between the walls and windows is achieved by reducing the brightness of the windows or increasing the brightness of the room generally. This latter point is achieved by providing surfaces with as high a reflectance as possible. Another method is to use splayed window reveals this creates a smoother transition between the bright windows and relatively darker walls as shown in figure 6.10.

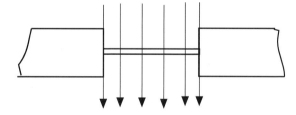

Square reveals creates sharp change in luminance

Splayed reveals reduces contrast between wall and window

Figure 6.10 Section through windows with square and splayed reveals.

As well as increasing the brightness of the room sur-faces, contrast can also be reduced by decreasing the luminance of the window. This can be achieved using blinds such as translucent roller blinds or part closed venetian blinds. This will reduce available daylight but on bright days when glare is a problem the reduction may still produce acceptable daylight conditions. Care should be taken to avoid leaving the blinds down when external daylight levels decrease as this could lead to an energy wasting "blinds down lights on" situation .

Avoiding glare by keeping windows out of principal fields of view requires some knowledge of the functioning and use of rooms. One example is not to position windows at the front of classrooms where the focus of attention lies. Computers on which glare is created by reflections of windows should be arranged so that the user sits side on to windows.

OVERHEATING

The key to avoiding overheating whilst still allowing in daylight is to separate the heat component of the sun's radiation from the daylight component. This occurs naturally on heavily overcast days. The amount of heat entering a building with the skylight is small. North facing windows receive scattered skylight only. This means the heat input through north facing glazing is low. On the east, west and south facing windows, where sunlight can accompany the skylight, louvered blinds can be used to separate the heat from the light as shown in figure 6.11.

These blinds can be used internally or externally. External blinds are better at rejecting heat than internal blinds. Internal blinds trap a proportion of the suns heat behind the glass. Unfortunately it is less easy to adjust and maintain external blinds and they are also susceptible to weather damage. Blinds should be retracted on dull days to maximise daylight entry.

A fixed shading device that aims to separate sunlight from daylight are brise solail (figure 6.12 and 6.13). This is an array of vertical plates fixed horizontally above a window. Direct sunlight is stopped but scattered daylight can still enter the window.

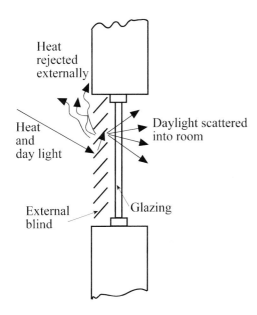

Figure 6.11 Blinds to prevent sunlight entry.

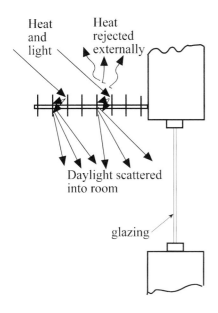

Figure 6.12 Brise Solail.

6.3 Side lit Rooms

The majority of rooms are daylit using vertical side windows. Figure 6.15 illustrates the problem of illuminating rooms in this way which is that daylight is mostly available near the window but finds difficulty in spreading to the points furthest from it.

Figure 6.13 Brise solail. (GPCS17) © Crown Copyright

Various methods have been proposed to improve the spread of daylight in side lit rooms. They are; light shelves, louvres, prismatic glazing and prismatic films. Each of these methods change the direction of light flow so that instead of pooling near the window it is projected up to the ceiling and then reflected to the rear of the room. The general principle is shown in figure 6.14 where an external light shelf is being used for this purpose. It can be seen from the overlaid daylight factor graphs that the total amount of daylight getting in to the space is actually reduced by the shelf. However, the amount at the rear of the room is slightly increased and the daylight spread has been made more even.

The uniform distribution of light within a space is particularly important in the psychology of switching on artificial lighting. What happens is that a person entering a room does not assess the overall amount of light in the room but compares where that person is stood, usually the door at a point away from the window, with the well lit area near the window. The person perceives it as being gloomy near the door in comparison to the window and so switches the light on, even though there may be adequate daylight for working. The effect of the light shelf is to make the spread of light in the room more even. A person entering the room now sees the entry point as being similarly lit as the rest of the room and so does not switch on the lighting.

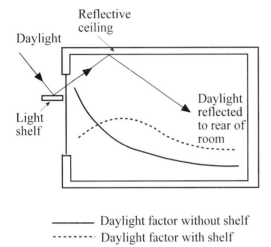

—————— Daylight factor without shelf
-------- Daylight factor with shelf

Figure 6.14 Daylight distribution in a side lit room.

LIGHT SHELVES

Light shelves can be either internal, external or both. External shelves (figures 6.14 and 6.15) have been found to have the most effective mix of daylight distribution combined with solar shading for the UK climate. There are a number of design issues related to light shelves;

- The shelf should be positioned above eye level to avoid obstruction of the external view.

- The higher the ceiling above the shelf the deeper will be the penetration of re directed light.

- The higher the reflectivity of the top of the shelf the better the light redirection.

- The underside of the shelf can also be reflective

to re-direct light from external paving into the room.

- The greater the area of the shelf the greater is the amount of light intercepted and therefore shaded and redirected.

Figure 6.15 Underside of external light shelf. photo from GPCS19: South Staffs water company (1991) © Crown Copyright

LOUVRES

Louvres are a form of multiple light shelf. Their benefit is that they can be adjusted to give optimum daylight redistribution throughout the day as the suns position changes. This would, however, require the operator to adjust them at regular intervals throughout the day. The louvres can be retracted on dull days to allow maximum daylight entry. One of the problems with louvres is that they can obstruct views out of the window. To overcome this, some systems form the louvre blades out of perforated aluminium sheet. This gives a combination of light re-direction, direct daylight entry and a view out (figure 6.16).

PRISMATIC GLAZING

Prismatic double glazing includes a layer of glass which has had one of its surfaces formed into a series of prisms the upper surface of which has a reflective coating deposited on it[2](figure 6.17). The glazing is no longer transparent and so is usually fitted above eye level in the glazed opening. Light hitting the prismatic glazing is reflected and refracted upwards on to the reflective ceiling.

When white light passes through a prism the individual wavelengths (colours) are refracted by differing amounts. This can lead to coloured fringes appearing around the pool of light redirected up on to the ceiling. This however is not usually a problem. Of more concern is that the optimum refracting angles in the prismatic glass are fixed. With sunlight, which is highly directional, this means that optimum refraction will only take place when the sun is at a particular angle of altitude. The problem can be improved by etching the glass to refract low angle sun on east and west facing glazing and higher angle sun on south facing glazing. An additional benefit of prismatic glazing is that it reduces the luminance of the sky seen through it. This helps to reduce glare.

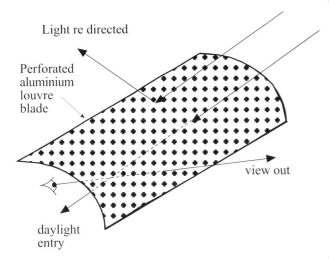

Figure 6.16 Perforated louvre blade

PRISMATIC FILM

A system which can accommodate multi directional sunlight is prismatic film. This is a plastic film which can be applied to glazing. The surface of these films has much finer prisms on it than prismatic glass. This means that in the space of one prism etched into glass a number of prisms can be etched into the film. Each prism has differing angles of refraction to accommodate changes in the suns altitude throughout the day or different days of the year.

PERFORMANCE OF SYSTEMS

A test comparing light shelves, prismatic glazing, louvres and prismatic films showed that prismatic glazing was the only system to increase light levels at the back of the room during periods of sunlight. However it did this on only a few days in the year. On overcast days prismatic film and light shelves performed better[2]. All of the systems reduced the daylight in the room but improved its distribution. They also reduced the likelihood of glare in the room.

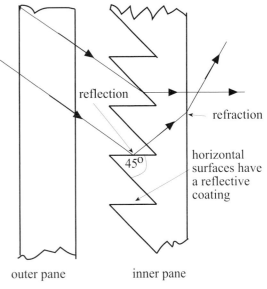

Figure 6.17 Prismatic glazing.

6.4 Roof Lights

Roof lights are very useful for providing daylight to the core of single storey or upper floor of multi storey buildings. They are horizontal windows whose main benefits are;

- They face the brightest part of the overcast sky (figure 6.3) as a consequence they let in three times as much daylight as the equivalent area of vertical glazing.

- The daylight from roof lights is less likely to be shaded by external obstructions, such as trees and other buildings or by internal obstructions such as posters stuck to windows or office furniture placed against windows.

- Daylight distribution below roof lights is in the form of a symmetrical pool reducing in illuminance towards the edges.

The two negative aspects of rooflights is that heat losses in winter and heat gains in summer through them are high. The heat losses are greater than through vertical glazing as warm air rises up to them creating an elevated temperature difference between inside and outside. However, since a view is rarely required through rooflights, transparent insulation as described in section 4.3 can be used. The second concern, high heat gains, is traditionally overcome by tilting the roof lights towards the north to create a north light (figure 6.18). This reduces the amount of daylight entering the rooflight but reduces heat gains and reduces glare.

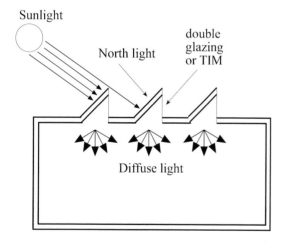

Figure 6.18 North light.

A second method is to attempt to separate the heat component of the solar radiation from the light. An example of this is shown in figure 6.19. The rooflight is made out of vertical glazing protected from direct sunlight by overhangs.

6.5 Lightwells and Atria

A lightwell is a vertical duct running through a multi storey building which is glazed on the top in a similar manner to a roof light. It also has vertical glazing

throughout its length. The aim is to extend the rooflight idea to provide daylighting to lower floors. Lightwells perform best when they are short and wide as opposed to tall and narrow. This is because windows on the upper floor absorb the daylight by allowing it to pass into the upper rooms adjacent to the light well. As a consequence there is less daylight available for the lower floors. One way of overcoming this is to reduce the size of windows on the upper floors and gradually increase them towards the lower floors. Any remaining structure should be smooth and painted white to ensure that light is reflected down the light well and not absorbed.

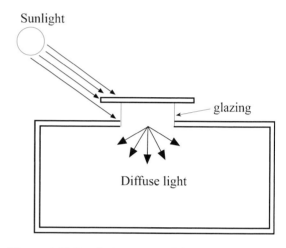

Figure 6.19 Rooflight protected from direct sunlight.

Lightwells are usually too narrow for useful occupancy to take place in them. However, they can have a dual function of acting as ventilation shafts for passive ventilation systems (see section 5.6)

Widening the lightwell so that its base can be used as an occupied space creates an atrium. The factors that affect the usefulness of an atrium for daylighting are;

- The atrium roof glazing system has a major impact on the amount of daylight entering the atrium. There are many devices which can obscure the sky. These include, structural elements, glazing bars, smoke dampers, ventilation dampers/fans, solar shading, fire detection equipment and acoustic absorbers (sound absorbers to reduce the high noise level arising from the hard, non absorbent, surfaces within the atrium). The effect of all of these can be to reduce the available daylight by 50% between outside and inside the atrium roof.

- Widening the atrium with successive floors improves the view that lower floors have of the sky and therefore improves daylight access (figure 6.20).

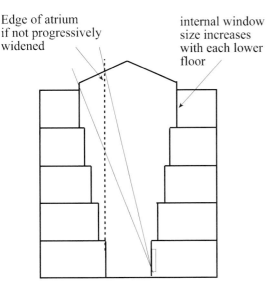

Edge of atrium if not progressively widened

internal window size increases with each lower floor

Figure 6.20 Stepped atrium design to improve daylight access to lower floors.

- As with lightwells the remaining internal structure should be finished in light reflective surfaces to encourage daylight distribution to the base of the atrium.

- Atria come in differing patterns. Some examples are shown in figure 6.21. The differences occur in the number of external surfaces through which daylight can enter the atrium and the arrangement between the atrium and the spaces adjoining it. The side atrium for example will reduce daylight entry into adjacent rooms when compared to having no atrium. The street type atrium will add some daylight to the deep plan rooms next to it.

6.6 Light Pipes

Light can be provided to interior spaces by guiding it along a light pipe. The actual system varies depending on whether it is based on sunlight or daylight. Sunlight systems tend to be complex, as they are based on a mirror which tracks the position of the sun and reflects the sunlight down a light guide to the room in which it is required (figure 6.22). The flow of light down the light guide is controlled using lenses. The light guide can be either a plastic rod, fibre optic bundle or a mirrored tube. A diffuser is fitted at the terminal of the light pipe to spread the light into the room beyond. The system is most appropriate to sunny climates and suffers from the need to have a solar tracking mirror which has high maintenance costs.

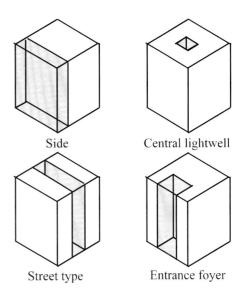

Side   Central lightwell

Street type   Entrance foyer

Figure 6.21 Various atrium positions.

A much simpler system which can guide either daylight or sunlight is based on a mirrored tube (figure 6.23). The diameter is larger than the solar tracking system described above. A window is fitted to the top end of the tube and a diffuser to the bottom end. Light enters the tube and is guided to the space below by reflections from the tube walls. Lower spaces in the building can be served by connecting more than one length of light tube together. Bends can be included but should be avoided if possible as they reduce daylight transfer.

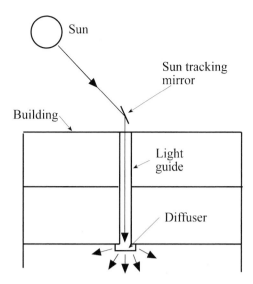

Figure 6.22 Solar tracking mirror.

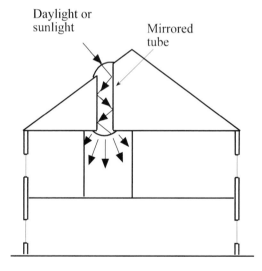

Figure 6.23 Light pipe.

6.7 Daylight Assessment

There are a number of methods that can be used to assess daylight in buildings. The majority are based on the standard overcast skies described in section 6.1.

ARTIFICIAL SKY

A useful tool, because of its simplicity, is to use an artificial sky chamber (figure 6.24). The chamber consists of a box approximately 1.5m square on plan. and 1.25m high. The walls of the box are lined with vertical mirrors. The roof of the box is fitted with lamps above a diffusing surface. When the lights are switched on reflections within the chamber produce a light distribution similar to a CIE sky. Scale models of the building under investigation are then placed at the centre of the chamber. The windows in the model are fitted with modelling materials with characteristics similar to that proposed in the full scale building. A light sensor outside the model measures the value of external illuminance E_o and an array of sensors inside the model measure the internal illuminance E_i over a grid of points. The data is fed into an analyser which compares the value of E_i at each point in the room with the value of E_o and outputs it as a daylight factor. Modifying the model by placing external obstructions, changing reflection factors of surfaces, type and size of glazing or adding lightshelves allows the effects of these changes on daylight distribution in the room to be assessed.

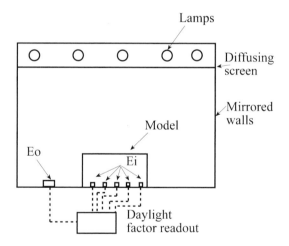

Figure 6.24 Artificial sky.

DAYLIGHT FACTOR PROTRACTORS

Daylight factor protractors are clear overlays, very similar to geometry protractors. They are used in conjunction with scale plans and sections of a room to determine the daylight factor at a particular point indicated on the drawings. Lines of sight are placed on the drawings between the point of interest and window reveals to determine the area of sky seen by the point of interest. The protractors have values of sky component based on the illuminance distribution of a CIE overcast sky printed on to them. Values of sky component are determined by reading off values where lines of sight from the point to the window opening on plan and section cross graduations on the protractor. The externally reflected component is determined using the same protractor and drawings. The variation is that the sight lines are drawn to the edges of the external obstruction and the values on the protractor are reduced by 80% to indicate the low luminance of external obstructions.

The value of the internally reflected component is obtained from tables.

The method is relatively simple, following basic instruction, but suffers from the fact that creating daylight factor contours requires the calculation of the daylight factor at many points in the room and is therefore time consuming. It is also difficult to predict the daylight factors when the building has been fitted with novel daylighting systems such as light shelves.

COMPUTER MODELLING

The physical processes behind the movement of light in spaces and its reflection from specular and diffusing surfaces of various colours are well known. The limitations on the use of computers has been that a large amount of data needs to be processed. However latest developments in computer hardware has made an analysis of how buildings interact with sunlight and daylight possible. The operator inputs data on the size, location and orientation of windows, glazing system light transmission factors, room dimensions and surface reflectances and colour. The computer then determines by geometry what proportion of the sky is seen by various points in the room and then calculates daylight entry and distribution within the room. The output can be in the form of daylight factor contours or 3D images rendered to show variations in daylight distribution within the space.

DAYLIGHT FACTOR METERS

A daylight factor meter is a light meter that has two sensors and so can simultaneously measures the illuminance at a point inside the building and outside the building. Internal circuitry then determines the size of the daylight factor from this data. The daylight factor meter is useful for determining daylight entry in existing buildings. It is not however very accurate as the value of external illuminance measured is rarely that of an unobstructed sky due to shadowing by nearby buildings.

REFERENCES

1. Crisp, V.H.C., Littlefair, P.J., Cooper, I. and McKennan G. Daylight as a Passive Solar Energy Option: An Assessment of its Potential in Non Domestic Buildings. Building Research Establishment Report 129. HMSO 1988.

2. Aizlewood, M.E. Innovative Daylighting Systems: An Experimental Evaluation. Lighting Research and Technology. 25(4) pp141-153. 1993

FURTHER READING

Good Practice Guide 245 - Desktop guide to daylighting for architects. 1998

General Information Report 35: Daylighting for sports halls - Two case studies. 1997.

CIBSE. CIBSE Applications Manual AM1: Window Design. 1998

The British Standards Institute. BS8206 Lighting for Buildings, Part 2: Code of Practice for Daylighting, 1992

BRE. BR209 Site Layout Planning for Daylight and Sunlight: A Guide to Good Practice. 1991

BRE. BR288 Designing Buildings for Daylight. Professional Studies in British Architectural Practice. 1995

BRE. Daylight design in Architecture. 1998

BRE. BRE Digest 309 (part 1) and BRE Digest 310 (part 2) Estimating Daylight in Buildings. 1996

07 A R T I F I C I A L . L I G H T

In this chapter we will find that;

- Daylight should be used to remove or reduce the need for electric lighting.

- The lighting design should provide the required lighting performance with a good energy effciency

- Lighting designs should achieve the recommended task illuminance and no more.

- The installed load can be reduced by providing a low background illuminance and increasing this to the task illuminance on the work surface using desk lamps.

- Lamps should be chosen with a high luminous efficacy.

- The three basic lamp types in order of increasing efficacy are incandescent lamps, fluorescent lamps and gas discharge lamps.

- The installed load gives us an indication of the energy efficiency of the lighting system. Low energy systems should aim for an installed load of less than 12 W/m².

- Luminaires that direct most of their light downwards help to reduce the installed load.

- Controls should be used so that the lights are not left on in an unoccupied room or when there is sufficient daylight.

- Reducing the use of artificial lighting also reduces the cooling load in air conditioned buildings.

- The building regulations part L place a requirement on buildings to use no more electricity for lighting than is required

7.0 Introduction

In the previous chapter it was stated that daylight should be used where possible because it has a range of psychological and visual benefits in addition to removing the need for electric lighting. Unfortunately, there are also concerns with natural light as it increases the risk of glare and over heating occurring. In addition, it cannot form a complete lighting strategy because it is variable and at certain times of the day disappears completely. At these times artificial lighting is required to supplement the natural light. Some spaces rely completely on artificial light, examples are basement rooms and auditoria in cinemas and theatres. Others have a continuous requirement for artificial light even if daylight is present. examples are, those buildings that have a specific requirement for display lighting such as shops, art galleries or museums.

The advantage of electric lighting is that it is available when required and in the quantities required. The disadvantage is that it requires electricity for its production and, as described in chapter 1, electricity is the most expensive and polluting form of energy. Note that artificial lighting is also referred to as electric lighting.

LIGHTING SYSTEMS

In domestic buildings the lighting system is based on individual lamps that create illumination within the room. Little attention is paid to lighting design in the home beyond aesthetic considerations. However, in commercial buildings there is greater emphasis on design to create the required light levels, avoid glare and generate a "work like" ambience. The two main types of lighting found in commercial buildings are accent lighting and task lighting.

Accent lighting is used to create interest or a focal point at a particular location such as a reception desk. It is based on individual or small groups of luminaires creating variations in the illuminance to draw the attention of the eye. A luminaire is a complete light fitting. It contains the lamp which creates the light from electricity (see IP6), a power supply and the casing for the lamp. The casing has a number of functions. It supports the lamp, holds the wiring to supply it with power, protects the lamp from dust and physical damage and, using reflectors, prisms and diffusers, controls the spread of light from the lamp.

Accent lighting design is based on data supplied by the luminaire manufacturer. The data gives details of the direction and spread of light and the illuminance created by it at certain distances from the lamp. An example of this is illustrated in figure 7.1. This information is known as photometric data. If the distance between the lamp and surface to be illuminated is known then the spread of light and the illuminance created on the surface can be determined from this information.

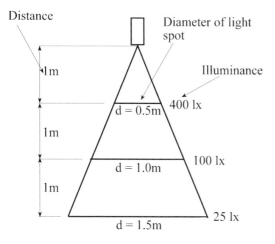

Figure 7.1 Photometric data for a display spot lamp.

Accent and display lighting is often based on tungsten halogen spotlamps. These have a low efficiency and so should be be used in a limited number of locations. Some retail installations use high pressure discharge lamps for accent lighting which are more efficient.

Task lighting is used to provide adequate light for carrying out tasks. It can be provided by a desk lamp but is more usually provided in commercial buildings by a number of luminaires arranged in a uniform grid

throughout the room (figure 7.2). In this way the light output from each lamp combines to create resonably uniform illuminance across the space.

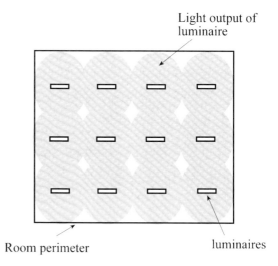

Figure 7.2 Uniform task lighting provided by an array of luminaires.

Three other categories of lighting can be identified that generally consume less electricity than accent and task lighting but should still be considered.

- **Emergency lighting.** This is intended to assist people to safely leave a building or close down dangerous processes in the event of mains power failure. The primary consideration with this system is therefore safety although energy efficient systems based on LEDs are avaiable.

- **Outdoor lighting.** This system should use energy efficient lamps and be controlled so that it only operates as required during the hours of darkness.

- **Process lighting.** This system is used to illuminate individual processes. One example is the provision of lighting in operating theatres. The limited use of process lighting means that the effective lighting of the process is the main consideration here.

To reduce the amount of electricity used for artificial lighting the following strategy must be adopted;

- Optimise the use of daylight.

- The lighting installation must be designed to give the required light conditions whilst consuming the minimum amount of energy.

- The lamps must be energy efficient.

- The lighting must be controlled so that it is on only when required and to the level required.

The first issue, optimisation of the use of daylight was addressed in chapter 6. This chapter will concentrate on the design of the lighting system the lamps, luminaires and the control of the lighting system.

7.1 Task Lighting

The lamps in a task lighting scheme consume electricity to provide light so, the more lamps that are required the more electricity that will be consumed. This section will consider the factors that determine the number of lamps required in a task lighting system, this is so that those aspects of the lighting design that influence energy consumption can be identified.

The method used to compare the energy consumption of alternative lighting designs is to compare their installed loads. The greater the value of the installed load the greater the electrical consumption of the lighting system when it is switched on.

The installed load is the rate at which electricity is consumed by the lighting system to illuminate each square metre of the room. It is determined by dividing the total power consumption of the lighting system (lamps, control gear and other items), measured in Watts (W) by the area of the lit space, measured in square metres (m^2). The units of installed load are therefore W/m^2.

$$\text{Installed load} = \frac{\text{total power consumption}}{\text{floor area}} \quad (W/m^2)$$

Lamp rating. The rate at which a lamp consumes electricity is known as its rating. The rating is measured as the number of Joules of energy that are consumed

per second. The unit Joules per second (J/s) or Watt (W). For example the rating of a typical domestic tungsten filament bulb is 100W.

Control gear. One of the requirements of gas discharge and fluorescent lamps is that they require electrical circuitry known as control gear to initiate and then control the gas discharge. This circuitry consumes electricity in addition to that consumed by the lamp. For example, each mains frequency fluorescent tube rated at 58W requires control gear that consumes electricity at a rate of 12W during the operation of the lamp. The total rating is therefore 58+ 12 = 70W.

Other items. There may be additional power consumption by transformers in low voltage lighting systems and by power factor correction equipment.

As an example, if a room 7m by 16m was fitted out with sixteen luminaires each having a total rating of 90 W (including lamp and control gear) . Then the installed load would be,

total power consumption	= number of luminaires x rating
	= 16 x 90
	= 1440W
floor area	= length x width
	= 7 x 16
	= 112m^2
Installed load	= $\dfrac{\text{total power consumption}}{\text{floor area}}$
	= $\dfrac{1440}{112}$
	= **12.9 W/m^2**

A typical installed load to provide an illuminance of 500 lx in an office is 25W/m^2. A low energy installation would aim for an installed load of less than 12 W/m^2. A low installed load has two benefits. Firstly, the electrical consumption of the lighting system is reduced and secondly, heat given out by the lamps is reduced so that the cooling load is reduced. This latter point assumes that most of the electricity consumed by the lighting system appears as heat within the space.

FACTORS IN THE DESIGN OF A LIGHTING SYSTEM

This section will concentrate on providing the recommended illuminance on the working plane within a space. However, it must be remembered that this is not the only criteria for producing a well lit room. For example, it is also necessary to ensure sufficient light falls upon the walls and ceiling of a room so that they do not appear gloomy and that glare is avoided. The CIBSE lighting guides give more information on good lighting systems for buildings[1].

The number of luminaires, spaced out in a grid, required to give a uniform illuminance across a large work space is determined using the Lumen method of design. The method is based on the following formula;

$$N = \frac{E \times A}{F \times UF \times MF}$$

where:

N = Number of luminaires required
E = Illuminance required (lux)
A = Area of working plane (m^2)
F = Total Luminous flux output of the lamps within each luminaire (lumen)
UF = Utilisation factor
MF = Maintenance factor

Since it is the lamps in the luminaires that consume energy we are interested in keeping the number of luminaires (N) small. It can be seen from the above formula that to do this we need to decrease the size of any of the terms on the top row of the formula or increase the size of any of the terms on the bottom row. The following sections will investigate each of the factors in turn and indicate how the lighting system might be optimised to reduce the number of lamps required and hence the electricity consumed by the system.

ILLUMINANCE (E)

The value of the illuminance for any particular space is recommended in the CIBSE lighting guides[1]. The figures given have been chosen to provide an efficient, safe and comfortable working environment based on the complexity of the task and age of the occupants. Complex tasks require higher illuminances and therefore a greater number of lamps. One example is in the parts of factories that are dedicated to inspecting products. Identification of fine detail is required and so high illuminances are recommended and therefore more lamps are needed. This is illustrated in the photograph of an inspection area shown in figure 7.3.

Figure 7.3 Large number of luminaires in the inspection area of a factory. photo from GPCS 174. Energy efficient lighting in factories. (1993) © Crown Copyright

Reducing the value of illuminance as a means of reducing the number of luminaires is unacceptable as this would result in poor lighting conditions. Our focus should instead be on the avoidance of over illumination as this does not create further improvements in working efficiency. This is illustrated in figure 7.4 which shows efficiency of office working against illuminance. As the illuminance increases the efficiency of working improves. However, the rate of improvement in efficiency with increasing illumination diminishes and illumination above 500 lx results in little further improvement.

Recommended levels should be achieved in lighting design but not exceeded. Some spaces however accommodate mixed activities and therefore require more than one illuminance level. One example is where

IP6 - Artificial Light Sources

There are three basic types of lamp; incandescent lamps, gas discharge lamps and fluorescent lamps. Each of them produce light by the excitation of atoms using electricity. When energy is input to an atom the electrons orbiting the nucleus rise to a higher orbit (figure IP6.1). At a later time the electron falls back to its original orbit and the energy is re released as a photon of light. The atoms may be material forming the filament of a lamp, the gas inside it or a phosphor coating.

Figure IP6.1 Excitation of atoms to create light

INCANDESCENT LAMPS

Incandescent lamps are the common light bulbs found in most homes they are also known as tungsten filament lamps or GLS(general lighting service) lamps (figure IP6.2). They consist of a glass envelope which is filled with argon (85%) and nitrogen (15%) gas. These gases are unreactive, their role is to prevent the fine tungsten filament from burning out when it gets hot. A cap at the base of the lamp provides electrical contacts to allow the current to flow through the fine tungsten filament. The filament is made from tungsten wire as this is a metal which can get very hot without melting. As the filament heats up it begins to glow with sufficient intensity that it emits light. This ability of hot objects to give out light is known as incandescence.

Tungsten filament lamps are very cheap to buy but are also very inefficient at producing light. Much of the

electrical energy is turned to heat. This makes the bulbs hot to the touch. The luminous efficacy of a standard tungsten bulb is 13 lm/W.

Tungsten halogen lamps are a special form of tungsten bulb. A halide gas, usually iodine is added to the nitrogen/argon mix. Iodine combines with tungsten evaporating off the hot filament and returns it back to the filament. This extends the life of the filament, avoids bulb blackening and improves light output. This type of lamp is used in display lighting, usually in the form of spot lamps. Tungsten halogen lamps have a slightly improved efficacy when compared with standard tungsten filament lamp at 17 lm/W.

Figure IP6.2 Tungsten filament lamp

GAS DISCHARGE LAMPS

Gas discharge lamps work in a completely different way to filament lamps. Here a glass envelope is filled with gas at a low pressure (figure IP6.3). The most common examples are sodium lamps which are the yellow lamps used for street lighting. A large voltage is placed across terminals either side of the tube. This causes electrons orbiting the gas atoms to be stripped off. The electrons move towards the positive terminal and the now positively charged gas atoms (ions) move towards the negative terminal. Collisions between the ions and electrons causes excitement of the gas atoms and the emission of light. Low pressure sodium lamps are very efficient at producing light but unfortunately they only produce yellow light. This is acceptable for street lighting but cannot be used for lighting interiors. Low pressure sodium lamps are also known as SOX lamps.

Figure IP6.3 Gas discharge lamp.

By increasing the pressure of gas in the tube the light emitted becomes more white. Unfortunately this also causes a reduction in efficacy. High pressure sodium lamps are known as SON lamps. They can be used in interior lighting, often as uplighters in offices and for lighting atria and tall spaces such as warehouses. Another form of gas discharge lamp used for industrial use is the metal halide (MBI) lamp. It has a lower efficacy than the sodium lamp but better quality light output.

One aspect of gas discharge lamps and fluorescent tubes is that they require additional electrical circuitry to initiate and then control the current flowing through the tube. This is known as control gear. It first applies a large voltage across the gas which is initially an insulator. The gas then breaks down and begins to rapidly conduct electricity. This rapid conduction would create a damaging surge of current if not controlled. Unfortunately, the control gear gets heated in the process. This heat is energy being wasted during the production of light and therefore control gear losses need to be considered when assessing the efficacy of the lamp.

FLUORESCENT TUBES

Fluorescent tubes are the lamps commonly found in workplaces such as schools, colleges and offices. They are a special form of gas discharge lamp. The filling gas is argon with a trace of mercury. When the gas discharge is created the gas does not emit useful visible light instead it emits ultra violet (UV) radiation. However, a phosphor coating applied to the interior of the tube absorbs the UV and re-emits this energy as visible light (figure IP6.4). The phosphor coating is similar to that used on television screens. This means that by mixing the phosphors a cool blue, warm yellow or daylight white light can be produced. Fluorescent tubes have a high efficacy but less than that of the sodium gas discharge lamp.

Figure IP6.4 Fluorescent tube.

there is an open plan office containing a circulation route (figure 7.5). The illuminance required for an office is 500 lx the illuminance required for a circulation route is 150 lx. Most lighting designs would provide 500 lx across the entire space. In an open plan office the lighting system cannot incorporate two very different illuminances as the contrast would be too great, the circulation route would appear very dull in comparison to the rest of the room. However, by partitioning off the circulation route the different illuminances could be achieved and therefore energy savings made.

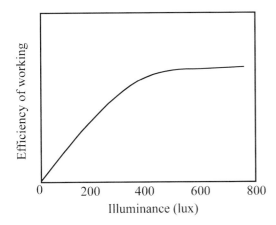

Figure 7.4 Graph of working efficiency against illuminance.

Figure 7.5 Open plan office incorporating a circulation route

Background illumination and desk lamps. A method of reducing the number of luminaires whilst maintaining the illuminance on the task is to provide a lower level of background illuminance in the room to say 300 lx and then install individual desk lamps to provide the additional 200 lx required on the desk. If high pressure sodium uplighters are used to create the background illuminance and compact fluorescents used to create the task illuminance then the installed load to provide 500 lx on the desks can be reduced to 8 W/m².

Pendant light fittings. In rooms with high ceilings the luminaires are usually suspended from the ceiling to bring them closer to the working plane. This is necessary because the spread of light from a luminaire follows the inverse square law of illumination. This is where the illuminance falls by a factor of four for each doubling of distance between a point source of light and the surface it is illuminating. This is illustrated in figure 7.6. It can be seen that as the distance is doubled the area over which the light is spread is four times larger. This reduces the flux density or illuminance to one quarter of its original value. The reverse is also true if you halve the distance between source and surface the illuminance will increase by a factor of 4. Therefore, bringing the light fittings closer to the working plane increase the illuminance they create. This will also diminish the spread of light from each luminaire and so care should be taken in any designs that the uniformity of light within the space is not too uneven. Using pendant fittings can reduce the installed load necessary to provide an illuminance of 500 lx to as low as 11 W/m² .

AREA OF WORKING PLANE(A)

Luminaires have a limited area beneath them which they can illuminate. It follows therefore that as the total area to be illuminated increases the number of lamps needed to cover this area also increases.

LUMINOUS FLUX OUTPUT (F)

The amount of light given out by a luminaire is specified by its luminous flux output measured in lumen (see IP5). The size of this is determined by the luminous flux output of the lamps and how much of this manages to escape out of the luminaire through the diffuser.

The light output of lamps is described in two ways. The first is the initial lumen output which is a measure of the light output when nearly new (1 hour old for incandescents and 100 hours old for fluorescents). The initial lumen output of a 100W incandescent bulb and a 50W fluorescent tube are approximately 1400 and 1900 lm respectively. The second method of describing light output uses lighting design lumens. This is the luminous flux output of the lamp measured under standard test conditions to represent a more realistic 'in use' situation. This is necessary because the light output of lamps decreases with age as shown in figure 7.7. As the name implies, lighting design lumens are used in lighting design. It follows therefore if the lamp light output depreciates quickly with time then a low value of lighting design lumens will be input to the formula and therefore more lamps will be required.

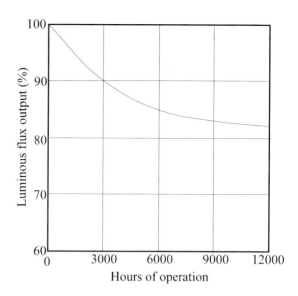

Figure 7.7 Decline in the luminous flux output of a fluorescent tube with age.

UTILISATION FACTOR (UF)

This is a factor that describes how well the light emitted from the luminaire is being used to create illumination. If all of the light were used perfectly the utilisation factor would be 1.0. In practice the utilisation factor is less than 1.0 indicating that the not all of the light from the luminaire is being used to illuminate the surface. The lower the value of utilisation factor the greater the number of luminaires that are required.

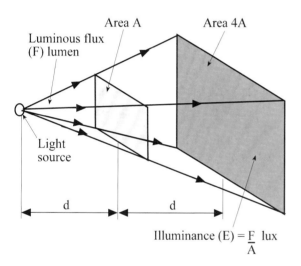

Figure 7.6 Inverse square law of illumination.

Not all of the light from the lamps leaves the luminaire. Some is reflected back into the tube itself and some is absorbed by the plastic diffuser (figure 7.8) or dust on the surrface of reflectors. The luminous flux outputs of individual luminaires fitted with different types of lamp is provided in trade literature produced by lighting manufacturers.

For energy efficiency, low lumen depreciation lamps should be selected as should luminaires without plastic diffusers.

Light that reaches the working plane directly is utilised to the best advantage. Light that reaches the working plane after reflection from a surface is degraded. The size of the utilisation factor therefore depends on the pattern of light distribution from the luminaire, the reflectance of the room surfaces and the dimensions of the room.

Light distribution of the luminaire. Luminaires vary in the way that they direct the light output from the tubes. Figure 7.8 shows a section through a general diffusing luminaire. The mirrored reflector at the top of the unit ensures that light moves predominantly downwards. The side diffusers scatter the light that hits it in all directions, this means that some light travels up away from the working plane. This creates a bright ceiling which results in a less oppressive environment.

Page 110

The prisms on the underside of the diffuser directs the spread of downward light into a well defined pool beneath the luminaire. For highest utilisation factor all of the light output should be directed downwards. Many modern luminaires have specular (mirrored) reflectors and no diffusers. Direction control of the light is carried out using polished anodised aluminium louvres below the tubes so that a maximum amount of light goes downwards. A softer downward light distribution with some sideways scatter can be achieved using a brushed aluminium finish.

The proportion of light output from the lamps that escapes from the luminaire is known as the light output ratio (LOR). The proportion of the LOR that travels downwards is specified by the downward light output ratio (DLOR) of the luminaire. For a general diffusing luminaire as shown in figure 7.8 the value of DLOR is approximately 75-80% for a luminaire with a specular reflector the value of DLOR is approximately 95%. It has been found during refurbishment that four tube diffusing luminaires can be replaced by three tube specular luminaires whilst still providing the same illumination level. This gives a energy saving of 25% for each luminaire. However, care must be taken to avoid creating too dark a ceiling and an uneven spread of light on the working plane.

In situations where visual display terminals are being used it is recommended that the luminance of luminaires and the direction of light output is controlled to prevent light falling onto the screens and causing glare. However this is not the only criterion for good lighting design and more information on this is presented in the CIBSE lighting guides.

Surface reflectance. Light which is reflected from a surface is degraded in two ways. Firstly the quantity of luminous flux leaving the surface is reduced. For example, the amount of light hitting a wall with a reflectance of 70% will be reduced by 30%. The second degradation occurs due to surface colour. In this case some of the incident wavelengths of light will be absorbed and light predominantly in the wavelength of the colour of the wall will be reflected onto the working plane. This will only cause a problem when highly coloured room surfaces are used. Smooth white surfaces are therefore important in increasing the value of the utilisation factor. It should be remembered that

high surface reflectance also assist in the utilisation of daylight.

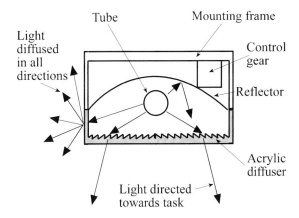

Figure 7.8 Section through a general lighting luminaire with plastic diffuser.

Dimensions of the room. The width and length of the room are important as is the height between the working plane and the luminaire. When the luminaire is high above the working plane and the room dimensions are small there is more chance that reflections will occur, reducing the utilisation factor.

To maintain a high utilisation factor;

- Choose a luminaire that directs most of its light downwards (with due regard to avoiding dark walls and ceiling).

- Keep surfaces light (high reflection factor).

- Keep luminaires as close to the working plane as possible (with due regard for head clearances and glare problems from lighting in the field of view).

MAINTENANCE FACTOR

This is a factor that tells us the average state of cleanliness of the luminaires and surfaces in the room. In dirty environments luminaire reflectors and diffusers will become dirty and therefore light absorbing. The reflectance of dirty room surfaces will also be lower. Typical maintenance factors are 0.9 for a regularly cleaned and maintained office, 0.8 for an office that is not regularly maintained and 0.6 for a factory.

7.2 Lamp Efficacy

Lamps are devices for converting electricity into light. Lamps are not perfect at this task as some of the electricity is turned to heat. The efficiency of a lamp is described by its luminous efficacy which is found by comparing its light output in lumens against the electrical input in watts. Circuit efficacy on the other hand includes the power consumption of the lamp plus associated control gear. The units of luminous efficacy are lumen per watt (lm/W).

$$\text{Lamp efficacy} = \frac{\text{Light output (lm)}}{\text{Electrical input to lamp (W)}}$$

$$\text{Circuit efficacy} = \frac{\text{Light output (lm)}}{\substack{\text{Electrical input to lamp and} \\ \text{circuit components (W)}}}$$

The actual luminous efficacy varies depending on the type of lamp (see IP6) and also the rating of individual lamp types. Table 7.1 shows the typical luminous efficacies of various type of lamp. The greater the luminous efficacy the better is the lamp at converting electricity to light.

Lamp type	Efficiency (lm/W)
Tungsten filament, GLS	13
Tungsten halogen	17
T12 - 38mm Fluorescent tube	55
T8 - 25mm Fluorescent tube	65
T5 - 15mm Fluorescent tube	96
high pressure sodium, SON	102
low pressure sodium, SOX	130

Table 7.1 Luminous efficacy of various type of lamp (including control gear losses)[2].

The efficacy of fluorescent tubes has been continually improving since they were commercially developed during the 1940's. This is illustrated in figure 7.9 which shows increases in tube efficacy over the past sixty years. In 1945 the maximum efficacy was 32 lm/W by 2002 this had increased to 105 lm/W.

The Building Regulations part L describe minimum lighting system efficacy in terms of initial (i.e. light output at 100 hours) lamp-lumens per circuit-Watt.

Figure 7.9 Improvements in fluorescent tube luminous efficacy over time.

HIGH FREQUENCY CONTROL GEAR

There are three types of control circuits which can be used to initiate and then control the light output from fluorescent tubes.

Switch start. Simplest and cheapest circuit consisting of a magnetic copper/ iron ballast, a capacitor and a glow starter unit. Currents flowing through the coil creates a magnetic field which induces a new current flowing in the opposite direction to the first. This prevents current surges because the stronger the current through the coil the greater is the induced current flowing in the opposite direction. It is here where the control gear losses take place.

Electronic start. This uses electronic starting which is flicker free. It does this by slowly warming the tube for a fraction of a second before starting. This reduces the discolouration of the end of tubes, increases life and reduces lumen depreciation.

High frequency electronic starting. A modern development in control gear is the introduction of electronic circuitry which replaces the control gear systems described above but uses the same tubes. The electronic circuitry operates at 20,000Hz whereas wire wound control gear operates at the normal mains frequency of 50Hz. The energy benefits of this system are;

- High frequency lamps operate at a higher luminous efficacy than mains frequency lamps.

- The control gear losses are reduced from 12W to 11W.

- One electronic circuit can control two lamps whereas a wire wound circuit is needed for each lamp.

- The lamps can be dimmed with an almost linear light output to energy consumption relationship i.e. as the light output falls the electrical consumption falls in proportion(figure 7.10). This is not the case with mains frequency fluorescents that reduce their power consumption when dimmed but to a much lesser degree. Dimming with comparable power saving is essential for incorporating the lamps in circuits that increase or decrease light output in response to daylight (see section 7.3).

- High frequency lamps have instant starting characteristics. This means that almost immediately after switch on they achieve maximum light output. Mains frequency fluorescents slowly build up light output after switch on. This means that high frequency lamps are appropriate in lighting installations where control systems switch them off at the end of occupancy. When occupants return to the room light levels can quickly be recovered as the lights switch back on again.

- The lumen depreciation when operating lamps at high frequency is lower than operating lamps at mains frequency. This is illustrated in table 7.2 which shows the luminous flux output of a high frequency and a mains frequency fluorescent tube at various ages.

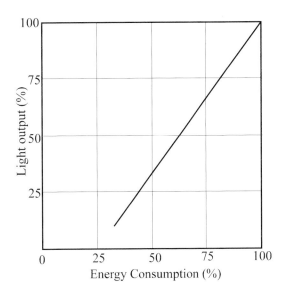

Figure 7.10 Reductions in energy consumption with falling light output due to dimming.

	Percentage of initial flux output (%)	
Age (hours)	mains freq.	high freq.
100	100	100
2500	90	97
5000	85	92
7500	83	90
10000	82	89

Table 7.2 Reductions in luminous flux output with age for HF and mains frequency lamps.

The main energy implications of the above are illustrated in table 7.3 which shows that the combination of reduced control gear losses and higher luminous efficacy of the HF tube result in a 21% energy saving for a twin tube luminaire. Further savings will then be achieved if the HF lamps are part of an occupancy and daylight controlled lighting system.

A non-energy benefit from using high frequency lighting is that it eliminates the flickering and mains hum associated with mains frequency fluorescents. The frequency of operation of HF tubes is above that which can be detected by humans. This may give benefits in reducing the incidence of sick building syndrome where lighting has been identified along with other factors in causing sick building syndrome.

Item	rate of energy consumption	
	Mains Frequency	High Frequency
Tubes	2 @ 58W	2 @ 50W
Control gear	2 @ 12W	1 @ 11W
total	140W	111W

Table 7.3 Energy savings arising from the use of high frequency control gear.

The Building Regulations Approved Document L2 describes high efficiency control gear as that having a power consumption not exceeding that shown in table 7.4.

Nominal lamp rating (W)	Control gear power consumption (W)
less than or equal to 15	6
greater than 15, less than or equal to 50	8
greater than 50, less than or equal to 70	9
greater than 70, less than or equal to 100	12
greater than 100	15

Table 7.4 maximum power consumption of high efficiency control gear.

T5 TUBES

The diameter of fluorescent tubes is identified by a T number. 38mm tubes are T12's, 26mm tubes T8 and the latest 16mm tubes are T5's. The latest and most efficient tubes are T5 tubes with a luminous efficacy of 106 lm/W.

The improvements in fluorescent tube efficacy have arisen as a result of;

- Improved manufacturing techniques which maintain consistent quality and tolerances.

- Modifications in the dimensions of the tube. This keeps the tube wall near its optimum operating

temperature of 45°C. Note it is important that luminaire design helps to maintain this temperature and avoids heat build up.

- Developing improved phosphor coatings. The cheapest phosphor coating is Halophosphate. This is used to coat older 38mm tubes. The most efficient coating is the triphosphor coating made up of red, green and blue rare earth phosphors.

- Changes to the gas filling. T8 and T5 tubes use a Krypton gas filling along with the mercury.

COMPACT FLUORESCENTS

Tungsten bulbs benefit from being cheap and small however they have a very low luminous efficacy. They are still widely used in domestic properties and for minor roles in commercial buildings e.g. stairwells, lift lighting hotel room lighting and the lighting of small rooms such as toilets and stores. They can however be replaced by fluorescent tubes that have been reduced in size and coiled so that they are only slightly larger than an equivalent tungsten bulb, known as a compact fluorescent lamp (CFL). A 60W tungsten bulb can be replaced by a 15W CFL. The spectral output is similar and an energy saving of 75% is achieved.

One of the problems with CFL's is that the control gear for the fluorescent discharge is contained in the base of the lamp. The life of the control gear is much longer than that of the tube. This means that when the tube fails the control gear must also be thrown away. This wastes resources and is costly. This is difficult to avoid in domestic lighting when the CFL is replacing a standard tungsten bulb. In commercial buildings new light fittings should be installed that have separate control gear within the fitting itself so only the tube is replaced on failure (figure 7.11).

7.2.1 New Light Sources

In addition to the three main categories of light source described in IP4 there are some significant new entries to the lighting market. Some are already commercially available and others are still under development.

INDUCTION LAMPS

Induction lamps are a development in the way that energy is input to the lamp to create light. The traditional method is to use metal electrodes which either penetrate the lamp via a sealed metal cap or through a seal in the glass itself. The problem with this is that the seal is a weak element in the tube. Heating and cooling of the tube creates mechanical stresses that can result in cracking around the seal leading to failure. The induction lamp has no electrodes penetrating glass envelope. Instead, a coil is used to create a magnetic field that induces current flow within the filling gas of the lamp. The lamps which are commercially available have a high efficacy and an extremely long lifetime. This makes them very suitable for locations which are hard to reach or difficult to access such as high places and subway lighting.

Figure 7.11 Compact fluorescent lamp (CFL) with cover on and off. Photo from GPCS 86 Low energy lighting in the community areas of housing. (1993) © Crown Copyright

LIGHT EMITTING DIODES

One of the most efficient sources of artificial light is the light emitting diode (LED). They use approximately 10% of the energy needed by an equivalent tungsten bulb. Individual LED's are inadequate for lighting interiors as they are too small and emit light in basic colours such as red, green, yellow and orange although white light versions are being developed[3]. They can be used to replace traditional lamps where a limited lighting area is required. The most important example is in emergency lighting systems where LED's are used to illuminate exit signs. However they can also be built up into arrays to produce accent and display luminaires. One of the main benefits of LED's is their long life. The typical lifetime of a LED light source is 100,000 hours.

ELECROLUMINSCENT PLASTICS

Certain specially developed plastics have been found to emit light when a voltage is applied across them. These plastics are only available in small quantities and are not commercially available for general lighting purposes. However, it may be possible in the future to coat a large area of the ceiling with this type of material to act as a source of light. This would give a much more even light distribution in the room than using an array of individual lamps that create peaks of illuminance beneath themselves and lower illuminances in between the luminaires.

7.2.2 Economics of High Efficacy Lamps

All higher efficacy lamps are more costly than the equivalent standard unit. Amongst the reasons for this is that both the improved triphosphor coating of high frequency tubes and the Krypton gas filling are more expensive than the basic coatings and gases used. A standard luminaire with twin 85W 26mm tubes would cost approximately £55. An equivalent fitting with high frequency tubes would cost approximately £83 i.e. an extra cost per fitting of £29. The extra cost involved must be recovered in the value of energy savings made before additional financial savings can accumulate.

The payback period of energy efficient lighting

depends on the number of hours over which it is run. The greater the number of hours the shorter the payback period as shown in figure 7.12 which shows the fall in simple payback period of high frequency fluorescents with hours of use.

However, it should be remembered that ultimately lighting energy savings are achieved by switching it off. The way that this is achieved is discussed in the next section.

Figure 7.12 Reduction in payback period with hours of use.

7.3 Lighting Control

No matter how efficient the lamps are, electricity is being wasted if the lamps are on when they are not required. The general rule is that "lighting should be on only when required and to the level required". What this means in detail is that;

- When the space is unoccupied the lighting should be off.

- When there is sufficient daylight the lighting should be off.

- When there is some daylight but not enough the

artificial light output should be varied to supply supplementary lighting up to the required illuminance.

There are a number of control methods that can be utilised to achieve these requirements including manual switching, simple time control, occupancy detection and daylight sensing.

ZONING

Before considering control in more detail it is worth considering zoning of the lighting system. Zoning is the wiring up of lights to switches and control devices so that they can be turned off or on within certain areas independently. The two reasons for switching off lights are for lack of occupancy and the presence of adequate daylight. This indicates that zoning requires a consideration of how natural light flows in to a room and patterns of occupancy. On this latter point it was found in chapter 2 that the energy consumption of an open plan office was greater than a cellular office. This, in part, was due to the ability to switch off lights in individual rooms without affecting the remaining occupied spaces. If this were to occur in an open plan office gloomy zones would be created leading to lights being turned back on again.

A small room with a single luminaire is treated as a single zone. However as the room becomes larger and requires two luminaires it is worth having the two luminaires switched separately. This means that the luminaire nearest the window can be switched off if there is sufficient natural light so saving 50% of the rooms lighting energy consumption. Figure 7.13 shows a lighting system zoned to take advantage of daylight.

It is known that light flows into a room from the windows and diminishes in quantity with depth from the windows. The lighting system should be zoned along the direction of diminishing light flow as shown in the diagram. In this example it may be possible to have zone 1 lamps off, zone 2 lamps at 50% of their output and zone 3 at 100%. If the room were switched as a single zone these savings would not be possible. Zoning requires the installation of additional wiring and switches/sensors which increases the capital cost of the system. However since electricity is a costly fuel these additional costs are quickly recovered in the value of electricity saved.

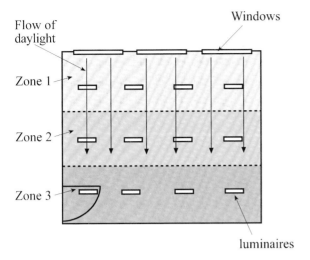

Figure 7.13Lighting system zoned to take advantage of daylight.

MANUAL SWITCHING

The simplest and most cost effective method of switching off lighting is by manual switching. This is very effective in domestic properties where the occupants have responsibility for the fuel bills but less effective in workplaces where lights are readily turned on in response to gloomy conditions but are not turned off again as the daylight returns. The situation can be improved by workplace awareness schemes. These use in-house magazines, posters and stickers by light switches to encourage occupants to switch off lights when they leave rooms. Unfortunately it has been found that the good practices encouraged by these awareness schemes soon wears off and the occupants return to their normal practices within a month or so. For this reason it is necessary to continually repeat the awareness message throughout the year.

SIMPLE TIME SWITCHING

Above it was stated that the occupants of work places readily turn lights on but do not turn them off again as daylighting improves. One way of overcoming this behaviour is to use simple time switching control. In this situation all of the lights in the building (where there is natural light)are turned off at certain times of

the day. The building occupants must then decide if they want to turn the lights back on again or not. If daylighting has improved then it is likely that the lights will remain off. In addition, there is evidence that the probability of switching lights on regardless of the amount of available daylight diminishes towards the middle of the day and then slowly increases again towards the end of the day as shown in figure 7.14. This may be due to the fact that there is an expectation that lighting is required at the start and end of the day. A feeling which is retained regardless of actual daylighting availability.

Figure 7.14 Graph of probability of switching on lights with time for various daylight factors.

Typical switch off times are morning break, 10:30am and lunchtime 12:00noon. A mid afternoon switch off time should be treated with care since the probability of switching back on is starting to increase once again (figure 7.14).Experiments have been carried out with switching off at short intervals such as hourly throughout the day. However, this simply creates annoyance amongst the building occupants who then demanded that the control system be removed.

It is possible that the simple timers switch off lights on a gloomy day when they are needed. In this case the lamps can be turned back on using wall switches, pendant cords hanging from the luminaires or hand held remote controllers. In some elaborate systems it is possible to turn the lights on over your desk by dialling your own internal phone number. In addition dialling in an further digit between 0 and 9 allows you to vary the light output of the lamp above your workstation.

OCCUPANCY DETECTION

One of the problems with simple time switching is that the lights can remain on between switching intervals even when there are no occupants in the space. One way of overcoming this is to use occupancy detectors as part of the control system that switchs the lights off when the space is vacant. The type of detectors used are passive infra red (PIR) detectors that sense body heat or ultrasonic detectors that sense movement. Both of these detectors can give a false reading that the space is unoccupied. If the person is at their desk but not moving or are sat outside of the detection area of the PIR then the lights may be extinguished. Occupants can then be seen waving their arms about to re-activate the lighting system. This creates dissatisfaction with the system. One way of avoiding false absences is to build a delay in to the unit so that the lights remain on for a further 15 minutes after an absence is detected. This usually gives sufficient time for any stationary occupants to be sensed and the lights will remain on.

Rapid switching of fluorescent tubes should be avoided as the regular heating/cooling of the cathode and tube reduces the life of the lamp. As a rule of thumb each start reduces the life of a tube by two hours. When limited to reasonable switching (less than 8 times per day) this does not have a significant effect on tubes for which the recommendation is that they should be replaced every 11 to 12,000 hours.

DAYLIGHT SENSING

One of the problems with occupancy detection is that the lights can remain on during occupation even when there is sufficient daylight entering the space. Daylight sensing uses photocells (figure7.15) to detect the combination of daylight and artificial light within a space. Control takes two forms, the simplest is when the lights are turned off when the quantity of light detected goes over a certain threshold. The switching is sudden and is more noticeable. This could lead to

the lights being turned back on as a reflex reaction. It is usually recommended therefore that the lights should only be switched off when the total light level exceeds the required illuminance by at least a factor of two. The second method varies the artificial light output so that a constant illuminance is maintained. This means that as the daylight levels increase the artificial light output is reduced and vice versa. This is illustrated in figure 7.16 where a constant room illuminance of 350 lx is maintained against reducing daylight levels.

Figure 7.15 Internal photocell. photo fromGPCS158. Energy efficient lighting in factories (1993) © Crown Copyright

SYSTEMS

A lighting control system requires sensors, wiring, a processor to determine actions from the sensed information and actuators to switch on/off or modify the light output of the lamps.There are a number of ways in which these components can be arranged;

- The simplest system is to install all of the control components into the luminaires themselves. Occupancy and light sensors being built in to one end of the luminaire. This simplifies and reduces the cost of wiring but requires a larger number of sensors and processors as one is required for each luminaire.

- The second method uses a wall mounted processor unit and one daylight and one occupancy sensor for each zone being controlled. The processor is accessible so that commissioning and changes to control strategy can be easily made. The number of sensors is reduced but more control wiring is required running from each sensor to the control unit and then back to each bank of luminaires.

- The third method is similar to the second in that single zone sensors and a wall mounted controller are used. However, the signals from the sensors and to the luminaires are carried by mains signalling. This is where a signal is carried in the mains electrical cable to each light luminaire. Each luminaire has an in-built control unit with a unique address so that the luminaire only responds to control signals that are meant for it.

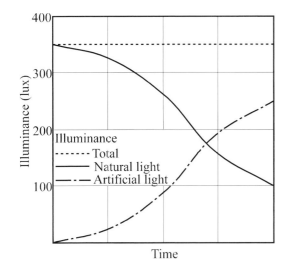

Figure 7.16 Control of artificial light output by daylight sensing

7.4 Building Regulations

The Building Regulations part L require that resonable provision be made for the conservation of power by providing appropriate lamps and controls. These requirement will be met by:

- Utilising energy efficient lamps and luminaires

- Having suitable manual and/or automatic switching controls (where the automatic systems have been suitably commissioned).

There are differences in the way that domestic and non-domestic buildings are treated.

DOMESTIC

Compliance with the building regulations can be demonstrated by providing fittings at locations that are expected to have the most use, that can only take lamps having a luminous efficacy greater than 40 lumens per circuit watt. Suitable locations are identified in GIL 20, Low energy domestic lighting, 1995. The regulations require that a resonable number of energy efficient fittings are provided. Recommended resonable numbers, depending on total number of rooms, are shown in table 7.5.

Number of rooms	Recommended minimum number of locations
1 - 3	1
4 - 6	2
7 - 9	3
10 - 12	4

Table 7.5 Number of locations to be equipped with efficient lighting.

In houses, manual control is considered acceptable but external lighting fixed to the building should have a minimum circuit efficacy of 40 lm/W and should go off when there is adequate daylight or it is not required at night.

NON-DOMESTIC

The regulations cover the efficiency of lamps and their control as described below. There are different requirements depending on building type

General lighting in office, industrial and storage buildings.

- Designing the lighting system to use lamps and control gear to give an average initial efficacy of 40 luminaire-lumen per circuit-watt or higher.

The formula used for calculating the luminaire efficacy takes into account the power consumption of the lighting system and also the way in which it is controlled. The formula is:

where:

$$\eta_{lum} = \frac{1}{P} \cdot \sum \frac{LOR.\phi_{lamp}}{C_L}$$

η_{lum} = the luminaire efficacy (luminaire-lumens/circuit watt)

LOR = Light output ratio

ϕ_{lamp} = the sum of the average initial (100 hour) lumen output of all the lamps in the luminaire (lm)

P = the total power consumption of all the luminaires (W)

C_L = a factor that is related to the reduction in power consumption of the lamp when electric lighting is not required (see table 7.6).

Control function	C_L
Luminaire is in a daylit space and its light output is controlled by a) a photoelectric switching or dimming control b) local manual switching (see figure 7.14)	0.80
Luminaire is in a space that is likely to be unoccupied for a significant number of working hours and where a sensor switches the lights off when the room is unoccupied and switching on is by manual switching	0.80
both of the above	0.75
non of the above	1.00

Table 7.6 Luminaire control factors

GENERAL LIGHTING IN OTHER BUILDINGS

The requirements would be met if the installed lighting capacity has an initial lamp plus ballast efficacy of at least 50 lumen per circuit watt. This can be achieved by selecting 95% or more of the lamps used to light the building from an approved list as shown in table 7.7

Light source	Types and ratings
High pressure sodium	all types and ratings
Metal halide	all types and ratings
Induction lighting	all types and ratings
Tubular fluorescent	16mm diameter (T8) lamps and 16mm diameter (T5) lamps rated above 11W provided with high efficiency control gear. 38mm diameter (T12) linear fluorescent lamps 2400mm in length
Compact fluorescent	all types and ratings above 11W
Other	Any type and rating with an efficacy greater than 50 lumens per circuit watt

Table 7.7 Approved lamp types.

CONTROLS

There is a requirement in the building regulation that suitable controls be provided to make effective use of daylight and limit operation when spaces are unoccupied. A way of meeting the requirement is to provide manual switches in easily assessible positions within the space being lit, usually near the entrance door. Maximum distances are set on plan between the switches and the luminaire it controls as illustrated in figure 7.17. Manual switches can be supplemented with occupancy and daylight based automatic controls.

OTHER TYPES OF LIGHTING

In addition to the general lighting system display lighting is also covered by the regulations. There are two ways of achieving compliance. The first involves selecting display lighting from an approved list, the second is that it should have an initial efficacy of not less than 15 lamp-lumens per circuit watt. Lighting such as emergency lighting and specialist process lighting are not covered by the regulations.

d < 8m or 3 x fitting height above floor

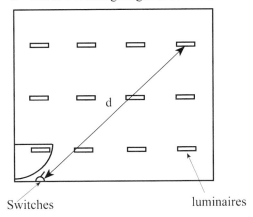

Switches

luminaires

Figure 7.17 Building regulation maximum permissible distance from switch to furthest luminaire

REFERENCES

1. Chartered Institute of Building Services Engineers. CIBSE Code for Interior Lighting. 1994

2. Philips Lighting. Indoor Lighting Catalogue (CI/ SfB (63) X. page 145. 1995.   Telephone 0181 686 1966

3. Richard Forster. The Challenge of LED's. Light and Lighting. pp14-15 September 1999.

FURTHER READING

GPG 160: Electric Lighting Controls - A Guide for Designers, Installers and Users. 1997

GPG 272: Lighting for People Energy Efficiency and Architecture - An Overview of Lighting Requirements and Design. 1999

08 RENEWABLE.ENERGY

In this chapter we will find that;

- Renewable energy is obtained by tapping into the earth's natural energy flows.

- The greatest benefit of renewable energy is that it produces no carbon dioxide or other pollutant gas emissions.

- Renewable energy only provides 3.5% of the UK electricity supply. This small proportion arises as a result of three factors; low energy content of renewable sources, inefficiencies in energy collection and low uptake of available technologies.

- Wind farming has become a mature industry. It provides useful amounts of energy and has the potential for further expansion.

- There are barriers to the further expansion of wind energy. These are mainly objections about intrusive visual impact. Offshore wind farms may provide a solution.

- Large scale hydro-electric power stations provide 2% of the UK electrical energy supply but future expansion is limited due to lack of additional suitable sites. Small scale hydro may provide further expansion.

- A few examples of wave energy schemes can be identified but they have not yet been developed on a large scale.

- Biomass is providing useful amounts of energy in waste fired power stations. Methane from landfilling and sewage digestion is used on a smaller scale to fuel gas fired CHP systems.

- Wood burning has traditionally been used as a form of space and water heating. It is now being re-discovered in efficient wood burning stoves.

- Geothermal energy is very important in some countries but in the UK its use is limited due the technical difficulties encountered in removing heat from hot dry rock.

- Geothermal energy can help to raise the efficiency of space heating heat pump systems.

- For passive solar energy to be effective a credit must be obtained in the balance between heat losses and heat gains through glazing.

- Optimum solar collection is obtained through south facing solar collectors

- Thermal mass present in the building structure and exposed to the room air improves the utilisation efficiency of solar gains and helps to reduce overheating.

- There are three concerns with passive solar heating systems. These are, summer overheating, high heat losses and glare.

- The two types of solar water heating collector are flat plate and evacuated tube collectors. Both are designed to maximise solar heat collection whilst minimising their own heat losses.

- Solar water heating can provide 50% of the hot water requirement of a typical household over the course of a year.

- Photovoltaics have a low efficiency in converting solar energy to electricity. At present, their high cost makes them an uneconomic form of renewable energy.

8.0 Introduction

There are two ways of reducing the carbon dioxide emitted as a consequence of building energy consumption. The first is to cut down on the amount of fossil fuels used, the second is to replace fossil fuels by renewable forms of energy that do not emit carbon dioxide when used.

Renewable energy is energy that is obtained by tapping into the earth's natural processes. Both electricity and heat can be provided by renewable energy. The majority of renewable energy forms can be traced back to energy released by the sun. The exceptions are tidal energy which is due to the rotation of the moon around the earth and geothermal energy which is derived from the energy trapped in the core of the earth during its formation. There are two main advantages to renewable energy. The first is that the use of renewable energy does not result in the release of carbon dioxide or other pollutant gases to the atmosphere. The second advantage is that it is continuous in the case of solar energy or regenerates within a short time such as the growing of crops for fuel.

Despite the advantages the amount of renewable energy utilised in the UK is small. This is because of a number of barriers to the uptake of renewable energy.

Energy content. Although the renewable energy potential is very large indeed, the energy content is low. The energy content is a measure of the amount of energy contained within the renewable source. For example, wind and a flowing river both contain kinetic energy. However if they were both flowing at the same speed the flowing water would have the greater amount of energy because there is more mass on the move than within the equivalent volume of air. With both air and water increasing the speed of flow increases the amount of energy available for collection. This is why wind farms are situated on hilltops where windspeeds and therefore energy potential are greatest.

Collection efficiency. The efficiency by which natural forms of energy can be collected and converted to forms useable in buildings (electricity and heat) is generally low. For example, crops used as biomass only collect 1% of the available solar energy. Man made devices are better with maximum collection efficiencies of photovoltaic panels and solar water heaters being 15% and 45% respectively. Typical values though are

10 and 30% respectively.

Environmental impact. We usually associate renewable energy as having a positive impact on the environment. However very few human activities leave the earth without change. Renewable energy is no exception and there are a number of negative environmental impacts associated with renewable energy some examples are listed in table 8.1.

Renewable Energy	Environmental Impact
Tidal Barrages	Damage esturine life by changing the tidal pattern
Wind Farms	Cause visual impact on hilltops
Waste burning	Releases pollutants such as dioxins

Table 8.1 Environmental impacts of some forms of renewable energy.

Some of the impacts listed in table 8.1 have serious implications for human health such as the potential for the release of cancer causing dioxins from the incineration of domestic waste. Others are subjective such as the visual impact of wind turbines. Some observers appreciate them in the landscape, others strongly object to their presence.

Technical difficulties. As with many technologies difficulties are encountered in converting a planned method of harvesting renewable energy into reality. An example is in collecting geothermal energy from hot dry rocks. Here the slow speed at which the rocks recover their heat content after it has been extracted from them limits the viability of this form of energy.

CONTRIBUTION OF RENEWABLES

As a consequence of the above barriers, renewable energies only make up about 3.5% of the UK electrical supply (figure 8.1)[1]. The total UK electricity consumption per year is approximately 250 Terra Watt hours TWh (T = terra = 10^{12}). However, It should be noted that the policy of the government at the time of writing is to increase the proportion of energy provided by renewables to 10% by 2010 and then 20% by 2025.

A large modern coal fired power station has a peak electrical output of approximately 2000MW, the peak output of a nuclear power station is approximately 1300 MW. Renewable sources of electricity cannot currently match the levels of electrical output provided by these conventional power stations. In order for renewables to make a rational contribution to UK energy consumption the following must be implemented;

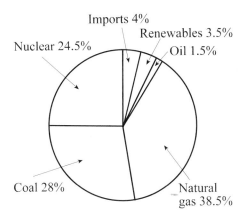

Figure 8.1 Breakdown of fuels used to provide the UK electricity supply.

- The energy consumption of buildings, their services and appliances must be reduced by low energy methods. In this way the energy requirement of the building will more closely match the limited output of renewable sources.

- Use of renewables must be further encouraged by government schemes such as the renewables obligation (RO). This requires electricity suppliers to work towards sourcing 5% of the electricity it sells to its customers from renewable sources by 2003 and 10% by 2010. In this way the renewable energy industry can develop mass production techniques which will reduce capital costs, raise efficiencies and help resolve technical difficulties.

This chapter will briefly describe forms of renewable energy but will concentrate on those forms which are particularly associated with buildings. These are in ascending order of importance; photovoltaic (PV) cells, solar water heating and passive solar space heating.

8.1 Wind Energy

Wind turbines use a propeller to catch the kinetic energy with in a moving air stream and convert it into rotational movement. This rotation turns an electricity generator connected to the propeller and mounted at the top of a tower inside a housing. The tower gives ground clearance for the blades and also lifts them up into the faster moving airstreams. The larger turbines have a small electric motor that turns the blades into the direction of the wind, guided by data from a small wind vane. When a number of wind turbines are grouped together a wind farm is created. The turbines are usually separated from each other by 10 blade diameters. This is because the turbines remove energy from the wind and so if too close together would deprive their neighbours further downwind of energy. A modern wind farm turbine typically has two or three 30 - 40 m diameter blades made out of glass fibre or wood-epoxy on a horizontal axis. The tower is 25 - 30 m high and is made out of steel. The output of wind farm turbines ranges from 400kW to 1.5MW each. A typical wind farm will have a total output of approximately 10MW. This output is only 0.5% of that from a coal fired power station, but of course produces no pollutant gases.

Figure 8.2 Wind turbine.

An environmental benefit of wind turbines is that farming such as animal grazing can continue right up to the base of the tower. They create a small environmental footprint on the ground but one of the main concerns of wind farms is their visual intrusion on the landscape. They are often sited on the top of hills within or visible from, areas of natural beauty as these are the places where windspeeds are greatest. As a consequence wind farm development must overcome strong opposition on visual impact grounds before planning permission is granted. To avoid this problem the next stage of development will be to construct offshore wind farms. One example is off the coast of Northumberland at Blyth where two 2MW turbines have been installed[2]. Remote areas are however more costly to develop as a lengthy connection to the grid has to be created.

As well as providing electricity to the grid, turbines can be attached to buildings themselves or, if land and space permits, be sited within the grounds. Turbines attached to buildings tend to be small since large units would create unacceptable stresses on the structure and would also contribute to airborne and structure born noise. One example of turbines attached to a building is the Green Building in Dublin[3]. This is a building whose aim is to demonstrate environmental technologies. It has three turbines attached to the roof. Each one is rated at 1.5kW. The total output of 4.5kW is said to contribute 80% of the buildings lighting energy consumption.

An example of a larger turbine sited near to a building is the Sainsbury's East Kilbride distribution depot in Scotland. Here a 600kW turbine has been installed to generate about one third of the electricity required at the depot.[4]

Wind power demonstrates one of the general difficulties associated with renewable forms of energy which is that it can be intermittent in delivery. The blades do not rotate when the windspeed is too low or so fast that damage would occur. As a consequence wind power could not form a complete electrical supply in itself. It would need to be supplemented by a more controllable and consistent method of power generation that can be used when wind generated electricity was insufficient or absent.

8.2 Water Power

The movement of water has traditionally been used as a mechanical energy source in mill buildings, collected using water wheels. However the movement of water can also rotate a turbine in order to generate electricity. The most impressive examples are hydro-electric power stations where water, held in a reservoir behind a dam is allowed to flow down to a lower level through ducts containing a turbine. Countries such as Canada and Norway have hydroelectric power stations with outputs of several thousand megawatts which is comparable to fossil fuel power stations. In the UK hydroelectric power contributes 2% of the UK electricity supply. The biggest hydroelectric power stations are found in high altitude regions such as Scotland where there are the necessary height differences through which the water can fall and plenty of rainfall. The potential for new large scale generation is very limited due to the lack of suitable sites. Future developments will be in small scale hydro power. This is defined as generation up to 5MW output. Small scale hydro turbines utilise the kinetic energy of fast flowing rivers or the potential energy built up in the head of water created by a small weir or reservoir. For example a unit at Roadford reservoir, Okehampton, Devon generates just under 1MW of electricity[5]. So long as there is sufficient and continuous rainfall the electrical output of hydro - electric schemes is continuous and therefore available when required.

TIDAL BARRAGES

A tidal barrage is a low dam constructed across the mouth of a tidal estuary. When the tide rises sea water is allowed to pass through a gate in the barrage and collects in the area behind it. At high tide the gates are shut and as the tide falls the sea water can only escape by passing through an opening in the barrage in which a turbine is placed. There are no tidal barrages in the UK although estuaries on the rivers Severn, Mersey, Wyre and Conwy have been considered[6]. There is a barrage at La Rance in France which generates electricity. The electrical output occurs twice a day during the ebb of the tide. The opportunities for future barrages is small in the UK. One of the reasons are the ecological concerns arising from altering the ebb and flow of tides in the estuary which would disturb estaurine life. Estuaries are the home to a great diversity of shellfish, sea weeds, marine and brackish water organisms and bird life that could be affected by this technology.

PUMPED STORAGE

Pumped storage is not a form of renewable energy but does allow the rest of the electrical generation network to operate more efficiently. At night surplus electricity is used to pump water from a low reservoir up to a high reservoir where it is stored. If there is a sudden demand for electricity such as can occur during commercial breaks in major televised sporting events when many kettles are switched on at once, water is allowed to fall back down to the lower reservoir through a turbine. This generates electricity needed for the surge in demand. This short term rapid generation of electricity is very useful since it avoids the need to fire up a conventional power station which is inefficient for short duration peaks in demand. There is an example of a pumped storage power station at Dinorwig in Wales.

WAVE POWER

Waves contain a large amount of energy. Many systems have been devised over the years to try and harness the energy in waves. Floating systems such as cam shaped buoys that rotate when a wave advances on them turning a generator had major maintenance problems and so have fallen out of favour. The current interest lies in coast based systems where access can be more easily obtained for maintenance and sea conditions are slightly less severe. Figure 8.3 shows a section through a system which is based on the compression of air when a wave enters a cave.

Figure 8.3 Wave power generator.

The generator is constructed to resemble a sea cave. As a wave enters the mouth of the generator the air within it rushes out of the only escape route which is a duct in the roof of the generator. A turbine in the duct, called a Wells turbine, rotates when the air passes through it generating electricity. As the wave subsides a negative pressure is created in the cavity and air is drawn in the reverse direction through the turbine. Gearing in the system ensures that regardless of the direction of air flow the electrical generator turns in the same direction. An example of this type of system is installed and operating on the isle of Islay in the inner Hebrides.

8.3 Biomass

Biomass is material derived from plants and animals. This material contains energy which can be released in a number of ways such as burning the raw material, burning waste from the material or processing it to produce new fuels. The use of crops to produce energy is considered to be carbon neutral as carbon dioxide released during combustion is re-absorbed when new plants grow. The use of animal litter as fuel is not carbon neutral as the animals emit metabolic carbon dioxide in life and burning of the litter also releases CO_2. However, burning organic waste is preferable to allowing it to decompose in an oxygen depleted environment. This is because the anaerobic digestion produces methane instead of carbon dioxide and methane is 30 times more potent than CO_2 as a greenhouse gas (see processed biomass below).

Wood burning has traditionally been used to provide energy and still represents the majority of energy released in the world. However it has been replaced as fuel for space heating and cooking in the UK by gas and electricity. There has however been a recent resurgence in interest in efficient wood burning stoves as a means of heating sustainable low energy housing and small commercial buildings.

COPPICING

Coppicing is the cultivation of crops to be burned as fuel. The most common example is the growing of willow trees. Willow is fast growing and after a few years the upper branches are cut off to be burned in solid fuel burning heaters. New shoots appear at the base of the cut branches and so new growth is regenerated. Rotation is needed so that the coppice is at various stages of growth. Areas are required to reach maturity each year to maintain the fuel supply. Large areas of land are needed to produce biofuels since only 1% of the solar energy is captured and converted to useable energy. However, in Finland in 1995 wood fuels accounted for 15% of the total energy requirement (heat and power) and 10% of the total primary fuel used to generate electricity[7].

WASTE

Waste can arise in a number of forms including thinnings and chippings from the timber industry, farming waste and also paper packaging which is found in domestic refuse.

There are a number of large scale example of energy from waste in the UK. For example Sheffield has a municipal refuse incinerator which burns 120,000 tonnes of waste each year and produces 28MW of heat which is used within a city wide district heating scheme[8]. Amongst the wide variety of materials contained in domestic waste are processed biomass products such as paper and plastics. As well as heat from waste there are also waste burning power stations. One example is in Humberside that burns straw waste from farming. Another at Eye in Suffolk burns chicken droppings mixed with straw and woodshavings. This latter example produces 12.5 MW of electricity. The plant burns 125,000 tonnes of poultry litter per year, approximately half of Suffolk's chicken farm output. The station produces power and avoids the problem of nitrates leaching out of the litter into river and groundwater systems.

PROCESSED BIOMASS

Biomass can be processed in a number of ways to make it into a more versatile fuel. One simple example is the chipping of timber to make it easier to feed in to a wood burning appliance. Natural processes can also be utilised. One example is the creation of methane gas from the anaerobic digestion of organic waste by bacteria. The most common examples are the collection of methane from the digestion of human sewage at sewage treatment plants, the digestion of animal sewage on farms and the collection of methane from landfill sites produced from the breakdown of organic material in the refuse. In each case the methane can be collected, cleaned to remove impurities, compressed and then used as a fuel in a combined heat and power plant. A typical medium sized anaerobic digestion chp scheme would generate 100kW of electricity. The combustion of methane means that this extremely potent global warming gas is not released to the atmosphere.

Crops can be grown specifically to be processed into a more versatile fuel source. Two important example of this is the growing of sunflowers so that the oily seeds can be utilised in the production of biodiesel. This is a fuel which is used extensively as a motor fuel but can also be used in building heating systems and power generation. The second example is the production of alcohol from the fermentation of biomass. This is used extensively in Brazil as a fuel for cars.

8.4 Geothermal Energy

The core of the earth is composed of molten iron and so is extremely hot. Some of this heat makes its way towards the earths surface by conduction. This heat manifests itself in three forms; hot aquifers, steam and hot dry rock. This section will also consider a method of extracting low grade geothermal energy using ground loop heat pumps.

Figure 8.4 Boreholes used to extract heat from hot dry rock.

Hot aquifers. At certain locations in the world ground

water passes through hot, porous rock and becomes heated. If a borehole is drilled to this porous rock the hot water can be extracted and used in a buildings heating system. This is common in places such as Iceland where water up to 100°C may be obtained. In the UK hot aquifers do not represent a significant heat source as the geological conditions which are favourable for hot water collection are not near major urban areas and it is impractical to pump hot water over large distances.

Steam. If the temperature of a hot aquifer increases above 100°C steam is produced. This can be collected and used in space heating or if passed through turbines can produce electricity. Unfortunately whilst geothermal steam is used to produce electricity in Iceland, Italy and New Zealand there are no geothermal steam resources in the UK.

Hot dry rocks. Hot dry rock is present everywhere in the world at depth. It is referred to as dry as it is solid and therefore has no water held within it which could be extracted. Instead two boreholes are drilled separated from each other. Water is injected into the first borehole at pressure which creates a crack pathway between it and the second borehole (figure 8.4). Water can then pass from the source borehole to the collection borehole and is heated en route.

Tests on hot dry rock have been carried out in the granite beneath Cornwall. So far technical difficulties involved with drilling to a depth of 2000m and creating fractured rock have meant that this source of energy has not been realised.

GROUND LOOP HEAT PUMPS

One method of extracting low grade energy from the ground is to utilise a ground loop heat pump system. In this method the geothermal energy compliments an electrically driven form of space heating.

Heat pumps are like a refrigerator working in reverse. A refrigerator removes heat from the ice box making it colder and discards the heat which has been removed as waste into the kitchen. The device is called a heat pump as it takes heat from a low grade source, a cold place, and converts it into a higher grade form by releasing it in a warmer place.

The basic components of a heat pump are shown in figure 8.5. The main components are an evaporator coil, a compressor, a condenser coil, and an expansion device. These components are connected together using copper pipe through which refrigerant circulates in a closed loop. Heating is achieved in the following way:

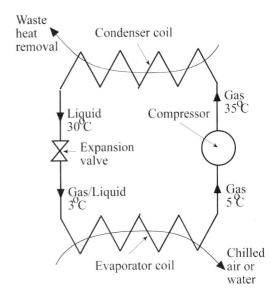

Figure 8.5 Components of a heat pump

Liquid refrigerant is forced through the expansion valve. As the refrigerant leaves the expansion valve its pressure is reduced. This allows it to evaporate which removes heat from the air flowing over the evaporator coil. The refrigerant, now in a vapour state, leaves the evaporator and passes through the compressor. The pressure is increased causing the refrigerant vapour to condense. This occurs at a relatively high temperature. As the refrigerant condenses it releases the heat it absorbed during evaporation. This heats up the condenser coil. Air passing over the condenser coil is heated and is used to warm the living space, while the refrigerant is cooled.

In terms of a domestic refrigerator the evaporator is situated in the ice compartment and the condenser is the grid of piping at the rear of the refrigerator. The evaporator and condenser coils are simply arrays of copper pipe with aluminium fins mechanically bonded to their surface to increase the area for heat transfer.

The efficiency of a heat pump is at its greatest when the evaporator and condenser coils are at similar temperatures. However, when space heating is required the condenser coil is in a warm room at 21°C and the evaporator coil is outside at temperatures below 0°C. This has two effects. The first is that the efficiency with which electricity is converted to space heating is reduced and secondly the evaporator coil can ice up, reducing its ability to transfer heat. As a consequence air to air heat pumps may incorporate an electrical heater to periodically defrost the evaporator coil. The use of electricity for defrosting also reduces the efficiency of the device.

The problems of icing up and low efficiency can be eliminated if the evaporator coil is placed in a warm environment. Examples of such environments are lofts heated by solar collection and ground waters heated by geothermal energy. One way of taking heat out of the ground is to bury a network of pipes which are filled with water, known as a ground loop (figure 8.6). During winter, the ground loop will always be at a higher temperature than air temperature as it is picking up geothermal heat from the ground. The water in the loop is pumped to a shell surrounding the evaporator coil thereby raising its temperature. Water leaving the evaporator shell will have been cooled, and so it is returned to the ground loop to pick up more geothermal energy. A large network of piping is required to absorb heat from the ground.

Figure 8.6 Ground loop heat pump system.

8.5 Passive Solar Heating

Passive solar space heating is simply the collection of solar energy by a building without utilising special devices, such as solar panels. However, elements of the building may be modified to optimise solar collection such as increasing the area of south facing glazing.

The usefulness of passive solar space heating varies depending on the type of building. In housing the entry of sunlight is considered psychologically pleasing and the heat it carries can offset the need for mechanical space heating. It is estimated that passive solar heating can reduce space heating energy consumption in a typical house by up to 10%. Small non-domestic buildings such as schools and health centres where space heating energy consumption is the predominant energy usage can also benefit from passive solar design. However, in commercial buildings, where heat gains from occupants, lighting and equipment are already large, the entry of solar energy can cause overheating leading to discomfort and, in extreme cases, to the use of air conditioning. In offices there is also a need for a good visual environment. Entry of sunlight can create glare either directly through windows or as reflections from computer screens. A common occurence associated with this is that blinds will be drawn and artificial lighting switched on leading to increased electrical energy consumption.

For a passive solar design to be successful the following must be considered:

- Availability of solar energy. The availability of solar energy varies depending on time of year and atmospheric conditions. These factors are beyond our control however the solar collector can be orientated to optimise solar collection when it is available.

- Solar collection systems - The most common collection systems are windows and conservatories. There are also less common systems such as Trombe walls. Each system has different solar collection abilities, heat loss characteristics and means of transferring the energy into the building. Problems of high heat losses, overheating and glare can arise and would reduce the effectiveness of the solar collection system unless eliminated at the design stage.

- Thermal storage - Solar energy is unpredictable both in timing and quantity. Thermal storage is needed to improve the utilisation efficiency of solar energy.

- Heat distribution - Solar energy is a south side phenomenon. Methods are required to re distribute some of the heat to the north side of the building.

- Mechanical heating system. Passive solar heating only saves energy if the mechanical heating system can reduce its output quickly in response to the incoming solar gains.

Each of these aspects will be discussed more fully in the following sections.

8.5.1 Solar Availability

A large amount of solar radiation is received by the earth. The solar constant, the amount of energy outside the earth's atmosphere, is equivalent to $1.2kW/m^2$. Some of this energy is removed by absorption and scattering in the atmosphere so that the maximum direct solar intensity falling on a horizontal surface in the UK is $0.8kW/m^2$. This will occur at noon on a clear day in mid summer . When averaged over a full day, to take the daily variation into account, the average solar intensity in the summer is $0.35kW/m^2$.

The total amount of energy falling on a surface depends on the number of hours of sunlight, the solar intensity and the orientation of the surface. As the suns position and number of sunlight hours changes with month of the year the average daily solar intensity also varies. This is illustrated in figure 8.7 which shows the average daily solar intensity on north, south and east/west facing vertical surfaces. The solar intensity on a horizontal surface is also shown. The following features can be observed:

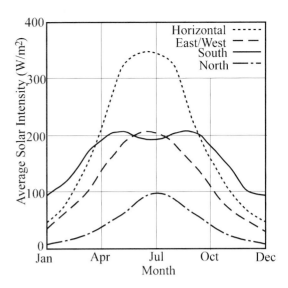

Figure 8.7 Solar intensities on various surfaces throughout the year.

- The highest value of solar intensity occurs on the horizontal surface in summer. This is because the solar intensity on a surface is greatest when the solar radiation falls perpendicularly onto the surface. In summer the sun is high in the sky and so is closer to this situation than in winter when the sun is lower in the sky. The low altitude of the sun causes a reduced solar intensity on the surface as illustrated in figure 8.8 This figure represents the solar radiation as a series of equally spaced parallel lines. It can be seen that more of these lines hit the given area (i.e. providing a high solar intensity) when the sun is high in the sky in June than when it is low in the sky in December.

- The curve for solar intensity on a north facing vertical surface is lower than the other curves at all times of the year. This is because it only receives direct radiation from the sun in the early morning and late evening in summer. The rest of the time north facing surfaces are in shade as the predominant direction of the sun is from south east to south west. When in shade north facing surfaces only receive solar radiation that has been scattered back on to it from moisture and pollution in the atmosphere.

- The solar intensity on east and west facing vertical

surfaces have the same curve. However, the curve does not show that the east facing surface receives its sunlight in the morning and is shaded in the afternoon and the west facing receives sunlight in the afternoon and is shaded in the morning. West facing glazing in office buildings exposed to the sun is of particular concern. This is because the sun will enter it at the end of the day. At this time the fabric of the building will have been heated up by other casual gains during the day. The additional solar gains cannot be absorbed by the fabric and afternoon overheating will occur.

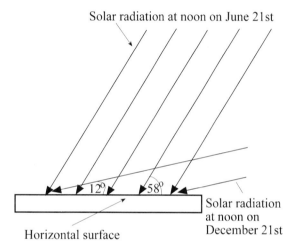

Figure 8.8 Diagram showing how solar intensity on a surface is reduced at acute angles of incidence.

- The solar intensity on the south facing surface follows a curve with two peaks. This pattern of solar intensity across the year is very beneficial to passive solar heating. The trough between the peaks occurs when overheating is of most concern and the peaks are moved out towards the start and end of the heating season.

It follows from the above that the optimum orientation for a solar collection system is facing south. However, it is usually assumed that a collector orientated within $^+/_- 30°$ of south will still receive the majority of available solar energy. Useful morning heating can be achieved using an east facing collector and evening warming using a west facing collector. This then dictates the orientation of the buildings themselves as shown in figure 8.9 that shows an estate of houses arranged to orientate their solar collectors towards the sun. Horizontal space heating solar collectors should be avoided as there is a peak during the summer when space heating is not required.

Figure 8.9 Estate layout for solar collection. diag. from GPCS 90 Lowri park road - passive solar design (1992) © Crown Copyright

8.5.2 Solar Collection Systems

The two requirements of a successful passive solar collection system are that it must transmit solar energy into the building when required whilst at the same time maintain the insulating properties of the fabric. The two most common collection systems are windows and conservatories. There are also a number of less common solar collectors such as trombe walls.

WINDOWS

The simplest solar collectors are the windows already present in buildings to provide daylight, views and ventilation. However since windows are the main route for fabric heat losses from the building care should be taken to ensure there is a net gain of energy through them during the heating season i.e.

$$\begin{matrix} \text{Heat gains} & > & \text{Heat losses} \\ \text{through glazing} & & \text{through glazing} \end{matrix}$$

This balance is very difficult to achieve. As is shown in figure 8.9[9] which shows the net heat gain over the heating season for south facing single glazing, double glazing and low emissivity glazing with night time insulated shutters. It can be seen that single glazing experiences a net loss of heat for about one half of the heating season. Net gains are confined to the early and late parts of the heating season. For double glazing the situation is improved but there are small net losses from November to February. The system which gives net gains throughout the entire heating season is low emissivity double glazing combined with night-time shutters.

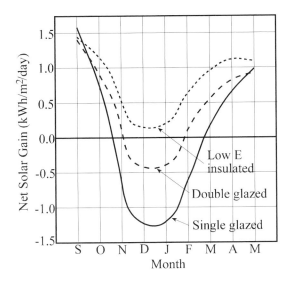

Figure 8.10 Net solar gains through various types of glazing[9].

It follows from the above that to be effective as a solar collector windows should;

- Have as low a U-value as possible i.e. double glazed with low emissivity coating and possibly argon gas filling.

- Be covered with insulation at night such as thick curtains or insulated shutters to reduce heat losses when no gains are available.

- Face within + or - 30° of south.

- The overall area of glazing on the building should not be increased. Instead glazing on the east, west and especially north facades should be reduced and an equivalent area transferred to the south facade. Note windows on east west and north faces should not be reduced to the extent that adequate daylighting is lost.

CONTROL OF HEAT GAINS

One of the problems with using windows as solar collection devices is that the energy is deposited directly in to the living spaces behind the glazing. Solar gains are very different to the heat input to a building by a mechanical heating system. A mechanical heating system releases heat into the room in a controlled manner. When the room is warm enough the heat output is stopped or reduced. With solar heating the quantity and timing of the heat gains are unknown. This can cause overheating in the living space and thermal discomfort. To avoid this some control of the solar gains is necessary. This is usually achieved using three mechanisms; solar blinds, ventilation and exposed thermal mass.

Blinds. Raising and lowering of blinds can vary the solar heat input to a space. When fully retracted full solar gains are achieved. If the temperature rises above comfortable limits then the blinds can be lowered to reduce the solar gain input. Varying the position and pitch of venetian blinds can give good control over solar gains. However adjustment is a manually intensive process which may not be appropriate in commercial buildings. Here motorised systems can be used which adjust the position of the blinds in response to data from indoor air temperature and external solar energy sensors.

Ventilation. Ventilation of a space can be used to carry unwanted solar heat out of the building in the form of hot exhaust air. This can be achieved by opening windows or by operating a mechanical extract fan. The fan should be controlled by an air temperature sensor so that it switches off when temperatures have returned to acceptable levels.

Thermal mass. The thermal mass of a building is a description of its internal fabric in terms of its ability to absorb heat.

When a material absorbs heat its temperature increases. Some materials can absorb more heat than others for each degree of temperature rise. Their ability to do this is described by the specific heat capacity (SHC). The SHC is a measure of the quantity of heat absorbed by 1kg of material in order to raise its temperature by 1°C. A material with a high thermal capacity can absorb a lot of heat and its temperature will only rise by a small amount. High thermal capacity materials are usually dense such as blockwork and concrete. Low thermal capacity materials have a low density such as timber, insulation and plasterboard.

A high thermal mass room would be one that had tiled solid concrete floors, blockwork internal walls and an exposed concrete ceiling. A low thermal mass room would have timber framed external walls, suspended timber floors and timber stud and plasterboard internal walls.

Thermal mass provided by exposed blockwork walls acts as a heat store. When the air temperature is higher than that of the wall heat moves from the room air into the walls. This reduces the air temperature. When the air temperature is lower than the wall temperature heat will move back out of the walls into the room air. This raises the room air temperature. The effect of this movement of heat into and out of the walls is to improve the utilisation of solar gains. This is because in a low thermal mass room sunlight entry would cause the air temperature to rise rapidly. Thermal discomfort would occur and windows would be opened to reject the solar heat gains. If thermal mass were present the peak temperature would be reduced, the windows would remain closed and the solar gains would be retained within the room air and fabric. Some of the heat absorbed by the fabric would reappear at a later time. By this process, thermal mass reduces peak internal air temperatures and raises troughs in temperature to give a more stable internal temperature profile.

The improved utilisation of solar energy by the provision of a thermally heavy building is illustrated in table 8.2[10]. The table shows the useful solar gains through one square metre of glazing for various orientations. The table illustrates two things. Firstly, that south facing glazing achieves the highest solar gains followed by east/west then north facing glazing. Secondly, that for all orientations of glazing the solar gains are improved as the thermal mass increases. The values given are for single glazing and should be reduced by 10% for double glazing. They are averaged over the heating season assuming space heating is operating between 0600 and 2300 hours.

Orientation	Solar gain (kWh/m^2/day)		
	Light	**Medium**	**Heavy**
South	0.75	0.90	1.04
North	0.23	0.27	0.31
East/West	0.45	0.54	0.62

Table 8.2 Average useful solar gains through one square metre of glass for various orientations.

HEAT DISTRIBUTION

One of the limitations of passive solar heating is that it occurs predominantly on the south side of the building. For most domestic buildings this is acceptable as heat can travel short horizontal distances towards the north side of the building and rising warm air will heat the upper floors. However, as the building becomes large such as a health center or school then clear north/south zoning occurs. The south side requiring no mechanical heating due to the solar gains but the north side requiring heating due to the absence of solar gains.

There are two methods for creating a more even horizontal distribution of heat through large floor plan buildings. The first is to provide solar collectors, such as windows, at more than one location as shown in figure 8.11. The second is to use ducting and fans to take warm air from the south side of the building and convey it to the north side (figure 8.12).

CONSERVATORIES

A more complex type of solar collector which has marginal energy saving benefits is a south facing conservatory (figure 8.13). Sunlight entering the conservatory raises the internal air temperature. Some of the solar energy is stored in the mass of the masonry outer wall and ceramic floor tiles on a concrete base. The elevated temperatures in the conservatory reduce fabric heat losses through that part of the outer skin of the building that is buffered by the conservatory. However as U values in the outer walls are reduced by Building Regulation requirements, the buffering effect becomes less valuable. The air within the conservatory can be used to ventilate the building. This air can move into the building via open patio doors, windows or trickle ventilators. More complex arrangements involving ducting and fans to move the heated air can also be used. The duct could be formed from a hollow core within an intermediate concrete floor slab, providing additional thermal mass to the system.

Figure 8.11 North side heating using multiple solar collectors.

Figure 8.12 Solar heat distribution using fans and ducting.

The benefits of a conservatory collection system are:

- It acts as a buffer between the solar collection and the occupied space. Gains can be accepted or if not required rejected.

- It avoids the need for large windows in the external shell of the building and so the thermal integrity of the building is maintained.

- It creates an extended living space. Shelter and solar gains make the conservatory habitable from early spring to late autumn

This latter feature is also the main cause for concern with conservatories. If they become important living spaces there may be a desire to fit them with space heating to be used in winter. This should not take place as the heat losses through the highly glazed structure would outweigh any gains made. In summer owners may wish to cool the conservatory using a portable air conditioner. This should be avoided and instead the temperature should be controlled using shading, thermal mass and ventilation.

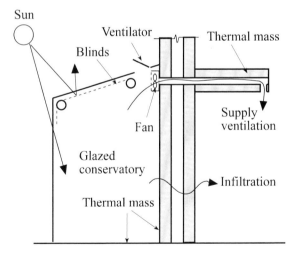

Figure 8.13 Conservatory as a solar collector.

OTHER COLLECTORS

A variety of other passive solar collection systems have been proposed one such example is the Trombe wall. Trombe walls form part of the south facing wall of the building (figure 8.14). Sunlight passes through a transparent outer panel, such as glazing or transparent insulation, and is absorbed by the structural wall at the back. The air in the cavity is heated by this action. If the house does not require space heating the warm air can be vented outside. This in turn draws ventilation air through the adjacent room, entering the trombe wall cavity from a low level vent. If space heating is required the external high level vent is closed and warm air will move out of the trombe wall into the living space by its own natural buoyancy. Convective cycling of air is created through the trombe wall via the high and low level room vents. The Trombe wall has thermal storage mass built into it as part of its construction. One of the disadvantages of Trombe walls is that they do not provide daylight or views out of the house. This can be overcome by forming the lower part of the wall as a solar collector and having standard windows within the remaining wall. Note if the trombe wall is created below sill height it must be at least 1m in height to set up a sufficiently strong convection current for heated air to escape from it.

Few examples of effective trombe wall heating systems exist due to the difficulty in designing the system for effective convective heat transfers integrated with opening/closing of vents as required.

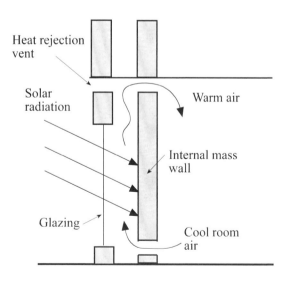

Figure 8.14 Trombe wall passive solar heating system.

LONG TERM HEAT STORAGE

One of the problems with passive solar heating is that the majority of solar energy appears in the summer when it is not needed for space heating. It has generally been considered impractical to collect and store heat in the summer for use in the winter. This is because a thermal store of similar size to the building would be required. However, a number of contemporary sustainable buildings have made an attempt at achieve this goal. One example is the conference building at the Doncaster earth centre this has a large water tank in its basement which is heated during the summer using evacuated tube solar water heating panels (see next section). In autumn the stored hot water is used in the heating system to provide space heating. Monitoring is at too early a stage at the time of writing to indicate how effective this system is.

In the above example water was used to store heat by virtue of its thermal capacity. Another storage medium is rocks, solar heated air is blown through spaces between the rocks heating them up. In the heating season air entering the building is pre-heated by passing it through the rock store. Research is continuing into phase change material as thermal storage media. These materials do not store heat by heating up but by changing state. For example they are a solid material and when they absorb heat they become liquid. This does not increase the temperature of the material and so sensible heat losses are small. When the phase change material changes back to a solid heat is released which can be used for space heating. Examples of materials that change phase around room temperature are inorganic hydrated salts such as calcium chloride hexahydrate, another are paraffin waxes. The latent heat of fusion is absorbed by a phase change material to melt it is much greater than that absorbed during temperature rise of a conventional sensible heat store. This means that the size of the thermal store can be greatly reduced.

8.5.3 Integration with Mechanical Heating

It was stated at the outset that passive solar space heating is only useful in reducing energy consumption if the output of the space heating system can be reduced or turned off in response to the entry of solar energy. This can only occur if the heating system has been designed to take advantage of solar gains and there are adequate control systems in place.

- **Control** The heating system must be zoned so that areas not receiving solar gains, such as the north side of the building can be heated independently from the south side. Sensors, placed out of direct sunlight, must be employed to detect solar gains as an increase in space temperature. In response, actuators are used to modify the heat output of the heat source and heat emitters.

- **Thermal response.** The heating system and in particular the heat emitters must have a quick thermal response time. This means that the time between receiving a command to reduce heat output and the commencement of reductions in heat output must be short. High thermal capacity systems such as underfloor heating, electric storage radiators or high water content radiators are unsuitable as they have a slow thermal response time. Even if the flow of hot water to them were to be stopped instantly the stored thermal energy within them would still be released for some hours before reducing significantly. Instead, low water content radiators or fan convectors should be used. Switching off the fan of a fan convector rapidly reduces its heat output. This means that if solar gains change as a result of movement of cloud cover, the heating system can respond to these changes quickly by turning the fan on as temperatures fall and off as temperatures rise above set point.

8.6 Solar Water Heating

Unlike space heating which is only required during the winter months, hot water is required all year round. This is useful as the sun's greatest availability is in summer when space heating is not required. A solar water heating system can provide all of the hot water requirement of a typical 2 adult, 2 children family during the summer months but only part of the hot water requirement in winter when the solar availability is

reduced. The system could be sized to provide full hot water delivery in winter but would then be greatly oversized in summer. As a consequence a typical solar water heating system based on 1m² per person provides approximately 50% of the annual hot water requirement of a typical family. The capital cost of a solar water heating system is between £1750 and £4000. If we assume the cost is £2000 to provide 4m² of solar collector and this provides 33,000 litres of hot water per year, normally heated by electricity, then the result is a simple payback period of approximately 15 years. The payback is considerably longer if the solar water heating system is displacing gas.

There are two main parts to a solar water heating system. The first is the solar collector that traps solar energy and transfers it into the water flowing through it. The second is the system that transfers the heat within the collector water to the water stored in the domestic hot water storage tank.

SOLAR COLLECTORS

Modern solar collectors take one of two forms. These are flat plate collectors and evacuated tube collectors. Both types of collector have to carry out the twin functions of maximising the collection of solar energy whilst minimising heat losses. Both types must also be extremely robust since they are mounted outdoors and have to withstand thermal cycling between low temperatures caused by radiant cooling to the night sky and high temperatures caused by the absorption of solar energy.

Flat plate collectors are rectangular and are typically 0.6m by 1.5m in size. Multiple collectors can be plumbed together in series to form a collector array which will increase the amount of hot water that is created. A typical flat plate collector is shown in figure 8.15. It is composed of a steel or aluminium frame which holds all of the components in place and allows the collector to be fixed to a suitable south facing mounting location such as the rooftop.

The uppermost layer in the flat plate collector is a sheet of glass. This allows the solar radiation to pass through to the collector plate below where it is absorbed. The glass sheet has two functions. The first is to create a greenhouse effect trapping heat within the air gap above the collector plate. The second is to reduce convective heat losses from the collector plate. This last function is necessary to increase collector efficiency since, in winter, the collector will lose heat to the cold surrounding air. Heat losses are reduced further if low emissivity double glazing is used. Instead of using a sheet of glass, standard thermal insulation forms a layer behind the collector plate to reduce backward heat losses. The collector plate is composed of a steel or aluminum panel onto which tubing is fixed. The tubing forms a close contact with the plate to ensure that solar heat absorbed by the plate is transferred into the water that circulates through the pipes. Low cost collector plates are simply finished in matt black. This finish is the most efficient at absorbing solar heat. More expensive units have collector plates coated in a metal oxide layer. This has a high heat absorptivity and a low heat emissivity. The coating therefore reduces radiant heat losses from the collector plate without affecting the absorption of solar energy.

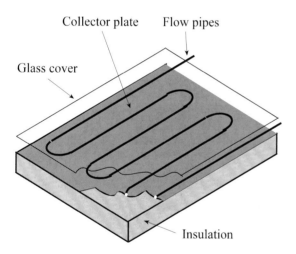

Figure 8.15 Flat plate solar collector.

Evacuated tube collectors have a collector plate similar to a flat plate collector but it is in the form of a strip that has the water circulation tubing running down its centre (figure 8.16). The tubing terminates in a connector which allows it to be connected to a header pipe. Other collector tubes are added to this header to form a collector array. Arrays can then be added together in series to increase the collector area. There is no thermal insulation at the back of the collector plate. Instead the glass envelope surrounding the plate

has had some of the air removed from it. This reduces the convective heat losses from the collector plate. This combined with a selective high absorbance/low emmissivity coating makes the evacuated tube collector the most efficient unit available for collecting solar energy.

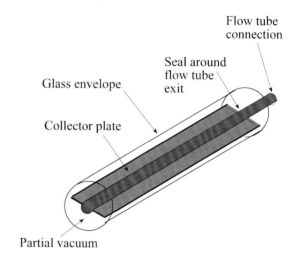

Figure 8.16 Evacuated tube collector.

Mounting angle. So that the sunlight strikes the collector plate at an angle that is close to right angles to the surface, both types of collector must be tilted towards the sun. The rule of thumb for the mounting angle is at latitude + 10° to the horizontal. At a latitude of 54° in the UK this would result in a mounting angle of 64° as shown in figure 8.17. It can be seen that this aligns the normal to the collector plate towards the noon winter solstice solar altitude rather than the noon summer solstice solar altitude. This is because there is less solar radiation in winter and therefore its collection must be optimised at this time.

One of the advantages of evacuated tube collectors is that the array can be mounted on a vertical surface such as a wall. Individual tubes are then rotated to the appropriate optimum collector angle (figure 8.18).

SYSTEMS

There are three basic solar water heating systems into which the solar collectors described in the previous section can be integrated;

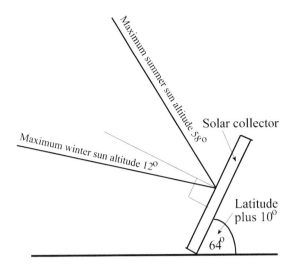

Figure 8.17 Tilt of solar collector to optimise collection in winter.

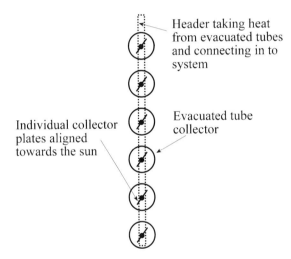

Figure 8.18 Vertical array of evacuated tube collectors.

- Low cost systems which use the buoyancy of warm water to circulate the heat to the hot water storage tank (figure 8.19). These are most often used as water heaters in developing countries as they do not require an electrical pump and have a low capital cost.

- Intermediate systems which use pumped circulation, minimal electronic controls and a single hot water storage tank (figure 8.20). The pumped

circulation means that the storage cylinder can be situated below the solar panel. These systems suffer from the fact that low grade heat from the panel cannot be used. For example if an immersion heater is used to raise the stored water temperature to 65°C, water coming off the collector at 35°C and circulating through the indirect coil would actually cool the stored water down.

- High efficiency systems with a pre-heat storage tank (figure 8.21). This system has the most components and is therefore the most costly. It does however use low grade heat coming off the collector to pre-heat incoming mains water as it passes through the primary tank.

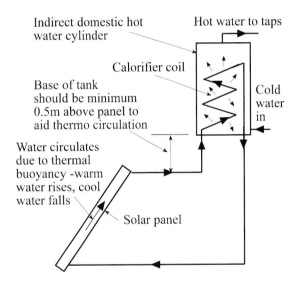

Figure 8.19 Low cost thermo-siphoning solar water heating system.

8.7 Photovoltaic (PV) Panels

The construction of a photovoltaic cell is shown in figure 8.22. The central component is a single crystal of silicon. Because of its atomic structure electric charge moves around naturally inside the crystal but in a random manner. The current can, however, be encouraged to flow in one direction by joining two types of silicon together one acting as a positive terminal (p- type) and the other acting as a negative terminal (n - type). The two forms are made by adding impurities to the silicon, called doping. n - type is formed by adding arsenic and p - type by adding boron. When sunlight falls on the p - n junction the energy contained in it causes more electrons to be released increasing the electric current available for collection.

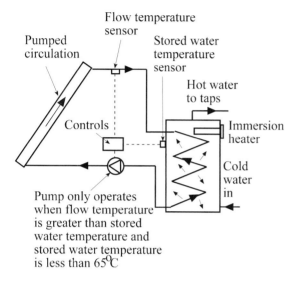

Figure 8.20 Single tank solar water heating system.

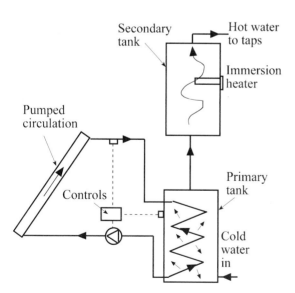

Figure 8.21 Dual tank solar water heating system.

As with all electrical devices connections are required

to pick up and channel the available electricity. The back of the crystal has a copper layer deposited on to it to make up the lower terminal. The upper terminal sits on the side of the semiconductor facing the sun. If the entire face were to be covered in copper the crystal would be shaded from the sun. To avoid this the upper terminal is made out of a network of extremely fine wires deposited onto the surface. Sunlight can pass between the gaps in the terminal grid and hit the crystal. The amount of semiconductor obscured from the sun by the upper terminal is one of the factors that reduce photovoltaic efficiency. Finally, the whole cell is protected by being encased in a glass sandwich. Small cells are used widely to power pocket calculators and watches. Larger arrays are now being manufactured to produce electricity for use in buildings.

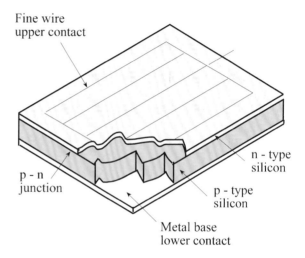

Figure 8.22 Silicon crystal PV cell.

The photovoltaic panels form part of a system as shown in figure 8.23 comprised of the PV panels, batteries, an inverter and an export electricity meter. The electricity produced by the panels is in the form of direct current (d.c.), like that obtained from batteries. Buildings use alternating current (a.c.) and so an inverter is used to convert the direct current to alternating current. If the electricity is not required at the time of generation it can be stored in batteries or converted to a.c. and exported to the grid. The export meter allows the building operator to charge the utilities for the electricity that has been supplied to the grid.

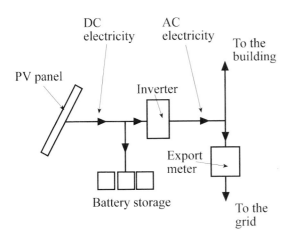

Figure 8.23 Components in a PV electrical system

PRACTICAL ISSUES

Photovoltaics remain an interesting concept for powering buildings. Unfortunately, the cost of photovoltaic arrays is too great for them to be economically viable. For example 10m² of PV cells would give a peak output of 1 kilowatt. This array would produce approximately 700kWh of electricity each year. If electricity for a house can be purchased from the grid at 7.0 pence per kilowatt hour then the value of this electricity is £49.00 per year. The capital cost of the PV array is approximately £400 for commercial and £600 for domestic buildings per square metre. The lower cost of commercial systems arises due to economies of scale. If we assume £6000 for our 10m² array. This results in a simple payback period of 122 years! But remember, no carbon is emitted from PV electricity generation.

Economic viability can be improved if;

- The unit cost of electricity from the grid, which is used to give a value to that supplied from the PV array, increases.

- The efficiency of the PV panels is increased. The efficiency of a PV panel is a comparison between the amount of solar energy hitting its surface and the electrical energy it produces. The maximum theoretical efficiency of a PV panel is approximately 28%. The actual peak efficiencies of a single crystal silicon array is 15% and that for an amorphous silicon array is 5%. Improvements in efficiency can be brought about by reducing the area covered by the upper electrical contact, keeping the PV panel cool and using multiple semiconductor materials which can absorb more of the solar spectrum. It is important that the PV panels are kept cool as their efficiency falls by 0.4% for every 1°C rise in temperature above 25°C. This usually means that the panels must be mounted with an air gap behind them so good air circulation is encouraged to remove heat from the panels.

- The capital cost of the panels is reduced. Single crystals of silicon, each up to 0.1m square, are very expensive to produce. Since they form the basis of PV panels, the panels themselves are also very expensive. Mass manufacturing techniques arising from increased uptake of the technology may help to reduce this high capital cost. It has been suggested that part of the capital cost of a PV array could be offset by replacing expensive cladding materials on commercial buildings with PV cells. So for example if the PV array costs £400 per square metre and prestige cladding panels cost £300 per square metre it could be argued that by replacing the cladding with PV the additional costs are only £100 per square metre. This creates a low 'apparent' capital cost but only for commercial buildings. An alternative is to create PV arrays from amorphous silicon. This is silicon which is not a single large crystal but is made up of numerous tiny crystals. These PV panels are much cheaper but unfortunately, as explained in the above bullet point, their efficiency is only 5%. It is possible that mass production techniques used by the glass industry to create float glass with specialised coatings could be used to make these panels extremely cheaply in the future. Their low efficiency would be offset by the ability to cover large areas of the building cheaply.

There are a variety of options for the integration of PV panels into buildings. They can simply be stand alone panels attached to south facing vertical surfaces of the building or mounted at an angle on the rooftop (figure 8.24). An interesting alternative in domestic buildings is the availability of PV roof tiles that have a similar appearance to traditional roofing tiles and when used to form a domestic roof avoid some of the visual intrusion created by the appearance of a stand alone panel. In commercial buildings it is common for the glass substrate onto which the silicon cells are placed to be coloured the same as the silicon cell. One alternative option that has been used is to leave the glass clear so that light can pass through it. When these panels are used as part of a glazing system the dual benefit of daylight, passive solar heating and electricity production is achieved.

Figure 8.24 Photovoltaic panels on the roof of a contemporary building. Photo from GPCS 361 Energy efficient lighting for houses - exemplars for builders, installers, owners and managers. 1996 © Crown Copyright

REFERENCES

1. Department of Trade and Industry. Energy Statistics

2.website of the British Wind Energy Association. www.bwea.com

3. Brister, A. Dublins Green City. Building Services Journal pp 32-33. August 1996.

4. Wind Power for Sainsbury's. Energy and Environmental Manager, p11. McMillan Scott 2001.
5. Department of Trade and Industry, Technology Status report 002. Small Scale Hydro Power, October 1993

6. Energy Technology Support Unit. Technology Status Report 003, Tidal Power. June 1993.

7. Anon. Renewable Energy is a Burning Issue. Energy in Buildings and Industry. p18. March 2001

8. Building Research Energy Conservation Unit. Case Study 81: Community Heating in Sheffield. HMSO. November 1994.

9. King, C. Passive Solar Heating. p10. Report written by the Energy Research Group Dublin for the European Comission Directorate General XII for Science Research and Development. 1995.

10. Uglow, C. E. The Calculation of Energy Use in Dwellings. BSER&T, Vol 2, No.4, pp1-14. 1981.

FURTHER READING

BRE CP75/75 Availability of Sunshine. 1975

GIR27: Passive Solar Estate Layout. 1995

GPG73: Energy efficient Housing Design - Exploiting Solar Energy.

GIL22: Passive Solar House design

09 MECHANICAL.HEATING

In this chapter we will find that;

- The period of the year over which mechanical heating is required can be reduced by insulating the building shell and taking advantage of solar and other casual gains.

- The release of thermal energy is necessary to provide space heating and hot water.

- The highest combustion efficiency occurs when the correct amounts of air and gas are mixed together in the heating devices burner.

- The efficiency of a typical boiler falls off at low loads, such as when it is only producing domestic hot water in summer.

- High efficiency boilers reduce the amount of wasted heat by using casing insulation, electronic ignition and a large heat exchanger.

- Condensing boilers have all the features of high efficiency boilers but have a very large heat exchanger to maximise the removal of heat from the flue gases.

- Condensing boilers cost approximately 50% more than conventional boilers. The additional costs are usually recovered in three years from the value of energy savings made.

- Multiple boilers are used in commercial buildings to increase system efficiency.

- Zoning allows the heating to be switched off in some areas whilst it remains on in others.

- The heat emitters must be selected to match the form of the building, its occupancy patterns and its heating strategy.

- The basis of heating control is that the heating should be on only when required and to the level required

- In domestic buildings simple on/off time and temperature control is usually sufficient to control energy consumption.

- In commercial buildings optimisers should be used to determine the best time to switch the heating on in the morning and off in the afternoon.

- In commercial buildings temperature control is achieved using a variable temperature flow circuit. controlled by a compensator unit.

- Most new commercial buildings have their heating systems controlled by an electronic building management system.

- In commercial buildings independent direct fired hot water heaters are the most efficient method of heating water.

9.0 Introduction

Thermal energy (heat) is released when fossil fuels are burned or when electrical current flows through resistive elements. This thermal energy is used in buildings to maintain inside air temperatures above outside air temperatures in the process of space heating and to heat water for cleaning purposes. Hot water is required all year round but space heating is only required during the winter months.

To achieve a reduction in the amount of energy used by combustion based space heating systems the following aspects require consideration;

- **Fabric.** Insulating the building and taking advantage of casual gains reduces the length of the heating season. Figure 9.1 shows that a poorly insulated building requires more energy and for a longer period than a well insulated building.

- **Combustion efficiency**. The fuel must be burned efficiently so that all of the energy contained in it is converted to heat.

- **Boiler efficiency**. The heat liberated during combustion must not be allowed to escape from the boiler. For maximum efficiency all of it must be collected and sent to the heat emitters.

- **System efficiency**. The heat emitters must be selected so that they release heat into the occupied space effectively and without wastage.

- **Control**. The heating should be on only when required and to the temperature level required.

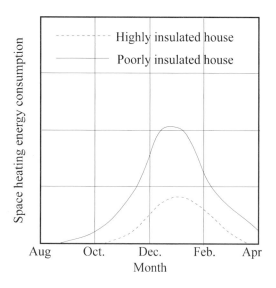

Figure 9.1 Space heating requirements of a highly insulated and a poorly insulated dwelling.

DIRECT AND INDIRECT HEATING

Combustion of fuels and electrical heating are used by two types of space heating device. The first are direct heaters, these are appliances situated in the room to be heated. The second are indirect or central heating systems that liberate heat centrally but use room based heat emitters such as radiators to supply heat to rooms. Direct heating systems have advantages and disadvantages in terms of energy efficiency. The main disadvantage is the difficulty of controlling their heat output centrally. although in-built controls provide effective local control. The main advantage is that they can be used to provide localised heating such as the use of a radiant heater to provide comfort over a workstation in an otherwise unheated space (see section 9.4 -zoning).

This chapter will focus on gas fired indirect heating systems as they are used in the majority of new homes and commercial buildings. However direct heaters are used extensively elsewhere such as in small industrial buildings and in peripheral buildings on large sites that are separated from the main complex of buildings and therefore the main indirect heating system.

9.1 Combustion Efficiency

The aim of combustion is to convert all of the energy contained in the gas to heat. To achieve this the burner must mix the gas with the correct quantity of oxygen, known as a stoichiometric mix. It is based on the fact that combustion is a chemical reaction and therefore the exact quantity of oxygen needed to combine with the gas can be determined. Insufficient air (the source of the oxygen) would result in incomplete combustion. Carbon monoxide would be produced and dangerous unburned gas would build up. Too much air and the combustion gases will be diluted and cooled. It is the function of the burner within the boiler (figure 9.2) to mix gas and air to give the most safe and efficient combustion possible.

In practice burners are set up to run with slight excess of air. This results in safe, complete combustion but at a slightly lower efficiency than maximum. To optimise the settings, flue gas analysis can be carried out. Here a probe is placed into the flue during combustion and a quantity of flue gas removed for analysis. The quantities of carbon dioxide, carbon monoxide and oxygen indicate the completeness of combustion and hence the efficiency of the burner. The burner can then be adjusted until the composition of the flue gases indicates optimum and safe combustion is taking place.

$$\text{Efficiency(\%)} = \frac{\text{Heat out}}{\text{Heat in}} \times 100$$

Figure 9.3 Boiler efficiency

Figure 9.2 Parts of a gas boiler.

ELECTRICAL HEATING

When heating is provided by electricity, combustion efficiency is dealt with remotely at the power station. As was stated in chapter 1 power station combustion efficiencies are low, typically around 35% for coal fired power stations and 43% for gas fired power stations. The efficiency with which electricity is used for heating in the building is 100%. However, the low efficiency in generation means that space heating using electricity should be avoided. It is theoretically possible to increase the utilisation efficiency by 250 - 300% using a heat pump but in practice this is difficult to achieve using an air to air heat pump. The system can be made to have comparable carbon efficiency as a gas heating system if a ground loop heat pump is used (see section 8.4)

9.2 Boiler Efficiency

The efficiency of a boiler is a measure of how well it transfers the heat liberated during combustion into the heating system. It therefore involves combustion efficiency and heat transfer efficiency. The quantification of boiler efficiency is illustrated in figure 9.3.

Boiler efficiency is a comparison between the heat input to the boiler and the useful heat output. Boiler heat input is in the form of gas or oil. When this is burnt the aim is to transfer all of the heat it contains into the heating circuit. A system that achieved this aim would be 100% efficient. However, for safety reasons, harmful waste combustion gases must be cleared from the boiler. This is achieved in natural draught boilers by allowing the natural buoyancy of the hot flue gases to carry them up and out of the flue. Unfortunately the heat contained in these gases is lost to the system. As a result all flued combustion appliances operate below 100% efficiency.

The energy content of the fuel is determined from its calorific value. Calorific value is usually measured in mega joules per cubic metre (MJ/m^3) for gas and mega joules per litre (MJ/l) for oil. Heat output from the boiler is determined by measuring the temperatures of the water flowing out of and returning to the boiler and its flow rate. The volume of water flowing and the temperature by which it is heated allows the heat input to be determined.

It can be seen from figure 9.3 that the key energy flows from the boiler are;

When firing

- Heat lost in the hot flue gases leaving the boiler

- Heat lost out of the boiler casing.

- Heat transferred into the heating system.

When not firing

- Heat from the burning pilot light which is lost by convection up the flue.

- Heat lost from the warm heat exchanger as cool air moves through the boiler by convection.

The balance of energy flows changes depending on whether the boiler is firing, has recently stopped firing or has been standing for some time. When the boiler is firing most of the heat enters the heating system, approximately 22% of the heat is lost from the flue and 3% lost from the casing. When the boiler has just stopped firing heat input to the heating system stops. Residual heat in the heat exchanger is lost by convection of warm air up the flue along with any heat given out by the pilot light. To avoid wasting all of the residual heat in the heat exchanger some control systems require the heating system pumps to run on for 15 minutes after firing stops to remove the residual heat from the boiler. When the boiler is standing, convective and casing losses slowly decrease as the heat exchanger cools until only pilot light energy losses occur.

BOILER LOAD AND EFFICIENCY

The efficiency of a boiler varies with the load upon it as this determines whether the boiler is firing or not and the rate of cycling between these two states.

High loads are when the boiler is being asked to do a great deal of work. An example of this state is first thing in the morning when the building and domestic hot water are both cold. To satisfy the demand for heat the boiler will fire continuously and the flue and casing losses will be small when compared to the heat being input to the rooms and dhw system. The efficiency at high loads will therefore be high.

Low load is when the boiler is being asked to do less work. An example of this situation is at the end of the day when the building has warmed through and the tanks are filled with hot water. The boiler will be cy-

cling, that is firing for short periods then stopping to keep heat levels topped up. In this situation it is possible that more heat will be lost by convection up the flue than is given to the heating system. Because of this efficiency will be low.

The load on a boiler changes throughout the day and season of the year. High loads predominate in the winter months and low loads in the summer. On a daily basis, high loads are more likely to occur in the morning and low loads in the evening. Figure 9.4 shows a graph of efficiency against proportion of full load for three boiler types including a standard boiler (dotted line).

Figure 9.4 Graph of efficiency vs load.

It can be seen from the graph that whilst standard boilers are effective when operated at high loads their efficiency falls off to as low as 35% when the load on them decreases. From the same graph it can be seen that high efficiency and condensing boilers have better efficiency against load profiles. The features of these boilers that cause the improvement are discussed below.

High Efficiency Boilers. These boilers are more costly than standard boilers because they include additional features to reduce wasted heat and therefore improve efficiency (figure 9.5). The features can include;

- Extra casing insulation and smaller physical size to reduce casing losses.

- Larger heat exchanger to remove more of the heat from the flue gases. This means more enters the heating system and less is lost up the flue.

- Spark ignition to replace the pilot light. This removes the heat wasted by the pilot during weekends, night time and other occasions when the boiler is not firing.

- Flue damper which is open during firing to allow flue gases to escape but is closed when the boiler is standing to retain residual heat within the heating system.

- Low thermal capacity heat exchanger that heats up and cools down quickly and so is responsive to changes in demand and does not contain large amounts of residual heat when firing stops.

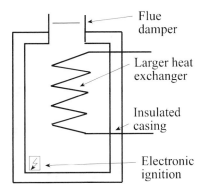

Figure 9.5 Features of a high efficiency boiler.

As a result of these features the seasonal efficiency is improved to approximately 85% with a reduced fall off in efficiency at low loads.

Condensing Boilers. These boilers have all of the features of the high efficiency boiler but have an even bigger heat exchanger (figure 9.6). This extracts the vast majority of the heat from the flue gases increasing the efficiency of the boiler. There are a number of consequences arising from this increased extraction of heat.

- The first is that water vapour in the flue gases is cooled so much that it condenses onto the heat exchanger (hence the name). This further increases efficiency because the latent heat of vaporisation that is released as the water vapour condenses is absorbed by the heat exchanger. In this way the heat exchanger recovers both sensible and latent heat from the flue gases.

- The condensate is slightly acidic and so the heat exchanger must be made out of a non corrosive material such as stainless steel.

- The condensate must be collected and drained from the boiler.

- The flue gases, having been cooled, lose their buoyancy and so must be removed from the boiler using a fan.

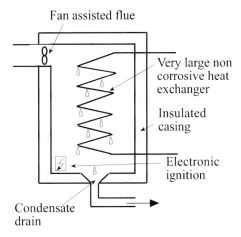

Figure 9.6 Features of a condensing boiler.

The additional features add about 50% to the cost of a condensing boiler in comparison to a standard boiler for the same rating. However, their peak efficiency is as high as 92% with a small fall off in efficiency with decreasing load (figure 9.4). This makes them economical with extra capital costs typically being recovered in the value of energy savings made within three years.

SEDBUK EFFICIENCY RATING

In recognition of the role that boiler efficiency has to play in reducing the energy consumption of buildings all boilers sold in Europe must operate to minimum efficiency standards. The classification used to compare boiler efficiencies is known as SEDBUK, seasonal efficiency of domestic boilers in the UK. Boilers are tested under standard conditions at full load and 30% load. The efficiencies found are used to calculate a seasonal efficiency based on typical load profiles. Boilers are then classified into one of seven bands as shown in table 9.1.

Band	SEDBUK efficiency
A	90 - 94%
B	86 - 90%
C	82 - 86%
D	78 - 82%
E	74 - 78%
F	70 - 74%
G	Less than 70%

Table 9.1 SEDBUK efficiency bands.

Section 4.1.1 indicates that the building regulations minimum SEDBUK rating for domestic buildings is 'D'.

CARBON INTENSITY

The Building Regulations part L2, for non-domestic buildings describes a method of complying with the requirement that the heating system is energy efficient based on carbon intensities. The carbon intensity of the heating plant is based on the carbon emitted per kWh of useful heat output. For compliance the carbon intensity of the heating system should not exceed the values shown in table 9.2 column a and b when operating at 100% and 30% heat output respectively. The figures are based on the carbon emission factors shown in table 1.2

Fuel	(a) at maximum heat output	(b) at minimum heat output
Natural gas	0.068	0.065
Other fuels	0.091	0.088

Table 9.2 Maximum carbon intensity (kgC/kWh) for different fuels at two heat outputs.

9.2.1 Multiple Boilers

In non-domestic buildings one way of ensuring that boilers fire near their high load rating is to provide the required load with more than one boiler. This is known as a multiple system of boilers. As an illustration, a multiple system of boilers used to satisfy a 100 kW load is shown in figure 9.7. It can be seen that the 100 kW load is provided by four 25 kW boilers feeding heated water into a common flow pipe. A common return brings water back to the boilers from the heat emitters. The first benefit of this arrangement of boilers is that there is back up if one of the boilers fails. It can be isolated and heating can still be provided, albeit at a reduced capacity, by the other boilers. The second benefit is that the boilers are fired in a progressive manner to satisfy demand. So for example, in the morning when there is a high load situation all of the boilers will fire. Later in the day when the building has started to warm through. Boilers 1 and 2 will fire continuously with boilers 3 and 4 shut down. At the end of the day, when heating is only required for topping up, boiler 1 will be firing on its own. The progressive mode of operation means that each boiler only fires near its full output rating. The system as a whole will therefore maintain a high efficiency even though the load is decreasing.

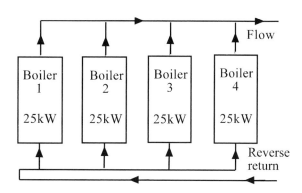

Figure 9.7 Multiple boilers for a 100 kW load.

A further refinement to the process is the introduction of two stage burners. In our example this would mean that each boiler would be capable of firing at 25 or 12.5kW output or would be turned off. The low setting would mean that heat could be input more gradually into the system and as a result there would be less cycling between the on and off states.

When a boiler is not firing heating system water will still be flowing through it. This means that the heat exchanger will be hot and so convective heat loss will take place as air currents move through the boiler. There are two ways of preventing this. The first is to close a valve on the return to the boiler heat exchanger. This however can upset the flows through the system. A better method is to allow the flow through the boiler to continue but to close a damper in the flue. This will stop convection currents through the boiler and does not upset the hydronic balance of the system.

CONTROL

Progressive operation of the boilers to match demand requires a control process known as boiler step control. It is based on boiler flow temperature. If this falls it is a sign that the water returning to the boiler is cooler having lost more heat to the spaces. This in turn indicates an increased demand for heating has occurred. As a result more boilers will be made to fire. Boiler 1 will be required to fire for more hours than any other boiler since it will operate during both high and low load situations. The boiler which is the first to fire up and last to switch off in any heating period is known as the lead boiler. To avoid unbalanced wear on the boilers the lead boiler will be cycled each week. So in week one boiler 1 will lead, in week two boiler 2 will lead and so on until after four weeks boiler 1 will once again be the lead boiler.

For optimum efficiency with moderate costs a typical arrangement is to have a condensing boiler as the lead. In this case the condensing boiler must always be the lead to achieve peak efficiency. The remaining boilers can still be cycled to reduce wear.

9.3 Combined Heat and Power

Gas or oil boilers are the primary source of heating in commercial buildings. However, in some buildings this may be supplemented by a combined heat and power (CHP) unit. These devices are based on internal combustion engines, similar to large vehicle engines (figure 9.8 and 9.9). They have all of the components of a vehicle engine but the differences are that instead of running on petrol or diesel they run on gas (natural, biogas or bottled) and that the drive rotates a generator rather than wheels. The generator produces the "power" part of the output. Instead of a radiator to exhaust the waste heat from the engine to atmosphere the CHP unit has a heat exchanger that transfers this heat into the heating system circulation. CHP units can also be based on gas turbine technology which gives much greater heat and power outputs.

Figure 9.8 Combined heat and power unit.

Figure 9.9 Combined heat and power unit - photo from GPCS 200. Energy Savings in Hospitals (1994). © Crown Copyright

A typical CHP unit would produce 120kW of heat and 70kW of electricity. CHP's are described in terms of their electrical (e) output and so this unit would be described as a 70kWe unit. The 60% efficiency with which the CHP unit produces heat is lower than that of a gas boiler. The efficiency can be increased by 5% if an extra heat exchanger is used to recover additional heat from the exhaust pipe and oil cooler. The overall efficiency would still be lower than that of a gas boiler. However, when the heat output is combined with the electrical output the efficiency is increased to approximately 85 to 90%. This is illustrated in the energy flow diagram of the CHP unit shown in figure 9.10.

The economics of CHP units is complex and involves a balance between reductions in energy bills against capital and running costs. CHP units produce electricity at a unit cost that is much cheaper than can be purchased from the grid. But for the savings from this to pay back the capital cost of the installation the CHP unit must run for the maximum number of hours possible. Balanced against this is the fact that the CHP unit, like any engine, requires periodic routine maintenance. This involves changing oil, filters and spark plugs. CHP maintenance is regular and labour intensive and so costs are high.

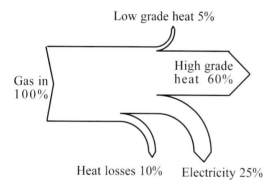

Figure 9.10 Energy flow diagram for a CHP unit.

Keeping the running hours to a maximum requires the following;

Firstly, the CHP energy output must be matched to the energy demand of the building into which it is to be installed. Specifically its output must be sized to satisfy the base heating and electricity requirements of the building. If the CHP gives out more heat than the base demand then at times of lower demand the system controls will switch it off to avoid over heating (figure 9.11). If the CHP gives out more electricity than is required by the building it will have to be used by

other buildings on the site or exported to the grid (figure 9.12). The export of electricity requires the installation of extra meters and unfortunately the price paid by the electricity companies for electricity deposited into the grid is low. The income it generates may not cover the hourly fuel and maintenance costs. It can be seen therefore that a high and consistent base demand is required for economic operation of the CHP unit. This tends to make them more suitable to buildings such as leisure centres and hotels with swimming pools and possibly, if demands indicate it is the case, nursing homes.

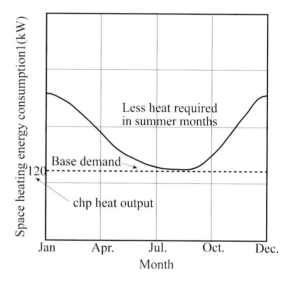

Figure 9.11 Heat demand profile showing sizing of CHP heat output to satisfy base demand.

Secondly, the CHP unit will be part of a heating system incorporating gas boilers to provide the remainder of the heat requirement. To make sure the CHP has the maximum chance to run it must be the first heating device the system return water encounters on its way back to the plant room.

Thirdly, the CHP must undergo routine maintained at specified intervals. If a fault occurs between routine intervals sensors, control devices and modems fitted to the unit allow it to auto-dial a maintenance company and give details of the nature of the fault. This will allow rapid attendance by a service engineer to rectify the fault.

Trials are now commencing on Stirling engine based CHP units that have much lower heat and power outputs than the CHP units used to date. Because of this they are referred to as microCHP units. The lower outputs and much quieter operation makes them potentially suitable for small commercial buildings and even housing.

Figure 9.12 Electrical demand profile showing sizing of CHP electrical output.

9.4 System Efficiency

Having liberated heat from fossil fuels in the most efficient way the next stage is to ensure that this heat is used effectively in the building. It is the role of the heat emitters, such as radiators, to release heat into a space to create comfort, without waste.

Heat emitters are available in a range of shapes and sizes, both of these variables have an effect on heat output. However, heat emitters can be categorised into two types. Those that give out their heat mainly by convection and those that give out their heat mainly by radiation. Convective heaters warm the room air first then the occupant. Radiant heaters warm the occupant and fabric of the room first then the room air.

The choice of heat emitter should reflect the form, characteristics and holistic low energy strategy of the building.

Form. The shape of a space affect how heat is distributed within it. Tall spaces for example are prone to stratification as described in section 3.2 as a consequence convective heat emitters should not be used in a tall space as the warm air emitted by them will rise to the ceiling. A more appropriate heat emitter would be a radiant heat emitter or underfloor heating. If warm air heaters are used it is advisable to use them in conjunction with a destratification fan.

Characteristics. Modern buildings should not be draughty and existing buildings should be draught proofed to avoid ventilation heat losses. However, some buildings naturally have a high air change rate. One example is car workshops where regular door openings as vehicles move into and out of the workshop results in loss of heated air. Here again convective heating should be avoided and radiant heaters used to heat the occupants rather than the air.

Strategy. Heat emitters should be compatible with the buildings low energy strategy. Two generalised low energy strategies can be identified. Climate accepting or solar strategy, and climate rejecting or highly insulated strategy. A climate accepting strategy requires large south facing windows to collect solar energy. As stated in section 8.5.2 solar heat gains are unpredictable and so it is essential to have a heating system that can rapidly respond to changes in solar heat input. Therefore a heat emitter with a quick response time should be used such as a low water content radiator. The radiator would also benefit from being made out of aluminium to reduce its thermal capacity further. Alternatively, fan convectors can rapidly vary their heat output by varying the speed or switching off the internal fan. Slow response systems such as storage heaters and under floor heating should be avoided in a solar house.

A building with a climate rejecting strategy has small highly insulated windows. As a consequence the solar gains are less important and less severe variations in solar energy input are obtained. Responsiveness of the heating system is, therefore, a lower concern than heating system efficiency. In this case it is beneficial if the heat emitters assist boiler efficiency. So for example over sized radiators or underfloor heating are recommended. Both of these use lower boiler flow and return temperatures that encourage condensing boilers to operate in condensing mode and therefore at a higher efficiency.

ZONING

Not all parts of a building need to be heated to the same degree at the same time. If the heating can be turned off in some spaces whilst being left on in others savings can be made. Differing heating demands within a single building occur for two reasons, these are differences in heat gains and differences in occupancy patterns.

Heat gains. South facing rooms will experience solar gains and the heating effect may be sufficient to remove the need for mechanical heating. In this situation the heating on the south side of the building should be shut off. Heating may still be required in north facing rooms. It can be seen then that the building can be split along an east/west axis into two zones one facing north and the other facing south. Further zones can be identified that are subject to other heat gains. For example, rooms with high occupancy levels or where extensive use of computers is being made.

Individual control of south facing rooms can be achieved using thermostatic radiator valves. An alternative method of zoning, which is more appropriate to larger buildings, is to install separate flow and return pipe work to each zone. A motorised valve, zone temperature sensors, pump and an appropriate control system are required to control the flow of heat into each zone. As a result there is a capital cost associated with zoning a building. However, these additional costs will be recouped over time in the value of energy savings made. There are also additional benefits to zoning a building such as greater degree of temperature control leading to improved thermal comfort and greater productivity of staff.

Occupancy patterns. Separate heating circuits can also be used to cater for differential occupancy of spaces within a building. One example is in the case of a school that holds night classes. Rather than heat the whole school for this event the school should be zoned and heating can then be supplied to the night school block only.

If the individual zones are being used on a commercial basis then heat meters can be fitted to the heating zone pipe work. These meters monitor how much heat is being taken by the zone from the central boiler plant. Knowledge of this allows accurate costing of out of hours use of spaces to be made. This information is also useful for energy management purposes (see chapter 11)

Direct heaters are useful for creating small heating zones within an otherwise indirectly heated space. For example, to provide heating to a workstation within a larger space.

SYSTEM COMPONENTS

There are a number of components in the heating system itself which can be optimised for energy efficiency.

- **Pipework**. The layout should be designed to be as simple as possible. Bends, reductions in bore and other components should be avoided where possible as these all add to flow resistance in the pipework. Resistance to flow must be overcome using energy in the form of electricity in a pump. The pipework must also be insulated. This is because the pipes are to carry the heat from one place to another and should not be a source of uncontrolled and unwanted heat input to rooms. Loss of heat from pipes can reduce the effectiveness of heat emitters and cause overheating in rooms through which the pipes run. Similar issues also apply to warm air heating systems that use warm air as the heat transfer medium and ducting to direct heat transfer. As with piping the number of ductwork components should be minimised, ducts insulated where appropriate and most importantly be made airtight.

- **Pumps** should be fitted with variable speed drives. This means that as zone valves close down and the demand for hot water in the building diminishes the speed and hence flow rate of the pumps can be reduced. Reducing the speed of pumps and fans results in significant energy savings.

9.5 Control

Controls are required to ensure that the heating system operates safely and efficiently and provides comfort for the building occupants. In terms of energy conservation the control system should ensure that the heating system only operates when required and to the level required. The two basic forms of control for any heating system are time control and temperature control.

DOMESTIC CONTROLS

Figure 9.13 shows a typical arrangement of controls for a domestic central heating system. It is comprised of the following components.

Figure 9.13 Domestic heating controls

Room Thermostat. Is a device that controls room temperatures. Control is made in relation to a preferred temperature setting made on the thermostat by the occupant. The thermostat is in fact a switch opened and closed as the room temperature rises above or falls below the temperature setting respectively.

The thermostat should be positioned in a representative room such as the living room at standing chest height away from sources of heat such as direct sunlight. This means it will accurately sense the air temperature experienced by an occupant in the room.

When the thermostat switch is closed, current can flow through it. This is interpreted by the control unit as a call for heat. The boiler will fire, the pump will run and the three way valve will direct hot water to the radiators. When the room temperature rises above the preferred temperature setting, changes within the thermostat, electronically sensed or due to the differential expansion of a bi metallic strip, cause the thermostat switch to open. As a result the control current will stop and the boiler and the pump will switch off. It can be seen therefore that room temperatures are controlled by stopping and starting the flow of heat into the room as required. The room thermostat is central to controlling space heating energy use in buildings. This is because the temperature difference between inside and outside is one of the factors that directly affects the heat loss rate from the building. For an average outside air temperature of 6°C, increasing the internal air temperature setting from 20 to 21°C results in an increased heat loss rate of 7.1%

Programmer. This is a time switch that determines the times within which the system will respond to a call for heat from the room thermostat. The start and stop times between which the heating will be allowed to operate are entered into the programmer. For example, heating may be required from 07:00 to 08:30 in the morning then 17:00 to 23:30 in the evening. Modern microprocessor controlled programmers allow multiple daily heating periods and the ability to programme each day of the week with a different heating programme. An example is that the first "on" period at the weekend may start at 8:00 and end at 12:00 to reflect the fact that the occupant is not in work on that day. Time spent setting up the programmer to accurately reflect occupancy times ensures that the building is not heated when unoccupied.

Cylinder thermostat. This is a temperature controlled switch similar to the room thermostat. The difference is that it is clamped on to the indirect domestic hot water (dhw)cylinder and therefore senses and controls the temperature of the dhw. When the switch is closed and therefore calling for heat, the three way valve will be instructed to divert boiler flow through the calorifier in the cylinder. This will cause the temperature of the water in the cylinder to rise. When the temperature reaches the setting on the thermostat the switch will open. The three way valve will then direct the flow away from the cylinder and back to the heating circuit.

Thermostatic Radiator Valve (TRV). This is a valve fitted to the inlet of the radiator. Gas in the TRV head (figure 9.14) expands with temperature and pushes a gate downwards blocking the inlet flow. This will restrict or even stop the flow of heat into the radiator. The heat output will then be reduced causing the room to begin to cool. As it does so the gas in the TRV head will contract and the valve will open up once more. TRV's allow room by room control of temperatures to be achieved. They are particularly useful in south facing rooms and rooms subject to casual heat gains. They give an extra layer of control in addition to the single room thermostat. At least one radiator should not have a TRV fitted to ensure that water flows through the boiler at all times.

Gas filled Belows

Gas expands as temperature increases

Figure 9.14 Thermostatic radiator valve

The domestic controls described above treat the house as a single zone. The room thermostat senses the conditions in one room. The assumption is that the radiators have been accurately sized and balanced so that if any one room is satisfied the others will also be satisfied. Low cost thermostatic radiator valves do give an extra layer of control and therefore energy saving. Controls for commercial buildings are more complex than those for domestic buildings. However, reductions in the cost of microprocessor based controls means that some of the ideas used in commercial controllers described below can be employed in domestic buildings. One example is the zoning of houses into two zones, one for the upstairs and one for the downstairs rooms.

COMMERCIAL CONTROLS

Large buildings cannot be controlled effectively using domestic control systems. The components must be scaled up and certain refinements made to provide adequate control. The difficulties encountered in heating control in large buildings arise due to the buildings thermal inertia, different heat loads/gains and differential occupancy of spaces. Both time and temperature control require more consideration than that given to domestic systems.

Time control in domestic buildings is adequately carried out using the fixed on/off time controller described previously. This is because even on cold days the time taken for the majority of domestic buildings to warm up to comfortable temperatures is unlikely to be more than twenty minutes. In this case the heating is simply set to come on 20 minutes before the start of occupancy. This period when the building is warming up to the occupancy temperature setting is known as the pre-heat period. Rapid pre-heating in domestic buildings is assisted by the fact that the boiler is often over sized. Whilst this rapidly heats the building it does reduce system efficiency as the boiler will be more prone to thermal cycling. In large buildings the pre-heat period will be considerably longer due to the thermal inertia of the structure and the heating system itself. The pre-heat period is also variable. It is longer in winter than in spring and autumn because the building cools more during the night. This means a fixed start and stop time would be wasteful. This is illustrated in figure 9.15. It can be seen that on a cold night the heating must come on at 1.0 a.m. to heat the building up to the required set-point by the start of occupancy at 8.00 am. If this fixed on time is retained on a mild night (dotted line) then the building is raised to the occupancy temperature at 5:30 am because heating commenced with a higher internal temperature. This is two and a half hours prior to occupancy and so is wasteful.

To overcome this problem an optimum start controller is used. This is a device that calculates when the best time is to switch on the heating. The times of the beginning and end of occupancy are input to the device, say 8.00 am and 5.00 pm. The optimum start controller then monitors inside and outside temperatures, combines this with a knowledge of the thermal inertia of the building and then determines at which time to activate the heating to achieve the desired internal temperatures by the start of occupancy. In the above example the optimum start controller would delay the onset of heating on a mild day until 3:30 am (dashed line). Thereby saving two and a half hours of heating which, for a large building, represents a significant saving in fuel costs and carbon emissions.

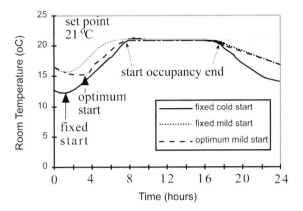

Figure 9.15 Graph of room temperature against time of day showing the benefits of optimum starting.

The optimiser can also use the thermal inertia of the building to switch the heating off mid to late afternoon. A slow decay in temperatures up to the end of the working day is unlikely to be noticed by the occupants and prevents the heating system from cycling.
The most difficult parameter to determine for the effective operation of the device is the thermal inertia of the building. Initial estimates of this may need to be modified during the commissioning stage to achieve accurate performance. Some devices monitor their own performance and carry out this adjustment automatically. They are known as self learning optimisers.

Temperature control is achieved in domestic buildings by simply switching on and off the flow of heat to the radiators. When the desired room temperature is achieved the boiler will be switched off and after a short run on period, to dissipate residual heat, so will the pump. This is not practical in large buildings because of the thermal inertia of the large volume of water circulating in the heating system. Swings in temperature about the set point would be too great as the water in the heating system was alternately heated and allowed to cool. Instead, large buildings vary the amount of heat energy entering the space as the demand for heating goes up or down. This process is achieved using a variable temperature (VT) compen-

sated flow circuit.

The parameter used by the system to signal an increase in the demand for heating is a reduction in outside air temperature. Figure 9.16 illustrates the principle of operation. The graph is known as a compensated flow curve. Moving from left to right on the graph, it can be seen that as the outside temperature increases the temperature of the boiler flow is progressively decreased. At 16°C outside air temperature the boiler flow temperature is equal to ambient temperature i.e. the heating is switched off. This temperature is known as the outside air cut off temperature. At this temperature no mechanical heating is required since 6°C worth of heating can typically be achieved from casual gains in the building such as passive solar energy, body heat, lighting and appliances.

Figure 9.16 Compensation curves.

The adjustment in flow temperatures with outside air temperature is achieved using a variable temperature (VT) heating circuit. This circuit is illustrated in figure 9.16. The boiler produces hot water for the constant temperature (CT) circuit at 80°C. Using a three way valve a proportion of this hot water is allowed to pass into the heating circuit. When the demand for heat is high such as on a cold day more hot water will be allowed into the heating circuit. On a mild day less heated water would be allowed into the heating circuit. The radiator temperatures will therefore be hot on a cold day and luke warm on a mild day.

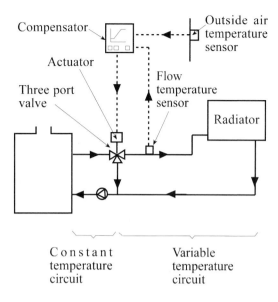

Figure 9.17 Variable temperature flow circuit

9.5.1 Building Management Systems (BMS)

All of the control functions discussed previously including boiler step control, optimisation, compensation and zoning can be carried out using a building management system (BMS). A BMS is a computer based heating, ventilation and air conditioning control system which offers a great deal of flexibility in the way it is set up and operated. It also offers the possibility of close interaction between the operator and the building services systems. The main components of a BMS are shown in figure 9.18 and are described below.

Outstations are small computers. Unlike dedicated hard wired controllers that only control the functions for which they have been purchased outstations can be programmed to perform a range of control functions. The outstation receives information about the status of the heating system and the building from sensors. The programme which decides what this information means and what to do as a consequence is called a

control strategy. A simple example is if the room temperatures are below the required temperature set point. Temperature sensors will signal this to the outstation. Using the logic contained in the control strategy the outstation will decide that heating is required and send signals to actuators to make the boiler fire and pumps operate to supply heat to the room. The control strategy refers to other rules before carrying this out for example heating will only be supplied if the time is within the occupancy or pre-heat period.

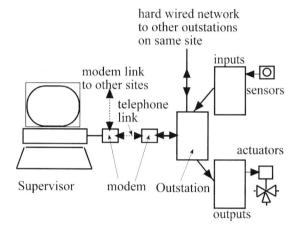

Figure 9.18 Building management system components

Sensors are the input devices for the outstation. They are transducers that convert a physical state into an electrical signal. There are two main types; analogue sensors and digital sensors. Analogue sensors return a varying signal to the outstation. For example, a signal in the range 0 to 5 volts from a temperature sensor can be set to represent the temperature range 0 to 25°C.

A digital signal can only take one of two values for example 0 volts or 5 volts. Such a signal can be sent from a switch to represent it being opened or closed. So for example if a boiler was firing a 5V signal would be returned if it had failed then a 0V signal would be returned.

Actuators are devices that turn electrical signals into the physical actions required by the control strategy using motors or solenoids. An example of an analogue actuator is one which sets the position of a motorised valve. The electrical signal to it may vary between 0 and 5V this corresponds to the fully shut and fully open positions. Hence a signal of 2.5V would cause the valve to be half open.

A digital signal can be used to open or close a solenoid. For example changing the signal to a pump from 0 to 5V causes a pump to operate. Changing the signal back to 0V causes it to stop.

The supervisor is a standard personal computer which allows human operators to interface with the system. It is loaded with the necessary software to interact with the outstations. The supervisor can be used to programme the outstation with its control strategy. Once this is installed it is possible to visualise all the information available to the outstation on screen. So for example room temperatures, the status of boilers, pumps and other equipment such as the position of valves or dampers can all be displayed. Values are displayed graphically so that their interpretation is easily understood with only a small amount of training.

The system constantly upgrades the information it presents and also stores data at the outstation for later inspection. For example, room temperatures over the last 24 hours can be displayed graphically. This is a most useful tool for diagnosing faults and commissioning the heating system following installation. The supervisor is also used to set variables. One example is the inputting of room temperature set points.

Buildings fitted with a BMS have been found to have lower energy consumptions than comparable buildings with dedicated controllers, provided that they are set up and operated effectively. There are a number of reasons for the savings that can be achieved. The first is the accuracy of control that can be achieved. The second is the ability of the system to signal heating system faults which may otherwise go undetected causing excessive energy usage. Finally, monitoring and management of energy consumptions is also facilitated by fitting sensors on to the utility meters. This allows logging of energy consumptions which can then be used to prepare reports and indicate excessive consumptions.

One supervisor can be used to control the operation of many outstations. The supervisor is typically located in the office of the energy or building manager. It can communicate with various outstations using modems and network cabling on site.

It is also possible for the BMS to communicate with other control systems in buildings. For example it is possible to integrate BMS systems with security systems. So for example access to spaces using key cards can be monitored. When it is known that all people have left a space the heating can be turned off or down to a set back position thus saving space heating energy.

One point of caution is that a BMS system can only save energy if it is designed and set up correctly in the first instance and is then used in the manner described above. If there are inadequate resources in terms of training and staff time to operate the system, it has been found that a simple control system that is used as it is intended is better than a complex system that is not.

9.6 Water Heating

Domestic hot water (dhw) provision requires that heat is input to cold mains water to raise its temperature. This heat can be taken from an indirect heating system or be provided by a direct water heater.

INDIRECT HEATING

Indirect Cylinder. Some of the heated water flowing through the heating circuit is diverted, using a three way valve, through a calorifier within the hot water cylinder (figure 9.19). The calorifier is a coil of copper tube through which the heating system water flows. Heat transfer from the calorifier warms up the cold water held in the cylinder. The sizing of the calorifier coil is critical to achieving good efficiency. If it is undersized there will only be a small transfer of heat from it to the stored hot water. This will cause high temperature water to return to the boiler causing it to cycle on and off, which is inefficient. It is preferable therefore to use cylinders with a large calorifier coil.

The heated water rises to the top of the tank where it is drawn off to the taps. The cold feed, which enters at the base of the cylinder, is from a mains fed tank which is often built in to the top of the cylinder to form an integral unit. Since the feed water tank is open to the air the system is referred to as a vented or non sealed system. Unvented indirect cylinders are available which are similar to the system described above except that the cold feed is from a direct connection to the water main instead of from a tank. As a result hot water from the cylinder is fed to the taps at mains pressure. This gives a higher flow rate than a tank fed system.

Figure 9.19 Indirect dhw cylinder.

The benefits of indirect water heating are that the central heating boiler performs two functions (space and water heating) and that there is a stored volume of hot water ready to meet peak demands. However, in summer the low loads encountered by a central heating boiler required to generate hot water only leads to reduced boiler efficiency. It is therefore recommended that indirect cylinders are used in conjunction with a condensing boiler. The cylinder itself must be well insulated (at least 35mm of factory applied PU-foam insulation) to reduce heat loss from the stored hot water. These heat losses are known as standing heat losses.

DIRECT HEATING

Immersion heater. The most common example of direct water heating is to use an electric immersion heater to heat water stored in a dhw cylinder. The immersion heater is a sealed resistive element through which electricity is passed causing it to heat up. The immersion heater penetrates the storage cylinder making direct contact with the stored water. A typical domestic immersion heater would have a power rating of 3 kW.

The immersion heater has an in built thermostat to control the domestic hot water temperature. This switches the current on or off, as required, to maintain the pre set temperature, typically 60-65°C. The duration of operation of the heater can be controlled manually using a switch or automatically using a time switch. Electricity is costly and polluting but short duration use of an electric immersion heater in summer can be more efficient that a poorly designed indirect heating system due to its poor low load efficiency.

Combination Boiler. A "combi" boiler is a combustion device that has two heat exchangers, one for the space heating system and one for the domestic hot water (figure 9.20). Cold water is fed into the unit directly from the mains. Turning on the hot tap allows cold mains water to flow through the boiler. The pressure changes cause the burner to fire. Hot water is therefore generated as needed. There is little or no stored volume of water which eliminates the standing heat losses associated with a storage cylinder full of unused hot water.

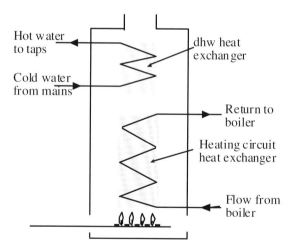

Figure 9.20 Combination boiler

The major benefit of this system is that it is simpler and less costly to install than an indirect cylinder system as a feed and expansion tank, indirect cylinder and cold water storage tank are not required.

DHW FOR COMMERCIAL BUILDINGS.

Hot water in commercial buildings can be provided by the methods used in housing discussed previously. The systems are however much bigger due to the increased demand for hot water experienced in larger buildings. Another method of indirect dhw production used in commercial buildings is to replace the indirect cylinder with a water to water plate heat exchanger. The source of heat is still the indirect heating system.

Water to water plate heat exchangers are built of a sandwich of convoluted thin plates (figures 9.21). Alternate voids created by the plates carry heating circuit and dhw flows respectively. Heat is transferred from the heating circuit flow to the dhw flow by conduction across the thin metal separating the two flows. This process is fast enough to produce hot water instantaneously.

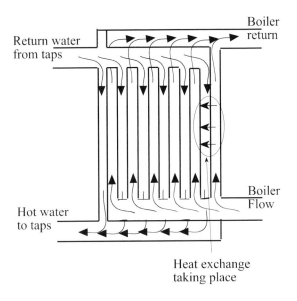

Figure 9.21 diagram showing principle of operation of a water to water heat exchanger

Plate heat exchangers have a number of advantages over storage systems;

• There are no standing heat losses since there is no stored volume of water to cool down overnight or at weekends.

• Legionnaires disease can arise where water is allowed to stand at the incubation temperature of the legionella bacteria. Since standing water is eliminated with plate heat exchangers the possibility of infection is avoided.

• Plate heat exchangers are physically much smaller than indirect cylinders. This makes them useful where space is limited.

Since there is no stored hot water, which is used to satisfy demand at times of peak usage, the heat exchanger must be sized to satisfy the peak hot water demand of the building.

DHW DISTRIBUTION

A significant difference between domestic and commercial dhw systems is the way in which the hot water is distributed to the taps. In domestic properties, a single pipe directs water from the cylinder to the tap. The length of pipe is known as a 'dead leg'. The length of the dead leg must be kept to a minimum. In large buildings the dead legs become longer due to the large distances between hot water production and use. Standing heat losses from these long pipes would result in tepid water being drawn off from these remote taps. Running off this tepid water until hot water was obtained and the heat lost from the pipes themselves would result in waste of energy. To provide a rapid response hot taps are usually supplied from a secondary hot water loop (figure 9.22). A secondary dhw pump continually circulates hot water from the cylinder or heat exchanger around this circuit. As a result hot water is always available at the taps. This system provides a good hot water service but can lead to high heat losses from the secondary distribution pipework. To overcome this and to avoid heat entry into spaces through which the secondary dhw pipes run, the pipes must be well insulated.

In commercial buildings that occupy a large site, it is common to decentralise the hot water system and to provide sources of hot water throughout the site corresponding to demand. This can avoid the need for long dead legs or a secondary dhw loop. Small storage or instantaneous heaters can be used as described above. For larger demands direct fired water heaters should be used. These devices are cylindrical in shape containing a small volume of stored water (figure 9.23). The gas burner is sited at the bottom of the unit. The heat exchanger and flue run up through the centre of the stored water volume and so excellent thermal contact is made between the source of heat and the water. Any heat losses from the flue also pass into the water. Since there is a stored volume there will be standing heat losses. To reduce these The exterior of the tank is well insulated and the volume of water stored is large enough to satisfy a surge in demand but small enough to reduce the standing losses. As a consequence of this and the other features described above direct fired water heaters operate at an efficiency of approximately 90%.

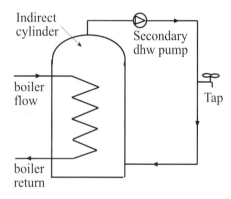

Figure 9.22 Secondary dhw circuit.

BUILDING REGULATIONS

It is a requirement of the Building Regulations Part L2 that the dhw services make efficient use of energy. Ways of achieving this requirement include:

- Avoiding over-sizing of hot water systems.

- Avoiding low load operation of boilers.

- Not using mains electricity (unless demand for dhw is very low).

- Using solar water heating panels.

- Reducing the length of secondary dhw loops and length and diameter of dead legs.

- Controlling the system so that hot water is provided only when required and to the temperature required

Figure 9.23 Direct fired gas water heater.

9.7 Commissioning

One of the key elements in the energy efficiency of mechanical systems whether heating, hot water, lighting controls, ventilation or air conditioning is the commissioning of the system. Commissioning is the setting up and adjustment of both the hardware, such as valves, dampers, pumps, boilers etc and software such as control strategies. Examples are that the combustion efficiency of boilers should be tested and thermostats should be confirmed to be turning off heating appliances and that BMS control strategies perform as expected. Badly commissioned heating, ventilation and air conditioning systems will be wasteful in energy and cause thermal discomfort. The bulding regulations part L require that a certificate should be issued on completion of the building stating that the commissioning has been successfully carried out. This certificate, including a record of system settings, should be included in the building log-book at handover.

10 COOLING

In this chapter we will find that;

- The air inside a building can become uncomfortably warm due to high outside air temperatures and/or high internal heat gains.

- Reducing the heat gains is the first stage in any cooling strategy.

- Warm air can be made to feel more comfortable by causing it to move over the occupants.

- Warm air can be cooled by bringing it into contact with the cool mass of the building structure.

- The building must be ventilated at night time to discharge the heat that the mass absorbs.

- The number and size of rooms treated by an air conditioning system must be kept to a minimum.

- The evaporation of water can be used to create chilled water and cool air.

- With a mechanical cooling system, energy is used by the refrigerant compressor and any pumps or fans used to deliver the cool air.

- The cooling apparatus and the cooling system should use energy efficient components.

- Absorption chillers use gas, solar energy or waste heat as an energy source instead of electricity.

10.0 Introduction

In winter, when indoor air temperatures are too cool for comfort, heat is added to the room air to increase its temperature. In summer the opposite can occur and air temperatures can become too warm for comfort. In this case energy must be removed from the room air to reduce its temperature. This is achieved using some form of cooling commonly referred to as air conditioning.

The cause of high internal air temperatures is a combination of high outside air temperatures and high internal heat gains. Whilst the UK is not known for its hot climate it is possible that in summer, daytime air temperatures can be in the high twenties for a number of consecutive days. This air enters the building and absorbs additional heat released from casual sources such as sunlight, lighting, occupants and equipment. The largest contributor of heat is the sun as shown in table 10.1 which lists the average daily heat gain rate per square metre of floor area for different heat sources. The values in table 10.1 are averaged over both the area of affected space and time of year. Variations will occur depending on the time of year and closeness to windows.

Heat Source	Gain rate (W/m^2)
Occupants	9
Lighting (typical)	20
Solar gains (south/east)	37
Equipment	25

Table 10.1 Sources of heat gain in a typical office building.

Closeness to windows. The figures for occupancy will be evenly distributed throughout the space. The solar energy gains will be greater near the windows than deeper parts of the space. Equipment gains will depend on where the equipment is positioned. Computers for example are usually fairly evenly spread out. Lighting gains may be reduced near windows if an effective daylight control strategy is adopted

Time of year. There may be greater gains from lighting in winter as a result of increased artificial lighting use on darker days. The gains from sunlight will be greatest in summer. However, sunlight is still present in winter and at this time of year it can be more difficult to shade since the sun is lower in the sky.

Causal heat gains in office buildings can be sufficiently high that air conditioning is required all year round. The energy used by air conditioning systems is the prime concern but an additional concern is that mechanical cooling systems are filled with refrigerants. In the past CFC's were used but are now prohibited as they were found to damage the ozone layer. Modern alternatives are much less destructive and in many cases ozone benign. However, many of the alternatives are greenhouse gases which, if they escape, add to global warming. Some refrigerants such as ammonia and propane are neither greenhouse gases nor ozone depleting gases. However they do carry risks of toxicity and flammability respectively.

The proportion of the total energy used in a prestige office for refrigeration is 11% with more added on for the fans and pumps used in distributing cold air or water around the building. In total, air conditioned buildings account for 2% of the UK annual CO_2 output. It is likely in the future that the amount of energy used in air conditioning systems will increase due to two factors; global warming creating longer and warmer summers and the move from an industrial economy to a service economy that makes greater use of information technology within office buildings.

Cooling a building using minimal energy requires the implementation of the following strategies:

- Eliminate or reduce heat gains.

- Design the fabric and form of the building to promote natural ventilation, daylighting and passive cooling.

- Adopt passive cooling strategies that utilise ventilation and exposed thermal mass.

- Use low energy mechanical systems such as air circulation fans and evaporative cooling.

- Restrict the area treated by air conditioning. The system should be constructed from energy efficient components and controlled to limit hours of use.

It is possible that the building will operate a mixed mode strategy to keep its occupants cool. This begins using passive techniques but may call upon mechanical systems to deal with cooling peaks during summer or when internal gains overwhelm the passive methods.

This chapter will begin by considering the range of casual heat gains in a building and how they can be reduced. It will then consider passive and low energy mechanical methods of cooling a building.

10.1 Heat Gains

This section will look at the various casual heat gains in descending order of size and consider ways of reducing them. This is particularly important since passive and low energy mechanical cooling methods have a limited cooling capacity that would not be able to satisfy the cooling requirement arising from unrestricted casual heat gains.

10.1.1 Solar Heat Gains

Solar heat gains were considered in chapter 8 as a useful way of reducing the space heating energy consumption of houses and small commercial buildings. However, in buildings with large glazed areas or those with other substantial heat gains the ingress of solar energy can cause overheating. Large glazed areas are the key risk factor for buildings especially when this is facing south or west. South because the solar intensity is at its greatest when the sun is in this direction. There are two problems when the sun is in the west. The first is that the sun is low in the sky and so is difficult to shade. The second is because the sun reaches the west in the afternoon and, the building fabric having heated up through the day, cannot be absorb any more heat and so the air temperature will rise.

It follows from the above that the first two recommendations for reducing solar gains is to reduce glazed areas on the west and south faces of the building. Glass is a popular material with architects and so a number of contemporary commercial buildings have facades with glazed proportions approaching 80%. This contrasts with the guidance given for offices in the LT method (see IP4) that indicates a glazing ratio of 40%

should not be exceeded on a south facing facade.

BUILDING REGULATIONS

The Building Regulations part L2 set a requirement to avoid overheating in commercial buildings due to solar gains. Methods of demonstrating compliance include:

- Designing elements containing glazing with glazed areas not exceeding the percentages of the internal area of the element as shown in table 10.2. It can be seen from the table that the greatest restriction on glazed area is placed on rooflights. This is because of the greater solar intensity on horizontal surfaces due to the high altitude sun in summer. This is followed in size of restriction for east, southeast, west and southwest glazed areas. This is because of the risk presented by the low altitude sun. The maximum permissible area of glazing on the south facade is greater than on the E/SE/W and SW. This is because it can be easily shaded from the high altitude noon sun using horizontal projections over the window.

Orientation of opening	Maximum allowable area of glazing (%)
North	50
NE/NW/S	40
E/SE/W/SW	32
Horizontal	12

Table 10.2 Maximum allowable areas of glazing in non-domestic buildings as a percentage of internal area of the element under consideration.

- Calculating the heat gain using the method described in appendix H of the building regulations. It must be shown that the solar heat gain per square metre averaged between 07:30am and 17:30pm is not greater than $25W/m^2$. This takes into account overshadowing of glazed areas.

- Using a detailed calculation procedure, such as that described in chapter 5 of the CIBSE guide A, to show that in the absence of mechanical cooling or mechanical ventilation that the space will not overheat when subject to an internal gain of $10W/m^2$

10.1.2 Solar Control

There are various systems available for controlling the entry of sunlight through glazing. These are: movable shading devices, fixed shading devices and special types of glazing. The choice of sun control system depends on the orientation of the glazing, the performance required, the need to maintain daylight levels and the aesthetics of the building.

MOVABLE SHADING DEVICES

Movable shading devices, commonly referred to as blinds, can be moved into place when required and retracted when the sunlight has gone. Retraction on overcast days allows adequate daylight levels to be maintained. Three forms of blinds can be identified; roller blinds, horizontal or vertical louvre blinds and shutters. An additional benefit of blinds is their ability to reduce glare caused by a bright window. Blinds were discussed in section 6.3 where they were considered as a method of alleviating overheating arising from adopting a daylighting strategy. This is added to below by describing a control strategy for the blinds.

Shutters, typically used in hot countries, are exclusively manual in operation. Blinds can be deployed manually or automatically. Automatic control requires a control unit such as a BMS connected to sunlight and internal temperature sensors and motorised actuators. The sensors detect a rise in temperature and if this occurs in conjunction with high sunlight levels, the blinds are made to descend. When internal temperatures decrease or the sunlight disappears the blinds can be re-opened. This avoids the blinds down lights on problem that can itself be a cause of unnecessary energy consumption and overheating when clouds obscure the direct sunlight.

A similar strategy can be adopted with horizontal louvre (Venetian) blinds. In addition to the capability of full or partial retraction they also have the facility for rotation of the blades. So for example as internal temperatures increase the blinds can descend down the glazing with blades in the horizontal position (figure 10.1). This allows some shading and maintains daylight entry. If the temperatures increase the blades can be rotated to the vertical position to totally obscure the sun. The reverse occurs as temperatures fall. Automatic control of blinds is particularly useful when the glazing is out of reach such as blinds protecting the roof of a glazed atrium or within double skin external glazed walling systems of office buildings. Any changes in blind position must be carried out slowly to be less noticeable and avoid disturbing the occupants.

Figure 10.1 Automatic blind control strategy.

FIXED SHADING DEVICES

Fixed shading devices form part of the structure or an extension to the fabric of the building and, as the name implies, they are fixed in position. Since no adjustment is available the shading device must be appropriate for the range of sun altitude and azimuth experienced by the facade to which they are part (see IP10). Generally speaking fixed shading devices fall into one of three categories; horizontal shading devices, vertical shading devices and combined horizontal and vertical shading devices. They differ from blinds in that they usually aim to cause little if any obstruction to the window so views and daylighting are retained.

Horizontal shading devices are typically found as horizontal shelves projecting externally over the window head (figure 10.2). They can be constructed out of lightweight materials such as aluminium, timber or fabric. They are suitable for shading high altitude

sun but not low altitude sun. This makes them useful for shading south facing glazing in summer but not for east or west facing glazing or south facing glazing in winter. Figure 10.3 is a shadow mask for a horizontal shading device over a south facing window. The grey area covers the parts of the sun path at the positions where the sun is obscured from the window. The upper semi-circle is fully obscured indicating that the building itself shades the window from all sun positions running from west to east through north. The shaded area in the lower semi-circle covers the parts of the sun path with the highest altitude indicating that the sunlight from low altitude sun will travel under the horizontal shading device and hit the window.

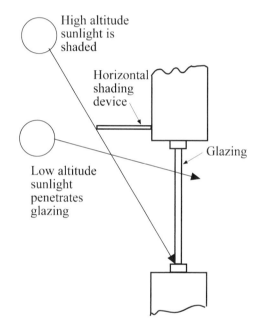

Figure 10.2 Vertical section through a window showing horizontal shading device.

Figures 6.12 and 6.13 show a horizontal shading device composed of vertical plates. The purpose of this is to shade the sun but allow scattered daylight to enter the window.

Vertical shading devices are most commonly encountered as the vertical part of the window reveal especially where the window is deeply recessed. Vertical panels are useful for shading low angled sunlight that strikes the window obliquely. For example figure 10.4

IP7 - Sun Path Diagrams

This information panel describes the path the sun appears to take across the sky and explains how the position of the sun in the sky at any time is specified using two angles.

The sun is stationary but the spin of the earth and its orbit around the sun gives observers on the earth's surface the impression that the sun moves across the sky. The path that the sun takes varies with each hour of the day and day of the year but the general pattern is well known. To an observer in the Northern hemisphere, such as someone in the UK, the sun rises in the east, reaches a maximum altitude at noon in the south and sets in the west (figure IP7.1). In summer the UK is tilted towards the sun and so the sun rises early towards the north east, has a high sun path and then sets north of west. The long sun path is experienced as a long day length. In winter the UK is tilted away from the sun so the sun rises towards the south east, reaches a relatively low maximum altitude at noon then sets in the south west. This low sun path gives a short length

of day. The position of the sun in the sky at any time of the year can be specified using two angles (figure IP7.1).

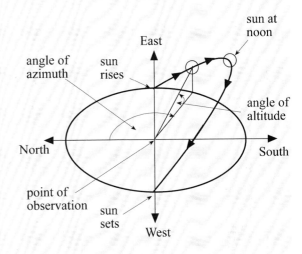

Figure IP7.1 General sun path showing angles of azimuth and altitude.

IP7.2 Sun path diagram

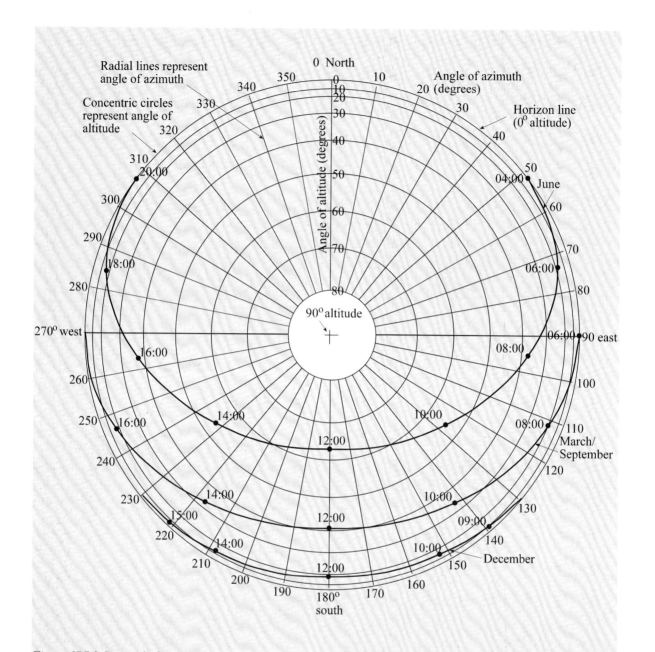

Radial lines represent
angle of azimuth

Concentric circles
represent angle of
altitude

0 North

Angle of azimuth
(degrees)

Horizon line
(0° altitude)

Angle of altitude (degrees)

90° altitude

270° west

90 east

180°
south

Figure IP7.3 Sun path diagram.

The first is the angle of azimuth. This is the angle
between the north point and a vertical plane passing
through the centre of the sun and the point of
observation. The second angle, the angle of altitude,
is the angle between the horizontal and a line passing
through the centre of the sun and the point of
observation. Tables of solar altitude and azimuth for
any given time of day and for 5° increments in latitude

on the earth are published in the CIBSE journal Part A.

SUN PATH DIAGRAMS

The sun path is three-dimensional however it can be
depicted on a two-dimensional chart called a sun path
diagram. There are two types of sun path diagram one
that projects the sun path information horizontally and
one that projects the sun path information vertically.

HORIZONTAL PROJECTION

An example of a horizontally projected chart is given in figure IP7.2 The y-axis represents solar altitude so the further up the chart a point is the higher the sun is in the sky. The x-axis represents the solar azimuth. Due south is in the centre of the chart. Three sun paths are shown for latitude 51° North. Other latitudes have a slightly different set of sun paths. The further north in the UK the lower the angles of altitude for any particular time of year.

The three traces shown represent the extremes and mid point of the sun path. The uppermost trace is the sun path for the summer solstice. This is the longest day of the year (indicated by the length of the sun path when over the horizon) and when the sun reaches its maximum altitude at noon. The lowest trace is the sunpath for the winter solstice. This is the shortest day of the year when the sun reaches its lowest altitude at noon. Finally, the central trace is the autumn and spring equinox. On this day the sun rises due east and sets due west. With each day passing from the summer solstice the sun becomes lower in the sky and the day begins to shorten. The autumn equinox position marks the mid point between the summer and winter solstice. Following the winter solstice the suns altitude increases again daily at any given time until it passes through a second mid position, the spring equinox.

VERTICAL PROJECTION

The vertically projected chart is shown in figure IP7.3. It can be seen that the graph paper used is different to the usual rectangular x - y arrangement. Here the outermost concentric circle represents the horizon or 0° altitude. Successive concentric circles represent increasing altitude in 10° intervals until the centre point represents 90° altitude, directly upwards. The building is considered to be under this centre point. The nearer a point on the graph is to the centre of the circle the higher it is in the sky. The radial lines represent angle of azimuth. These begin with the vertical radial line which represents north. Successive radial lines moving in a clockwise direction are 10° increments of solar azimuth. 90° azimuth represents east, 180° represents south and 270° represents west. The same three sun paths as depicted on figure IP7.2 are also shown on this sunchart.

USE OF SUN PATH DIAGRAMS

Both types of sun path diagram show the same information - angles of altitude and azimuth. However the horizontal projection of figure IP7.2 is better for visualising solar altitude whereas the vertical projection in figure IP7.3 is better for visualising solar azimuth.

USING THE CHARTS

The sun path diagrams are useful in studies of passive solar heating and passive cooling. The former by attempting to encourage the entry of sunlight into the building the latter by preventing the entry of sunlight into the building. A simple example using the circular sun chart shown in figure IP7.3 is the determination of which face of a building the sun falls on at a particular time and date of the year. A small outline of the building under investigation is placed at the centre of the sun path and is rotated to the correct orientation. The chart requires a sun path that relates to the latitude of the site and the day of interest. By connecting a point on the sun path at the time of interest to the centre point, the surface that this line crosses will be that which is affected by the sun.

The information carried on the sun path diagram is also used in environmental design software. The size, position and orientation of windows are defined either in terms of data or as a CAD image file. The software will then call upon inbuilt sun path information to determine external overshadowing of the site by adjacent structures, shadows cast by the building itself and finally, if data is also available on solar intensity as well as position, heat gains to the building through the glazing. Most software systems also have the benefit of being able to repeat these calculations at different times of the day, such as at hourly intervals. The daily heat gain can be calculated and animations created showing the movement of shadows and pools of sunlight within and surrounding the building.

shows a horizontal section through a south facing window that is protected from afternoon sunlight by a vertical projection.

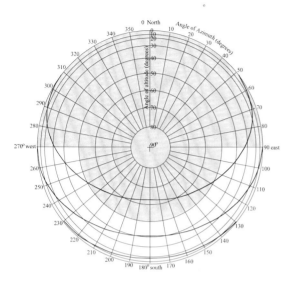

Figure 10.3 Shadow mask for a horizontal shading device over a south facing window.

Figure 10.4 Horizontal section through a window showing vertical shading device

Figure 10.5 shows the shadow mask associated with two vertical shading devices one on each side of a south facing window. It shows that the shading system obscures low angled sun coming from the east to south east and west to south west.

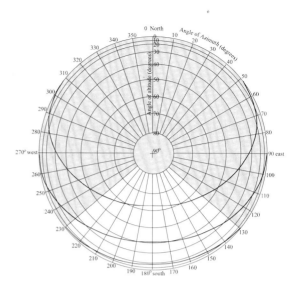

Figure 10.5 shadow mask for a vertical shading device placed at both sides of a south facing window.

Combined vertical and horizontal shading devices are encountered as either the reveals of small windows or as egg crate shading devices as illustrated in figure 10.6. Depending on the spacing of the elements the shading device gives a good degree of shading for most sun positions except for those where the sun is positioned on a line normal to the window i.e. is low altitude and opposite the window. However, views through the window are restricted in direction and the shading device is more noticeable both externally and from within the building. This form of shading device is common in hot countries appearing as perforated and carved timber screens in front of windows called mashrabiya.

The shadow mask for this device is the combination of both the horizontal and vertical shadow masks.

SPECIAL GLAZING

When sunlight hits a sheet of glass some of it is reflected, some absorbed and some transmitted (figure 10.7).

The absorbed component raises the temperature of the glass and this energy is then re-released both internally and externally. More tends to leave the glass outwards than inwards as it is usually cooler outside than inside.

The quantities of the incident solar energy that are reflected, absorbed or transmitted depend on the clarity and reflectivity of the glass and the angle of incidence of the sun's radiation striking it. For example if the solar radiation hits the glass at an acute angle to its surface more will be reflected. If the radiation hits the glass at 90° to its surface then more will be transmitted. Taken over a whole day with varying solar angles the components for clear 6mm float glass are transmitted 78%, reflected 7% and absorbed 15%. Of the 15% absorbed component10% is re-released externally and 5% enters the building. The total transmission is therefore 83%. By adding an extra sheet of glass to create double glazing the total transmission is reduced to 72%. Once inside the building the short wave solar radiation is absorbed and re-radiated at a longer wavelength. Glass is not transparent to long wavelength thermal radiation and so it cannot escape back out through the glass.

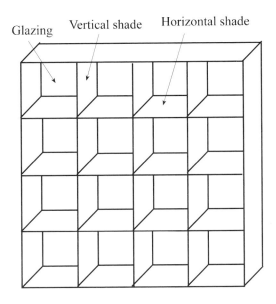

Figure 10.6 Combined vertical and horizontal shading device.

There are special types of glazing whose aim is to reduce the transmitted component and therefore reduce the solar cooling load. These two types are solar reflecting glass and solar absorbing glass.

Solar reflecting glass has a very fine metal coating applied to its outer surface to increase its reflectivity,

like the silvering that is applied to glass to create a mirror(figure 10.8). The amount of reflectivity can be varied depending on the thickness of the applied coat. It must be remembered that as the reflectivity of the glass increases the daylight transmission decreases. Table 10.3[2] shows that as sunlight transmission is reduced by increasing the reflected component from 7% to 45% the daylight transmission is also reduced by 67%. Daylight is useful in that it allows artificial lighting to be turned off thereby reducing the cooling load arising from lighting.

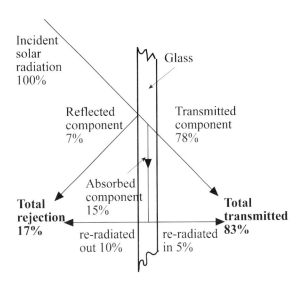

Figure 10.7 Reflection, absorption and transmission of solar heat through 6mm clear float glass.

In existing buildings reflecting films are available that can be cut to size and applied to glazing to reduce solar gains.

Solar absorbing glass protects the building by absorbing the incident solar heat within the glass itself. It is created by mixing additives to the glass during manufacture that darkens its structure. This type of glass is also known as body tinted glass. Most of this trapped heat will be lost outwards rather than inwards reducing the size of the overall transmitted component. Figure 10.8 illustrates the principle.

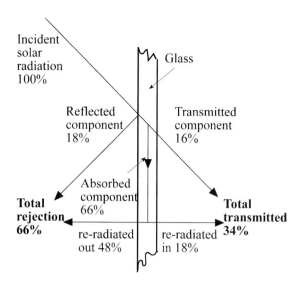

Figure 10.8 Reflection, absorption and transmission of solar heat through solar reflecting glass.

	Factor (%)		
	Heat		Light
Type	Trans	reflect	Trans.
10/23 silver	23	32	10
20/34 silver	34	18	20
30/42 silver	42	15	30

Table 10.3 Solar heat transmitance and reflectance and light transmission of solar reflecting glass.

Table 10.4 gives details for four thicknesses of body tinted glass. It can be seen that increasing the thickness of glass increases the absorbed component. A change from 6mm glass to 12mm glass reduces the solar heat transmission from 60 to 45%. However this change also reduces the daylight transmission from 42 to 19%. The absorption of solar heat increases the temperature of the glass. This can cause thermal discomfort to occupants working near to the glazing due to radiant heating. The use of solar absorbing glass is a less satisfactory solar control strategy than rejecting the solar energy immediately by reflection. One benefit of the reduced daylight transmission of both solar reflecting and solar absorbing glass is that it reduces glare from windows.

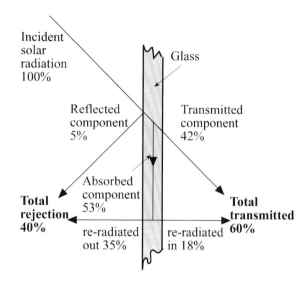

Figure 10.9 Reflection, absorption and transmission of solar heat through solar absorbing glass.

The above examples relate to single glazing. Both solar reflecting and solar rejecting glass performance is changed when it is incorporated into a double glazed unit. For example, 6mm 10/23 silver solar reflecting glass when incorporated into a double glazed unit with a low emissivity inner leaf, has its total transmission reduced from 23% to 14%.

	Factor (%)		
	Heat		Light
Type	Trans	Absorb	Trans.
4mm grey	68	40	55
6mm grey	60	53	42
10mm grey	49	71	25
12mm grey	45	77	19

Table 10.4 Solar heat transmitance and reflectance and light transmission of solar absorbing glass.

A variation on the above glazing systems is 'fritted' glass. This is glass that has been screen printed to produce a grid of opaque dots on its surface. If the dots are white the glass becomes partially solar reflecting glass. If the dots are black the glass becomes partially solar absorbing glass. Both types give a degree of internal shading that helps to reduce the effects of glare. The amount of shading and solar rejection can be increased or decreased by printing a closer or more spaced out arrangement of dots respectively.

FUTURE SYSTEMS

Research is continuing on special forms of glazing that change their solar characteristics in response to changing environmental conditions. There are three such types of glazing; photochromic glass that darkens as sunlight levels increase, thermochromic glass that darkens as its temperature increases and electrochromic glass that darkens in response to an electrical signal applied to the surface coating. All of these types of glazing have been produced in small scale samples but as yet are too expensive to be used practically in mainstream buildings. As with other technologies such as photovoltaics mass production techniques may make these glazing systems viable in the future.

10.1.3 Lighting Gains

Artificial lights are devices for converting electricity into light. Unfortunately this conversion process is not 100% efficient and heat is emitted as well as light. The heat output from lighting can be reduced by selecting energy efficient lamps and also controlling their operation to times when they are required. This has been considered previously in chapter 7. Virtually all of the electrical energy that goes in to a lamp to produce light makes its way into the building as heat. Therefore reducing the amount of electricity used by artificial lighting using efficient lamps, system design and control will reduce the cooling load. For example the heat gain to a building from a typical lighting installation giving 500 lux on the working plane is 20W/m^2. An equivalent low energy lighting system would contribute a heat gain of 11W/m^2.

One system that was not considered in chapter 7 is the use of remote lamps and fibre optics to convey the light to where it is needed without conveying the heat. In this situation a powerful light source produces light in an environment where thermal comfort is not an issue, such as a plant room, or where cooling can be achieved by rapid ventilation. Fibre optic cables collect the light and convey it to rooms where it is needed. This allows light to be provided without the associated heat gains that may otherwise cause the room to overheat. This system can also be used in environmentally controlled display cabinets to reduce or eliminate the need for them to be mechanically cooled

10.1.4 Occupants

Building occupants are a source of heat. A person sitting at a desk will be giving out almost 100W of heat derived from metabolic activity. An active person gives out more heat depending on the amount of muscular exertion. Table 10.5 shows how metabolic heat output increases with increased activity.

Activity level	Heat Output (W)
Seated at desk	90
walking in office	110
light work	150
heavy work	200

Table 10.5 Heat gains from occupants

When people congregate in large numbers the combined heat gain can be substantial. Given that occupants are the reason for most buildings to exist it is difficult to justify eliminating the occupants to reduce heat gains! In hot climates, rooms in which large numbers of people congregate are often adjacent to courtyards. If overheating is a concern the doors connecting the room to the courtyard are opened and the gains can escape outside the building. This is difficult to achieve in modern commercial buildings but the technique is partially adopted by increasing the volume of rooms in which lots of people congregate. Warm air will rise to the ceiling and will be diluted in the large volume of room air (see section 3.2.1).

10.1.5 Appliances

Office buildings house a large amount of equipment such as personal computers, printers, fax machines, drinks machines and photocopiers. All of these pieces of equipment will give out heat whilst performing the function for which they are intended. Normally the equipment used by the building occupant is outside of the control of the building designer. However, if the elimination of mechanical cooling is part of the buildings design strategy then it is important that the building users are made aware of this and adopt methods that would reduce the cooling load arising from small power consumption. These are:

- Choose efficient equipment that consumes the least amount of electricity to perform a given task. A good example of this is the choice of LCD computer visual display terminals (VDT) as opposed to cathode ray VDT's. A typical cathode ray device consumes 200W of electricity whereas a LCD screen consumes 28W.

- Switch off the equipment when it is not being used. Much computer equipment now has this capability built in. In equipment where this is not built in the occupants should be encouraged to switch off unused devices themselves. Where this is not practical and the hours of non-usage are well known, simple time switches can be used (whilst ensuring essential supplies are maintained such as those for refrigerators or data storage devices).

These suggestions should form part of the "user manual" that is a requirement of the Building Regulations to be supplied to the building management when a new building is handed over upon completion (see section 11.8).

10.1.6 Cooking

The heat liberated during cooking can be substantial. If this is released into the kitchen of a low energy house overheating will quickly occur. Traditionally in hot climates cooking was undertaken outdoors and so no heat entered the building. Modern societies cook inside and so to emulate the traditional means of avoiding

cooking gains an extract fan should be used to remove the heat along with the cooking smells and odours at source. This is best carried out using an extractor close to the source such as an over the hob extract unit. If this unit incorporates an air to air heat exchanger, it should be fitted with a by-pass for summer operation so that it does not pre-heat incoming air. Commercial kitchens will incorporate extraction as the norm. Extract fans should be fitted with suitable controls to limit their operation to times of cooking so that only excessively heated and polluted air is removed from the kitchen.

10.1.7 Summary

The techniques used to reduce the cooling load arising from casual heat gains in buildings are:

- Prevent the entry of solar energy

- Utilise daylight rather than artificial light

- Choose energy efficient equipment (including lighting).

- Control the hours of use of the equipment

- Extract the heat gains at source before they can raise room air temperatures for example extract luminaires or cooker extracts.

- Increase the volume of the room so that the heat gains are absorbed by a larger volume of air and surface mass. This reduces air temperature rises.

- Do not compound cooling loads for example by placing computer rooms on the south side of the building where solar gains also occur.

10.2 Improving Comfort

Mechanical cooling is required in response to complaints by occupants of feeling too warm. This can be avoided by increasing the temperature at which occupants begin to feel thermal discomfort using psychological and mechanical means. This allows the cooling set point to be raised and may mean that the cooling system is not required at all.

Psychology. The idea is to encourage the occupants to accept and tolerate higher temperatures. This occurs naturally to an extent since higher internal temperatures are expected and tolerated to a greater degree in summer than winter. Acceptance of higher temperatures is most effective when the occupants are well informed and are aware that they occupy a building with a low energy strategy. They also need to have a degree of control over their environment. This typically requires access to openable windows. The building also needs to be shallow in plan so that more people are near to the windows. The use of vegetation and cool colours in a building has also been suggested as a way of psychologically creating a cooler impression of an environment without actually reducing air temperatures.

Mechanical. The second method of improving comfort whilst not reducing air temperatures is to move the room air over the occupants. Moving the air creates additional evaporative and convective cooling of the occupants bodies. This acts to reduce core body temperature and helps in providing thermal comfort. This air movement can be achieved using desk or ceiling fans or a ducted ventilation system. This is not free cooling since electricity is being consumed by the fan. In addition, the heat liberated by the fan motor will create a small rise in air temperature however the fact that it is moving will make it feel cooler to the occupant's.

10.3 Passive Cooling

Passive cooling is the process of reducing air temperatures without using refrigeration equipment. Three techniques can be identified; free cooling, exposed mass and night time ventilation and evaporative cooling. Each of these will be discussed in the sections below. However, it must be stated at the outset that all passive methods have a limited cooling capacity and therefore it is essential to reduce the cooling load by reducing casual heat gains first as described in section 10.1

FREE COOLING

When overheating occurs as a result of internal heat gains it is usual for the outside air temperature to be cooler than inside. If this is the case an amount of free cooling can be achieved by simply replacing hot internal air with cool fresh outside air. At its simplest this is achieved using openable windows. This can be enhanced using mechanical window actuators controlled in response to increasing internal air temperatures. Air based air conditioning systems can also be used. The heater and chiller batteries must be switched off and any heat recovery system by-passed. This can form part of a staged cooling strategy where gains are controlled first by causing blinds to descend. Then if temperatures continue to increase the ventilation system is activated. If temperatures continue to rise the chiller plant is activated to reduce ventilation air temperatures. Free cooling by ventilation is only possible when outside air temperatures are lower than inside temperatures. A comparison of these temperatures should be built into the building management system control strategy. If outside temperatures are higher than inside then ventilation should be restricted to that required for good air quality and alternative cooling methods sought.

EXPOSED MASS AND NIGHT TIME VENTILATION

Reference was made in section 8.5.2 to the thermal mass of a room. It was stated that exposed dense structural elements such as concrete floors, blockwork walls and concrete ceilings improves the utilisation of solar energy by acting as a short term energy store. This mass can also be used as a passive cooling method to reduce air temperatures during the day. The principle is illustrated in figure 10.10 and 10.11. During the day heat gains cause the room air temperature to be higher than the structural temperature. Because of this heat flows from the room air into the structure raising its temperature whilst at the same time reducing the air temperature. It is estimated that if sufficient exposed mass is available air temperatures can be reduced by 2 to 3°C. On a daily basis it is only the first 100mm depth of mass that is involved in this process.

If nothing further is done the system will not work again the next day because the structure will still retain heat from the previous day. To re-cool the mass the room must be ventilated at night with cool outside air as shown in figure 10.11. The structure, being warmer than night-time air loses heat to the room air which is then discharged outside in the ventilation process. This super cools the structure so that next day it is cooler than the room air and is once again ready to absorb excess heat and reduce air temperatures.

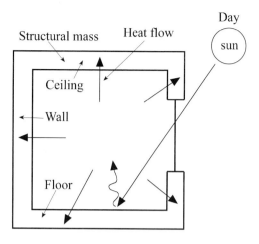

Figure 10.10 Section of a room showing that during the night exposed mass absorbs heat from the room air.

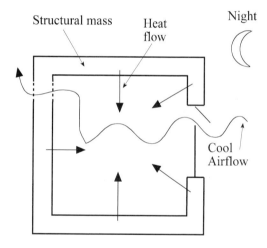

Figure 10.11 Section of a room showing that during the night exposed mass loses heat to the ventilation air.

There are a number of issues that must be addressed for the exposed mass and night time ventilation strategy to cool effectively:

- **Admittance.** Materials have a property known as admittance (Y). This is a description of the materials ability to exchange heat with the surrounding air as air temperatures change. The value of admittance, measured in W/m²K, is dependant on a combination of thermal conductivity (how well heat moves into and out of the material) and thermal capacity (the ability of the material to store heat). Dense materials such as concrete, ceramics and marble have a high value of admittance. Low density materials such as plaster, carpets and insulation have a low admittance value. To be effective the surfaces in a room being passively cooled should have as high a value of admittance as possible. The movement of heat into the mass depends on the size of the variation in air temperature from the average air temperature. A positive temperature difference moves heat into the mass, a negative temperature difference causes heat to move out of the mass. Movement of heat into and out of the mass is restricted by the internal surface resistance (see IP2) it can also be restricted by surface coatings such as lightweight plaster.

- **Control.** With a mechanical cooling system the chiller can be operated as and when required to satisfy changing cooling loads within the building. With exposed mass the chilling capacity is continuous at a low level and gradually decreases towards the end of the day. The overall capacity for cooling depends on the size of the temperature difference between the mass and the room air and the area of material exposed and therefore available to absorb heat (note on a daily cycle heat absorption and loss takes place in the first 100mm depth within the exposed mass). Control of the passive system is achieved by varying the degree to which the mass is cooled overnight. This is achieved by monitoring outside air temperatures, the trend in this temperature and the temperature of the structure. The basic control strategy is that at night openings in the envelope are opened or fans are operated to increase the ventilation rate of the building. For example, if the daytime ventilation rate is 4ac/h then at night this may be increased to 8ac/h. If the trend in outside temperatures is for a prolonged hot spell the ventilation is allowed to continue longer to give deeper cooling of the fabric. If cooler days are predicted then the ventilation will be activated for a shorter period. In either case temperature sensors embedded in the fabric indicate the degree of structural cooling achieved and if it is considered sufficient (usually based on operating experience) then the night time ventilation is terminated. This is necessary to avoid over-cooling the structure so that the heating system is required at the start of the next working day.

- **Exposing the mass** One of the problems with mass in office buildings is that it is traditionally covered up[3]. Overhead the mass is covered by suspended ceilings, the walls by lightweight plaster and the floor by a raised floor system. Figure 10.12 shows how the mass can be exposed to the room air. The suspended ceiling can be omitted. This requires high quality in the creation of the concrete work that forms the ceiling so that it can be painted and left exposed without being unsightly. Service runs also become exposed and again should be boxed in neatly. It is possible to distract attention from the exposed ceiling by using a suspened ceiling with lattice type ceiling panels. This forms a visual barrier but allows air to circulate easily through the panel. Internal walls should be formed from dense blockwork. These should be fair faced and joints finished neatly before painting. In office buildings, with the necessity for flexibility in the distribution of computer networks, communication and power cabling, it is difficult to omit the raised floor that normally covers these items. Air can be supplied to the building via the void beneath the raised floor (figure 10.12). This brings it into contact with the thermal mass of the floor. The cooler air then enters the room via floor outlet diffusers.

- **Acoustic environment.** One of the problems with exposed structural mass is that the materials are dense and therefore do not absorb the ambient sound that is naturally present in offices. This can lead to high ambient sound levels that interfere with work by masking telephone and other conversations. One way of overcoming this is to reintroduce some absorbent surfaces into the room. This could take the form of sound absorbent screens between workstations or the use of suspended ceiling tiles that have ventilation slots created in them so room air can move behind them to come into contact with the ceiling mass. Sound passes through perforations in the underside of

the panel and is absorbed by a layer of fibrous sound absorbing material above. This is illustrated on the right hand ceiling coffer in figure 10.12.

Figure 10.12 Exposing structural mass.

- **Security.** Night-time ventilation requires that ventilation devices are opened when the building is unoccupied. In many cases the ventilation openings are motorised windows. The opening of these can be a security risk unless smaller sections of larger windows are used and the open panels are above normal access heights.

- **Pollution** A barrier to passive cooling that was raised as a siting consideration in section 2.6 is that it necessitates the opening of windows. Many offices are in urban areas that suffer from noise and air pollution. This can be a serious disincentive to open windows. Consideration should be given to creating openings on faces of the building away from areas of traffic. The creation of internal courtyards in the building can be a useful way of achieving this. High level openings experience less air pollution but require fans and ducting to deliver the air to where it is required. The problem of noise ingress can be reduced by creating purpose built openings that contain an amount of sound absorbent material. Air can pass through the short length of ducting but the traffic noise and other external sounds are absorbed.

As was stated earlier the cooling capacity of exposed thermal mass and night time ventilation is limited. The capacity can be increased by cooling the mass to a greater degree over night or by increasing the area of exposed mass. A number of systems have now been utilised in various buildings throughout the UK to achieve this.

COOLING THE MASS USING WATER

It is possible to cool the exposed mass by means other than air brought in during night ventilation. The BRE Environmental Office Building utilises an embedded underfloor cooling system. This is formed from a network of plastic piping built into the floor slab during construction. By passing cool water through the pipes the slab is cooled. This system also allows the mass to be cooled during the day as well as during the night. In the case of the BRE office cool water is obtained from a borehole in the ground. It could also be obtained from an evaporative cooler (see section 10.4)

INCREASING THE AREA OF EXPOSED MASS

There are a number of ways in which the area of mass available for cooling can be increased. These include the use of earth tubes, hollow floor slabs and basement cooling.

Earth tubes. In this system a series of ducts are buried in the ground. One end is open to the outside air the other terminates at an air handling unit inside the building (figure 10.13). At night fans are operated that draw air through the earth tube into the building. This cools the lining of the earth tube and any exposed mass in the building. During the day the building is once again mechanically ventilated by drawing air in via the earth tube. Contact of the daytime air with the walls of the earth tube cools it before it enters the building. There is a risk of condensation occurring on the surfaces of the earth tube. This could lead to mould growth and ill health amongst the building occupants. Monitoring of intake air temperature and moisture content and earth tube wall temperature can alert the building management system when the walls of the earth tube are at or below the dew point temperature.

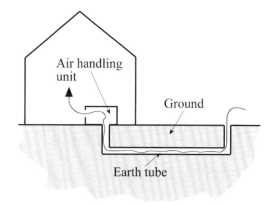

Figure 10.13 Earth tube.

Cellar labyrinth. This system utilises the exposed mass of a basement in addition to that exposed in the rooms themselves. In the example at the Earth Centre, Doncaster[3] a basement room composed of concrete is constructed with a number of concrete partition walls. Within the walls are mechanically operated doors (figure 10.14). Outside air is brought in at the far end of the basement and as it makes its way into the building it is cooled by contact with the basement walls, floor and roof. By opening or closing various doors within the labyrinth the path length and hence degree of cooling experienced by the incoming air can be varied.

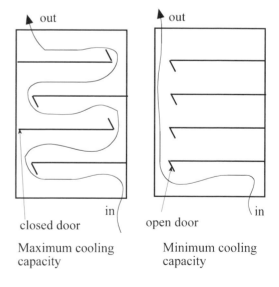

Figure 10.14 Plan of cellar showing labyrinth layout.

Thermodeck system. This method of increasing the area of exposed mass utilises concrete floor slabs containing hollow bores (figure 10.15). The bores are opened at the start and finish point to give an entry and exit point for the ventilation air. Intermediate bores are connected at the ends to give a continuous air flow path. The slab is cooled overnight using night time ventilation. The next day air is brought into the building via the bores in the slab. Contact between the warm incoming air and the walls of the bores causes it to become cooler. It has been found that the more turbulent the airflow across the surface of the concrete the greater is the heat transfer. It is for this reason that the greatest cooling effect occurs at the ends of the bores where there is a change of direction and turbulence occurs.

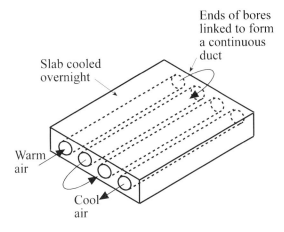

Figure 10.14 Thermodeck system.

10.4 Evaporative Cooling

When water evaporates it changes from a visible liquid to invisible vapour. For this to happen the water must absorb energy. It takes this energy from its surroundings and therefore the surroundings, having lost energy, become cooler. The amount of energy absorbed during evaporation of water is substantial. To illustrate this the amount of energy required to raise the temperature of 1 litre of water from 0°C to 100°C is 0.42 megajoules (MJ). The amount of energy required to change 1 litre of water at 100°C to vapour at 100°C is 2.26MJ.

The evaporation of water can be used for direct or indirect cooling. Direct cooling involves evaporating water in the space that is to be cooled. Traditional systems in hot countries use fountains, water trickling down ornate stonework or terracotta pots filled with water. Evaporation occurs more readily in a dry environment than a humid one and so these techniques work more effectively in hot dry climates. The reduced evaporation rate in hot humid climates means that evaporative cooling is of limited use there. Direct evaporative cooling is seen in the UK within air handling units. Here the incoming airstream is passed through a water spray. Evaporation of the spray droplets occurs and this cools the airstream. The airstream will also be humidified in the process. Care needs to be taken with direct systems that bacteria and algae are not allowed to thrive within them. Otherwise the organic matter can become airborne in water droplets and if inhaled cause infections and allergies within the building occupants.

Indirect evaporative cooling involves the production of chilled water by evaporation. This water is then pumped through a cooling coil in an air handling unit through which incoming air is passing. The water is chilled in a cooling tower as shown in figure 10.16 . The device shown is a forced draught cooling tower. Water is sprayed into the top of the device and droplets tumble downwards whilst at the same time air is forced upwards through the cascading water by a fan.

The tower enhances evaporative cooling by increasing the surface area of water exposed to air. Evaporation is a surface effect so increasing the surface area of the water in contact with the air increases evaporation. This is achieved by firstly injecting the water into the tower as a spray. It then tumbles down splash bars or coats a PVC matrix. Not all of the water evaporates. That which collects in the base of the tower will have been cooled.The cooled water can then be pumped through a cooling coil in an air handling unit or used within a chilled beam or chilled ceiling static cooling system.

It is important that the cooling tower is designed to minimise the escape of spray droplets and is regularly cleaned and treated to avoid the danger of the bacteria that causes legionnaires disease thriving in the water and escaping into the local environment.

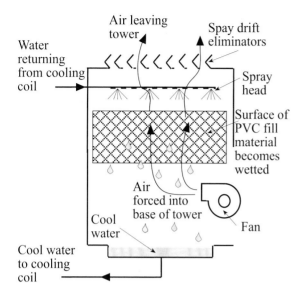

Figure 10.16 Forced draught cooling tower.

10.5 Mechanical Cooling

Refrigeration plant is equipment that uses electricity to cool air or chill water. The majority of refrigeration systems are based on the vapour compression cycle. This system was described in section 8.4 in relation to heat pump technology. In that section the heat pump was used to remove geothermal heat from the ground and place it into a building for space heating purposes. The ground becomes cooler and the building becomes warmer. In refrigeration heat is removed from an air or water stream, causing it to cool. The heat that is extracted is rejected outside the building as waste. It is the chilled air or water that is used within the building for cooling purposes.

The energy consumed by a cooling system is taken up by two components. The first is the compressor that is the electric pump used to circulate the refrigerant around the system. The second are the fans and pumps used to move the cold air or chilled water away from the system and into the building. Figure 10.17 shows a diagram of a split air conditioning system, a simple method of providing direct cooling of room air. The compressor consumes the majority, approximately 95%, of the electricity used by simple refrigeration equipment.

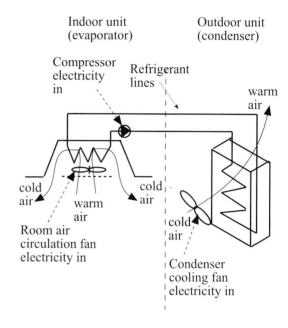

Figure 10.17 Split air conditioning system.

COEFFICIENT OF PERFORMANCE (COP)

The efficiency of a cooling system is normally called the coefficient of performance or COP. The COP of an actual cooling system is given by a comparison between the energy value of the electricity put into the equipment and the energy value of the cooling got out of it. Mathematically this is:

$$COP = \frac{\text{Cooling Capacity (kW)}}{\text{Total Power Input (kW)}}$$

Typical COP's for cooling are between 1.5 to 2.0 which indicates that you can achieve 2kW of cooling for the consumption of 1kW of electricity. This compares with a COP of 2.5 to 3.0 if the refrigeration equipment is being used as a heat pump. To study factors affecting performance more clearly it is useful to look at the formula for the theoretical COP. This is given by;

$$COP = \frac{T_1}{T_1 - T_2}$$

where 　T$_1$ = Evaporator ambient air temperature (K)
　　　　T$_2$ = Condenser ambient air temperature (K)

From this it can be seen that for the COP to be high the difference between T$_1$ and T$_2$ should be small. Since T$_1$ is set by system requirements the variable is T$_2$, the ambient temperature surrounding the condenser. Taking a split cooling system as an example, what this means in practice is that when the outside air temperature increases the efficiency of the system will fall. This is unfortunate since most cooling is required in summer when high ambient condenser temperatures prevail. However, there are a number of things that can be done to reduce the condenser coil temperature. The first is to increase the size of the air-cooled condenser and ensure that there is good airflow through the device. The next is to consider the use of evaporative condensers, these spray the condenser with water to use latent heat removal, during evaporation of the water, to reduce ambient temperatures. Finally, The condenser can be immersed in water and therefore water-cooled. The water should be obtained from a large body of low temperature water such as a canal, river, lake or groundwater.

ICE STORAGE

The COP of refrigeration equipment varies with the amount of work it is required to do. At low loads the efficiency will be reduced. One way of overcoming this problem is to use an ice storage system. Ice storage involves using an undersized chiller to produce ice slurry during the night. The ice is formed and stored in an insulated tank (figure 10.18). During the day, the chiller would not have enough cooling capacity on its own to satisfy the cooling demands of the building. However, by operating the chiller at full load and drawing additional cooling capacity from the ice store the building cooling demand can be satisfied.

The advantages of the system is that the chiller operates most of the time at full load and hence peak efficiency, it also provides a good proportion of the cooling requirement of the building using cheaper night time electricity tariffs. Both of these contribute to reducing operating costs.

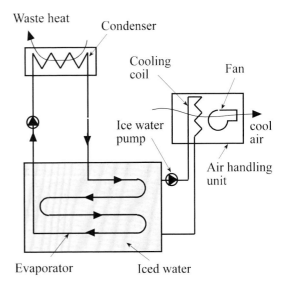

Figure 10.18 Ice storage cooling system.

ABSORPTION CHILLING

There is growing interest in a method of cooling buildings that uses gas as a fuel instead of electricity. The technology is known as absorption cooling. The biggest difference between this and vapour compression cooling is that the compressor and refrigerant are replaced by a gas fired generator and a refrigerant/absorber mixture respectively. A diagram of an absorption chiller is shown in figure 10.19. The generator is filled with a mixture of refrigerant and absorber (solvent) which can be either water/lithium bromide (>100kW cooling capacity) or ammonia/water. (30-800kW cooling capacity). The way the system works can be illustrated using the ammonia/water pairing as an example. In this case water is the absorber and ammonia is the refrigerant. The water is the absorber, giving the process its name, as it is so chemically attracted to ammonia vapour that it absorbs it out of the atmosphere.

A concentrated solution of ammonia in water is heated in the generator using a gas burner. The ammonia component vaporises first, as it has a lower boiling point than water, and passes into the condenser. The water that is left behind passes back to the absorber. The ammonia vapour condenses back to liquid ammonia in the condenser giving out heat, this is taken away for rejection outside the building by a water filled condenser cooling system. The ammonia now passes from the condenser into the evaporator via an expansion valve. In doing so its pressure drops and so it can evaporate once more. It does this by absorbing heat from the chilled water circuit. Chilling has therefore, been achieved. The ammonia vapour now passes into the absorber where it is absorbed by the water from the generator to create a concentrated ammonia solution. Heat is given out when the two chemicals combine. This waste heat is removed by the condenser cooling coil circuit. The ammonia solution is pumped back to the generator where the cycle continues once more.

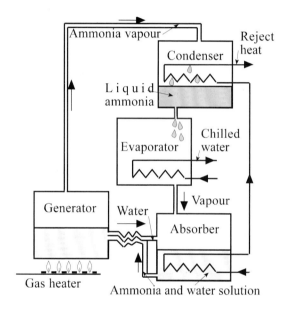

Figure 10.19 Absorption Chiller.

The above device is known as a single effect absorption chiller. Double effect units are also available which pre heat the ammonia solution on its way back to the generator by passing it through a heat exchanger. This improves the efficiency of the unit. Double effect units require a higher temperature heat source (>140°C) usually derived from direct gas fired burners or pressurised hot water.

Absorption chillers are less efficient than vapour compression chillers with a COP of approximately 0.7-1.2. It follows that more gas energy will be required than an equivalent electric chiller (COP = 1.5 to 2.0). However the gas chiller will be less costly to run and emit less

pollution per unit of cooling than an electrically driven chiller due to the high cost and pollution output arising from the use of electricity.

As well as direct gas firing some absorption chillers can be operated using waste heat. One form of surplus heat is that generated by combined heat and power units. In winter their heat output is used for space heating. In summer this heat is surplus to requirements and so can be used to drive the absorption chiller. This is known as trigeneration or combined cooling and power. When heat which would normally be wasted, is used absorption chillers emit much less CO_2 into the atmosphere than a vapour compression chiller for a given cooling effect. Research is currently underway which is investigating the linking of absorption chillers with solar panels as a source of generator heat. It is an advantage that the appearance of large amounts of solar energy coincides with the increased need for cooling.

10.6 Systems

Various systems are available to transfer the cooling effect of refrigeration equipment to the spaces that require cooling. Systems fall into two categories, direct expansion systems and indirect systems.

Direct expansion systems cool the room air by passing it directly over the evaporator coil.

- **Split systems,** as illustrated in figure 10.17 are the simplest cooling system and the most common type of device currently being installed in the UK. Manufacturers data should be considered along with a knowledge of the ambient operating conditions to select a devices with the highest operating efficiency. Milti-split systems are also available that use one outdoor unit connected to multiple indoor units. The use of electrical re heaters on individual indoor units to provide heating alongside cooling should be avoided.

- **Variable Refrigerant Flow.** A type of multi-split system using reverse cycle heat pumps so indoor units can operate in either heating or cooling mode. Heat recovery is possible if some units are operating in heating mode whilst others are operating in cooling mode. This is achieved by the re-direction of hot and cold refrigerant fluids.

• **Versatemp System**. This system uses room based water to air heat pumps to either extract heat from or deposit heat into a water loop circulating around the building. When simultaneous heating and cooling of rooms is required e.g. cooling on the south side of the building and heating on the north the system acts as a heat recovery and redistribution system (figure 10.20).

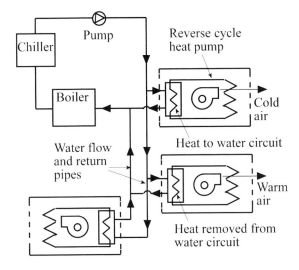

Figure 10.20 Versatemp cooling system.

Indirect, air based systems where air is cooled in an air handling unit and then sent to the rooms via ducting.

• **Dual duct system.** Two air handling units are used one to produce cold air the other to produce heated air. Both air streams are mixed on entry to the room to create the desired temperature with constant air supply volume. Uses a great deal of energy due to the need to both cool and heat air at the same time and so should be avoided.

• **Variable air volume system**. Chilled air at a constant temperature is sent in varying amounts to the room depending on room temperature. The hotter the room the greater the volume of cooled air that is supplied. As lower volumes of air are required the fan speed should be reduced to significantly reduce fan energy consumption. Some

systems use electrical heaters on the cold air terminals in case there is a joint need for cooling and heating. This should be avoided.

Water based systems.

• **Fan coil units.** This system chills water using a chiller and then circulates it to room based fan coil units. warm roof air is circulated through the fan coil and becomes cooled. Some units can also be supplied with ventilation air.

Radiant cooling - Where surfaces are cooled and comfort is achieved more by body radiant heat losses than contact with cool air.

Chilled ceilings are composed of an array of purpose built suspended ceiling panels. The panels are of a standard size and made out of perforated aluminium sheet (figure 10.21). A coil of copper pipe is fixed, in close contact, to the back of this panel. When chilled water is circulated through this pipe the ceiling panel becomes chilled. Any occupants in the room below the panels will feel cooler because their bodies will radiate heat to the chilled ceiling, the opposite effect to being stood next to a hot radiator. In addition to the radiant cooling effect air in contact with the ceiling will become cooled and descend into the room.

Figure 10.21 Chilled ceiling panel.

There is a risk that condensation will form on the chilled ceiling. To avoid this the chilled ceiling control system must monitor humidity levels within the space. If the humidity levels indicate a risk of condensation occurring then either the incoming air must be dehumidified or the chilled ceiling surface temperature must be raised. Chilled ceilings have a smaller cooling capacity than the cooling systems described earlier.

Chilled beams are an alternative to chilled ceilings. A passive chilled beam is shown in figure 10.22. It can be seen that the chilled surface is formed into a linear finned coil, this coil is then surrounded by a pressed steel casing and is suspended from the ceiling. Warm room air rises to the ceiling and enters the top of the beam. It is then cooled by contact with the cold coil. The cool air descends into the room through outlet slots on the underside of the beam. It can be seen that chilled beams cool a room entirely by convection and provide comfort by bringing the occupants into contact with cold air.

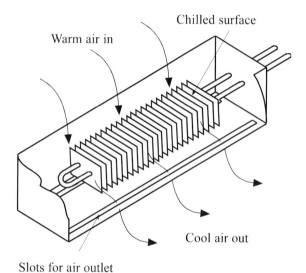

Chilled surface

Warm air in

Cool air out

Slots for air outlet

Figure 10.22 Passive chilled beam.

As the cooling output of a chilled beam increases by reducing the water flow temperature through the device, there is a possibility that the beam will create uncomfortable cold down draughts. One way of overcoming this problem is to use active chilled beams. In these devices tempered ventilation air is supplied through ducting within the beam itself. The air leaves the supply ducting through slots or nozzles with sufficient velocity that it drags warm room air into the beam and through the cooling coil reducing its temperature. The supply and chilled room air mix and enter the room via outlet slots on the underside of the beam. The outlet slots are arranged to avoid the cooler airstream causing a cold draught in the occupied zone.

The benefit of systems incorporating chilled ceilings and chilled beams or active chilled beams alone is that they are an energy efficient method of cooling. This arises due to the operating parameters of the system. The chilled ceiling and beams operate at a relatively high chilled water flow temperature. This means that the chiller has less work to do and therefore will consume less electricity. The coefficient of performance of the chiller is also improved by approximately 20% due to the higher evaporator temperature. When external conditions allow, the relatively high flow temperature water can be provided using the cooling effect of an evaporative cooling tower.

Chilled ceilings and chilled beams are often used in conjunction with a displacement ventilation system. This is a low energy mechanical ventilation system that was previously described in section 5.4.1.

REFERENCES

1. The building regulations, Part L;Conservation of fuel and power. HMSO 2000

2. Pilkington United Kingdom Ltd. Solar control glass data sheet. CI/SfB (31) Ro6 (M5), May 1997

3. BRE Digest 454 Thermal mass in Office Buildings: Part 1 An introduction

FURTHER READING

General Information Report 31. Avoiding or Minimising the Use of Air-Conditioning - A research Report From the EnREI Programme (1995)

Good Practice Guide 280. Energy Efficient Refrigeration Technology - The fundamentals

Good Practice Guide 279. Running refrigeration Plant efficiently - a Cost Saving Guide for Owners

Good Practice Guide 248. Strategy for Major Cooling Plant replacement

11 ENERGY.MANAGEMENT

In this chapter we will find that;

- The performance of a low energy building cannot be guaranteed. Energy consumption could increase unless it is monitored and managed.

- In energy purchasing decisions consideration should be given to 'green tariff' electricity.

- BMS systems are not 'fit and forget' devices. The information accessible by them should be regularly checked and acted upon. In this way they become an essential tool in energy management.

- The energy consumption of a building can be reduced by encouraging the occupants to perform good housekeeping measures such as turning off lights in unoccupied rooms.

- Baseline energy consumption data should be established and used to set energy reduction targets.

- Regular monitoring of energy consumption gives the data to check that it remains within acceptable limits. Software is available to assist in carrying this out.

- Energy efficiency measures range from no/low cost to very high cost. A knowledge of where the energy is used in a building and the cost and effectiveness of energy saving devices allows energy investment decisions to be made.

11.0 Introduction

Having designed a low energy building there is no guarantee that if it is left alone its energy consumption in use will remain low. Some of the low energy aspects are more robust than others. For example insulation will carry out its role of reducing the heat loss rate from the building without any kind of interaction or adjustment for many years. However, sensors may malfunction and controls may lose their adjustment causing services to operate when not required and/or to inappropriate levels. One example is when heating systems operate in unoccupied buildings at night-time. Another significant factor in excess energy use are the building occupants themselves. For example windows may be opened to reduce temperatures rather than switching the heating off. It is for these reasons that the energy consumption of buildings should be continually monitored. This ensures that it is consistent with pre-set targets and past performance. Any divergence from target energy consumptions must be investigated and remedial actions taken to return the building to acceptable levels of performance.

Energy management involves gathering data on the size and destination of energy flows and then taking steps to minimise these flows. Most large organisations such as local authorities, hospitals, universities and industry employ energy managers to carry out this function. It is also possible to contract out this work to outside energy consultants. This is known as contract energy management (CEM). The staff in these businesses have responsibility for managing the energy consumption in a wide range of organisations. They work on the basis of a fixed fee or alternatively take a percentage of the estimated savings in energy costs that they achieve.

This chapter will investigate the various aspects of energy management by considering the range of duties that are part of the energy managers job description. These are;

- Energy purchasing.

- Operation of the Building Management System (BMS), (if one is installed)

- Troubleshooting of energy consuming system faults

- Running energy awareness schemes

- Setting targets for energy consumption.

- Monitoring energy consumption.

- Making investments in devices that save energy.

- Preparation of reports on energy and environmental issues.

It has been found that for the effective management of energy in a large organisation it is necessary to have a key member of staff who has responsibility for and is the focus of energy issues. This is because energy can be overlooked when the focus is on completing the main activities of the organisation such as making and selling products and services. As well as the energy manager the duties may also be undertaken by a general manager with responsibility for energy issues, a facilities manager or building services engineer.

11.1 Energy Purchasing

This role of the energy manager is a financial one. It involves reducing the cost of fuel used by the buildings under the energy managers control. With the de regulation of fuel supplies there is great scope for negotiating lower unit energy costs from energy suppliers by competitive tendering. However, care should be taken that the lower fuel costs are not cancelled out by the additional energy usage that usually accompanies lower fuel prices. One way of avoiding this is to earmark any reductions in fuel and power costs towards energy efficiency investments. In this way cost reductions due to both reduced unit costs and due to energy savings can be utilised for further investment in energy saving items. In this way the energy management department can become self supporting.

The energy manager should also give consideration to the purchase of electricity from renewable sources such as 'green tariff' electricity (see section 1.1.1).

The unit cost of fuels will have an impact on energy efficiency investment decisions (see section 11.5). If fuel costs are high then there are more valuable savings to be made by investing in energy saving equipment than when fuel costs are low.

11.2 Operation of the BMS System

Building management systems (BMS) were described in section 9.5.1. They are flexible building services control systems that allow a high level of user interaction. This gives the energy manager the ability to:

- **Commission the system.** Following installation all building services systems require commissioning to ensure that they are providing the necessary environmental conditions, are operating efficiently and functioning within prescribed limits. Commissioning should be checked across a range of operating conditions to ensure that the operating characteristics are maintained when the requirements on the system change.

- **Fine tuning.** Following commissioning the initial settings may require fine tuning in the light of operational experience. The BMS system logs environmental data such as room temperatures so that for example set points can be refined and the effects of the changes closely monitored over time. It is also possible to modify the control strategy. This is a more technical process involving software changes. It can be carried out by appropriately trained energy managers or instructions given to the BMS installer to write the modifications.

- **Modifying operating parameters.** It is unlikely that the operating parameters of the system will be fixed 24 hours a day and 365 days a year. Making sure the BMS controls to the actual requirements of the building can save energy. Changing temperature set points to set back positions when spaces are unoccupied for example in empty hotel rooms. A second example is varying the heating programme so that heating is only provided when required, for example, restricting heating in schools during holiday periods and evening classes.

- **Monitoring energy consumption.** A large estate of buildings may have a small number of utility meters recording energy consumption for the entire site. There is a requirement in the building regulations that came into force in April 2002 to install sub meters to give more detail on where the energy consumption is going within the site. Examples are recording the consumptions of individual buildings and individual large loads within buildings e.g. catering or chiller energy use. However, these meters are no use unless they are read and the information obtained is acted upon. To aid this sensors can be affixed to gas, water and electricity meters that allow remote reading by the BMS. The information obtained can then be exported to other spread sheet and word processing software installed on the energy management PC for analysis and report writing.

11.3   Troubleshooting Faults

Faults in energy consuming equipment and their controls can lead to excess energy consumption in a building. Examples are over heating or cooling rooms and conditioning to occupancy standards when the rooms are empty. There may also be less noticeable faults such as a variable speed fan unit causing the fan to operate at high speeds at all times rather than reducing fan speed as the need for ventilation falls.

The energy manager can be made aware of the presence of faults from the observations of staff. An effective reporting procedure is necessary to obtain this information and act on it otherwise they appear as complaints. A second source is the BMS system. The BMS software allows the setting up of routines that monitor operational parameters of the building services systems. These routines check the data and look for readings that are outside normal operating limits. One example is a threshold set on boiler flow temperatures of say 85°C. The software continually monitors boiler flow temperatures and if the flow temperature exceeds 85°C an alarm message is displayed on the BMS supervisor screen. This may be caused by failure in the control system which must then be investigated and corrected.

11.4 Energy Awareness

One of the problems with non domestic buildings is that the occupants have no personal involvement with the energy bills levied on the organisation. This means that there is a tendency to be profligate with energy. Some examples are: lights are left on in unoccupied rooms, lights are left on when there is sufficient daylight, windows are opened whilst the heating is on and computers left running overnight. These actions also occur in peoples' own homes but likely to be prevented by higher personal energy costs. There are two ways in which the behaviour in the workplace can be modified. The first is to raise awareness of energy issues amongst the building occupants. The aim is to encourage them to adopt energy efficient behaviour such as turning off lights in unoccupied rooms. The second is to provide incentives for them to reduce energy consumption.

RAISING AWARENESS

Raising energy awareness is achieved using two methods;

- **Training sessions.** Small groups of staff are gathered for instruction on the importance of saving energy and how energy can be saved in the workplace.

- **Publicity.** Various types of publicity material can be created such as posters, articles in in-house magazines and stickers suggesting that equipment should be turned off when not needed. Stickers should be placed near occupant operated equipment such as light switches.

It has been found in practice that staff who have been made aware of energy issues do adopt energy saving behaviour. Unfortunately, it has also been shown that the majority of these staff revert back to their original profligate behaviour within four months. It is for this reason that awareness schemes should be repeated throughout the year. The challenge is to raise awareness without creating over familiarity that could lead to an eventual disregard of the message. One way of overcoming this is to use a variety of awareness publications and continually be innovative in the way they are presented to staff.

INCENTIVES

People are more likely to carry out an activity if there is an incentive for doing so. Whilst there are real incentives for cutting energy consumption to protect the environment and conserve fuel resources this tends to be detached from commercial building occupants. As a consequence some organisations provide financial bonuses to staff in line with the size of energy savings made. This could be restricted to key staff involved in energy savings such as caretakers or alternatively can be distributed amongst all staff say in the form of a free staff outing or meal. This latter form is the most preferable as it encourages the motivation of all staff within the organisation.

One example that illustrates that energy consumption is reduced when people make the connection with use and costs is seen in multi-residential properties using district heating. In many dwellings such as these the heating costs are included as a fixed sum in the rent. As a consequence there is no relationship between energy consumption and costs. This has led to high energy consumption due to heating being uncontrolled resulting in high internal temperatures. These temperatures may then be reduced by opening windows. This can be avoided by restoring the link between use and cost. For example, installing heat meters (figure 11.1 and section 11.5) that monitor the amount of heat taken by each property from the district heating scheme. Energy can then be charged for as used rather than as a fixed sum in the rent. In case studies where heat meters have been installed overall energy consumption falls and so does tenants expenditure each month.

11.5 Targeting

The energy manager needs to have a method of defining what represents a good energy consumption. This is necessary so that actual energy consumptions can be compared against the target to assess if the building is consuming energy at, above or below acceptable limits.

Target energy consumptions can be determined in a number of ways. The first is to use historical energy consumption data for the building. This data is then normalised by dividing it by the treated floor area of the building and the number of degree days over the year. Treated floor area is the area of the building that has its environment changed using energy consuming services. This gives a normalised performance indicator (NPI) measured in kilowatt hours per square metre per year (kWh/m^2/y). Occasionally it is worth dividing the energy consumption by a different parameter if that would give a better indication of performance. For example if school catering energy is being gathered for comparison with other schools then annual energy consumption per pupil taking school meals per year may be a more appropriate indicator. Another way of setting a performance indicator is to predict it by calculation at the design stage (see IP11). Another alternative is to obtain the energy performance indicators of comparable buildings within the same area. For example if you are setting energy targets for a primary school, data for other primary schools within the local authority should be consulted. If local data is not available then national figures can be used such as those presented in the CIBSE application manual on energy auditing[1] or the Energy Efficiency Best Practice programmes energy consumption guides.

Figure 11.1 Heat meter components.

Long term targets for energy reductions can then be set. Studies have shown that in existing buildings the potential for energy savings ranges from 10 to 60%. Typical average potential savings are of the order of 30%. Most organisations set modest targets, aiming to achieve 15% energy savings within the first 3 years of activity. The scope for savings will be less in a new low energy building, the key issue in energy management here is to maintain the initial low levels of consumption in the long term.

11.6 Monitoring Energy Consumption

The amount of energy consumed in a given period is determined from the difference between energy meter readings at the beginning and end of the period. For domestic customers meters are read quarterly i.e. three monthly intervals. For commercial customers monthly or possibly weekly readings should be taken.

Meters can be read manually and the data input into analysis software. Alternatively, it may be read using electronic readers with the facility for automatic data input. On a large site with many sub meters and short reading intervals, an automatic system will reduce the manpower required for data collection and storage. Some meters have transducers built into them so that an electrical signal representing the rate of energy consumption can be obtained. Other meters must have transducers attached to them. For example optical pulse counters can be used to log the number of rotations per minute of the rotating disk or flashing LED that indicates current flow in an electricity meter. The electrical signals can be returned via radio links, the mains cables themselves or communications cabling such as the BMS network (figure 11.2).

Sub meters should be used to measure the energy consumed by individual large loads within a building. However, if it is a large heat load that is satisfied by a central boiler system, it is only possible to measure the gas input to the central boilers. To be able to determine where the thermal energy is going from the boilers heat meters are required (figure 11.1). These measure the temperature of heated water entering the zone (°C), the rate of flow of heated water entering the zone (m³/h)

and the temperature of water leaving the zone (°C). From a knowledge of the thermal capacity of water and the volume that has flowed through the zone pipework over a given period, the amount of energy required to heat the volume of water and therefore that taken by the zone can be determined.

On some occasions it is not necessary to monitor the energy consumption if the equipment operates at a constant known load. In this case it is simply necessary to monitor the hours run by the piece of equipment and multiply this by its power rating in kiloWatts. The outcome is an energy consumption in kilowatt hours.

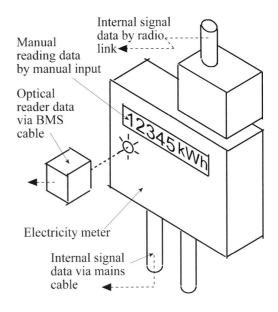

Figure 11.2 Alternative methods of collecting meter data.

BUILDING REGULATIONS

It is a requirement of the Building Regulations part L2 that suffcient meters and sub meters are installed to provide the information to attribute energy consumption to end uses. A resonable provision is for 90% of the estimated annual energy consumption of each fuel (electricity, oil, gas, LPG and heating and cooling from district heating schemes) to be metered.

Resonable provision of meters is to provide an incoming energy meter on all buildings greater than

500m² gross floor area, with sub meters for each separately tenanted area, for each piece of equipment with input powers shown in table 11.1 and any process loads. This latter category is necessary to distinguish building energy consumption from that used to make products in the factory during industrial processes.

Plant item	Rated input power (kW)
Boiler installations or CHP plant feeding a common distribution circuit	50
Chiller installations feeding a common distribution circuit	20
Electric humidifiers	10
Motors for fans and pumps	10
Final electrical distribution boards	50

Table 11.1 Size of plant for which separate metering would be resonable

ENERGY MONITORING SOFTWARE

Having taken the meter readings it is necessary to manage the data and analyse it to achieve some meaningful information. Software is available to assist with this that has a database at its core. Details about the locations of the meters are entered into it such as building address and, if there is more than one meter, the location of further sub meters. The meter reading and time that the reading was taken can then be input to the database. Having stored the basic data the software can then perform various analytical subroutines, such as:

- **Calculation of annual, monthly or weekly energy consumption**. Note that the accuracy of this depends on the amount of energy consumed and the frequency of meter readings. The greater the rate of energy consumption the more frequent the readings should be taken. Most software systems divide the energy consumption by the number of days between meter readings to give an average daily energy consumption. If the meter readings are taken at weekly intervals this gives a fairly accurate measure. If the meter readings are taken at quarterly intervals the accuracy of energy

consumption calculated for the quarter will be accurate but for any given week within this period will be low unless the energy consumption is similar each day.

- **Analysis of usage patterns**. The stored data cane output in graphical form. For example a bar chart of energy consumption per month across a year. This is the method that allows the most rapid assessment of usage patterns. In its simplest form a visual check can be made to ensure expected patterns are occurring. One example is confirming a significant dip in space heating energy consumption in summer.

If the data is being continuously monitored by electronic means, the hourly energy consumption over the last seven days can be output. This will allow a check that energy is not being used when it is not required such as in the evening or at weekends.

- **Normalisation of energy consumption using degree days** (see section 2.2). The space heating energy consumption of a building varies depending on the outside air temperature. The lower the outside air temperature the higher the space heating energy consumption. This makes the comparison of successive annual energy consumption's difficult to make as one year may have been particularly mild and the next particularly cold. Increased energy consumption in any particular year may be due to a faulty heating system or could simply be due to the lower outside temperatures. To eliminate this variable the energy consumption for each year must be divided by the number of degree days in that year to give an energy consumption per degree day (kWh/y/ degree day). Degree day data for each year must be entered into the system.

- **Statistical analysis of the data can be carried out such as regression analysis**. This is where one variable is compared against another that is related to it to check if the relationship is as expected. One example is in the comparison between outside air temperatures and space heating energy consumption. It is known that heat loss is directly related to outside air temperature so a graph of

IP8 - Assessment Methods

A number of methods exist for calculating the predicted energy consumption of a proposed building at the design stage. Some of these methods have been extended to form a full environmental impact assessment incorporating energy, health, pollution, material resources and the global environment. This type of information is useful in three ways;

- It can be used to compare the energy consumptions of alternative designs or the impact on energy consumption of modifications and new equipment.

- The information related to the final design can be used as a standard against which the actual energy consumption in use can be compared for monitoring and targeting purposes.

- The information related to the final design can be used as evidence to obtain Building Regulations part L approval

ENERGY ASSESSMENT

A range of energy assessment techniques are available, all of which are based on the basic principles of heat loss calculations and energy efficiencies of lighting, heating, cooling, ventilation and domestic hot water systems. The differences between assessment methods occur in two principle ways. The first is in the level of detail used in the calculation. The more detail the greater the accuracy but more time consuming the process. The second is the method by which the calculation is carried out. This can either be by manual calculation, simplified tabulated methods using pro-formae or computer based software where a range of options are available from an associated database.

Some of the methods available are;

ENVIRONMENTAL DESIGN SOFTWARE

Comprehensive building services design software is commercially available that is based on standard CIBSE calculation methods. Data, for example on wall/window dimensions, construction details, orientation of buildings and shading are input manually on a room by room basis or can be imported from other software such as computer aided design (CAD) packages. The in-built calculation routines will then calculate heating, cooling, lighting and domestic hot water energy loads. The software can then go on to assist in designing the services installation necessary to achieve the internal standards that were used within the energy calculations. The output is in terms of tabular quantities of energy and also graphical profiles. Some systems also convert the energy use into an emission of carbon dioxide based on energy to CO_2 conversion factors. Powerful software systems can have hourly weatherdata installed in their databases. This allows the system to carry out a dynamic calculation. For example determining how cooling load changes throughout the day as the sun position changes.

BREDEM - Building Research Establishment Domestic Energy Model

This energy calculation method it is now taken as the standard method of calculating the energy consumption of domestic buildings. BREDEM forms the basis of the Standard Assessment Procedure (SAP) which rates a house in terms of the **cost** of energy consumption. The final output is a rating from 0 to 100. The higher the score the lower the energy costs per year. SAP rating was used to demonstrate compliance with part L of the Building Regulations for many years. A rating of 60 was required. Low energy homes should have a rating over 80. The latest edition of the Building Regulations still incorporate a calculation method based on BREDEM but the energy consumption is converted into a carbon index (CI). This gives a better description of the energy consumption of the building in terms of its impact on the global environment rather than the householders pocket. Electric heating for example would fare much worse in a CI assessment than an equivalent gas heated house.

NHER - National Home Energy Rater

This is a calculation method similar to the SAP rating scheme except it also takes into account degree days so that comparisons of energy consumption's can be made throughout the country. Aspects of occupancy behaviour are also taken into account. The outcome of the method is a rating between 0 and 10.

LT - Lighting and Thermal Method

This method of energy calculation was described in section 3.1.2. Based on a simplified graphical technique it reduces the number of calculations involved in determining a building's energy consumption by making generalisations about the internal conditions required. The method is a useful tool for comparing the energy consumption of buildings with different plan shapes at the design stage.

ENVIRONMENTAL ASSESSMENT

In recent years energy calculation methods have been extended to cover a range of environmental impacts. The main versions of this type of assessment are;

BREEAM - Building Research Establishment Environmental Assessment Method

BREEAM is a comprehensive assessment tool for analysing and improving the environmental performance of buildings. Assessments are carried out by a network of registered assessors. The assessors consider the building design and allocate points if it satisfies certain environmental criteria. To achieve the points a range of values are compared with set criteria. Parameters range from the energy consumption per square metre to the provision of bicycle racks. Versions exist for a range of building types including offices and supermarkets. A version also exists for housing called Ecohomes.

ENVEST - ENVironmental impact ESTimating design software

Software developed by the Building Research Establishment for estimating the life-cycle environmental impacts of a building at the early design stage. It considers the environmental impacts of materials used during construction and maintenance and energy and resources consumed over the buildings life. All environmental impacts are assessed using 'ecopoints' derived from a consideration of total environmental performance. Data is entered as choices from a database within the software. Alternative choices

exist for

- Building and element dimensions

- Building plan shape

- Specification of building materials

- Installed building services

Environmental Management Toolkits

These toolkits have been developed by the Building Research Establishment to help energy managers make decisions regarding energy saving steps in existing buildings. The system uses a computer programme that guides the user through the stages necessary to reduce both the running costs and environmental impact of their buildings. It does this by assessing alternative strategies in terms of both financial savings in pounds and environmental impact in terms of eco points. Three versions are available, for schools, local authorities and offices.

FURTHER READING

CIBSE AM11, Building energy and environmental monitoring. 1998 energy consumption against outside air temperature should be a straight line as shown in figure 11.3. It can be seen that as the outside temperature rises energy consumption falls as expected. However it can be seen that the predicted reduction in energy consumption to zero at 15°C outside air temperature is not realised. This could be base line energy consumption due to hot water usage or could indicate a control fault causing the heating system to run when not needed.

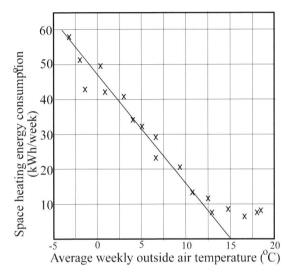

Figure 11.3 Regression graph of space heating energy consumption against outside temperature.

Another statistical technique is called the cumulative sum analysis (CUSUM). This method uses past energy consumption data as base line information and then sums any deviations from this on a weekly basis. The effect is to amplify changes in energy consumption so that they can easily be identified. An example of this is shown in figure 11.4. The average space heating energy consumption is calculated on a weekly basis for the building over the previous year. This is then compared with each new weeks energy consumption as it occurs. If the energy consumption has remained the same as last year there will be little or no change as indicated in weeks 1-4 of the graph. However, at the end of week 4 a new control unit was added to the heating system this resulted in a small saving in energy in week 5 compared to the same week in the previous

year. These savings continued in following weeks and each week's saving is added to the previous one causing the line on the graph to descend. All energy consumption's were corrected by the software to take into account variations in outside temperature one year to the next. The cumulative savings can be converted into an amount of CO_2 which can be used as part of an environmental audit. It can also be converted into a cost saving and an accurate calculation of the payback period of the control device can be worked out.

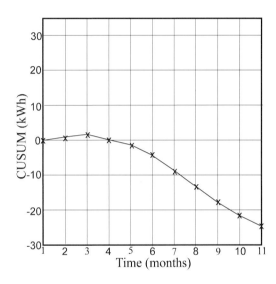

Figure 11.4 CUSUM plot.

ENERGY AUDITS

Energy audits are a systematic method of identifying where and how much energy is being consumed in a building. It is usually carried out by analysing fuel invoices. This is useful information in itself but it can also be used to identify major sources of energy consumption so that they can be earmarked for the application of an energy saving measure. Another important aspect of energy auditing is the 'walk around' this is where the energy manager tours the premises to visually identify sources of waste. Examples are seeing lights left on in well daylit spaces. It is recommended that energy audits are repeated at regular intervals such as every three years.

11.7 Energy Saving Investments

In large organisations the cost of implementing energy saving schemes can be high especially where this involves the purchase of large items of equipment such as combined heat and power units. However, it is also possible to implement no or low cost measures such as fine tuning of controls and energy awareness schemes. Large schemes can often be funded under a leasing arrangement where a contract energy management organisation pays the capital and installation costs of a device. It recovers its initial investment by taking a share of the value of energy savings until the costs and a profit are recovered. The value of energy savings to the business are much lower but at zero capital cost. However, the full value of reduced emissions of carbon dioxide belong to the organisation and so can appear as a positive element in an environmental audit.

The decision to invest in an energy saving feature is usually based on a comparison between financial costs and benefits. The costs are: the capital cost of the device, the installation costs and annual running costs (maintenance and any power input). The benefits are fuel cost savings. If installed at the outset there may also be cost savings available from reducing the size of the heating plant and lower maintenance costs as the plant has to run less often. There may also be non energy benefits such as increased comfort and productivity of the building occupants.

SIMPLE PAYBACK

The simple payback period is defined as the time taken for fuel cost savings to pay back the initial capital cost of the device. It is calculated by dividing the initial capital cost by the net annual running cost savings.

$$\text{Payback Period (y)} = \frac{\text{Total capital cost of item (£)}}{\text{Net annual savings (£/y)}}$$

The simple payback method is easily understood and is one of the most widely used methods of assessing financial viability. Most schemes that are approved have a payback period of less than three to five years. There are two main criticisms of the simple payback period. The first is that no account is taken of interest that you would have to pay on a loan taken out to fund the project or the value of other ways of making income from the initial capital sum such as interest from simply investing the money. It may be possible for example that investing the money in shares could provide sufficient income that equalled or exceeded the value of energy savings made. To allow for this criticism various accounting methods are available that take into account aspects such as taxation, depreciation of equipment and interest payments. The second criticism is that the simple payback does not take into account savings that occur beyond the payback period.

CARBON PAYBACK

The decision on whether or not to expend money on installing an energy efficiency measure is still largely decided on financial grounds. It was stated in chapter 1 that reduced energy costs and increased capital costs can make investments in energy saving devices difficult to justify on financial grounds. In any assessment of benefits arising from energy savings strong consideration should be given to environmental benefits such as reduced emission of pollutant gases. A carbon payback for example would compare the carbon dioxide emitted in the production of an energy saving device, known as the embodied carbon, with the net annual carbon savings made by having the device. i.e.

$$\text{Carbon payback Period (y)} = \frac{\text{Embodied carbon (kgCO}_2)}{\text{net annual carbon reductions (kgCO}_2/\text{y})}$$

11.8 Reporting

Reporting begins when a new building is completed and handed over by providing a building log-book.

BUILDING LOG-BOOK

The Building Regulations part L2, section 3 require that the owner and/or occupier of a building be presented with the log book which should include details on:

- Whole building energy strategy.

- Description of services installed and their function on a zone by zone basis illustrated by simple schematics.

- Installed capacities of the energy consuming plant.

- Copies of commissioning reports.

- Operating instructions and maintenance intervals.

- A description of the location of each meter and sub meter, the fuel type it monitors, plant or space it monitors and the method for using the information as part of an energy management strategy.

- Copies of any measurements taken such as air permeability or thermographic studies.

- Copies of any energy calculations made such as predicted energy consumption and carbon emissions.

It is essential that the log book is added to as necessary for example recording the activities of the energy manager in respect of any additions or adjustments that affect energy consumption.

On a day to day basis adjustments to controls, installation of new equipment and rectification of faults should all be logged. This good practice will ensure that new staff within the organisation have access to all the information that is necessary to ensure that the building and its services operate effectively.

Annual energy management reports give senior management the opportunity to judge the value of energy conservation work. As well as financial savings and energy usage reductions. The energy reductions should be converted into a carbon reduction figure. This can then be used in an overall environmental audit of the business.

REFERENCES

1.CIBSE (1991) Applications Manual AM5:Energy Audits and Surveys.

FURTHER READING

GPG165: Financial Aspects of Energy Management in Buildings.

GIL 65: Metering Energy Use in Non-Domestic Buildings. 2002

12 INDEX